SATHER CLASSICAL LECTURES

VOLUME FIFTY

PAUSANIAS'
GUIDE TO ANCIENT
GREECE

PAUSANIAS' GUIDE TO ANCIENT GREECE

Christian Habicht

With a New Preface

University of California Press

Berkeley   Los Angeles   London

This book is a print-on-demand volume. It is manufactured using toner is place of ink. Type and images may be less sharp than the same material seen in traditionally printed University of California Press editions.

University of California Press
Berkeley and Los Angeles, California

University of California Press, Ltd.
London, England

First Paperback Printing 1998

Library of Congress Cataloging in Publication Data

Habicht, Christian.
    Pausanias' guide to ancient Greece.
    (Sather classical lectures; v. 50)
    Bibliography: p.
    Includes indexes.
    1. Pausanias.   Description of Greece—Addresses,
essays, lectures.   2. Greece—Description and travel—
To 323—Addresses, essays, lectures.   3. Greece—
Antiquities—Addresses, essays, lectures.   I. Title.
II. Series.
DF27.P383H33 1985   913.8'049   84-16243
ISBN 0-520-06170-5 (alk. paper : pbk.)

Printed in the United States of America

The paper used in this publication meets the minimum
requirements of ANSI/NISO Z39.48-1992(R
1997)(Permanence of Paper)

FOR FREIA

CONTENTS

LIST OF ILLUSTRATIONS

ix

PREFACE TO THE 1985 EDITION

The pages that follow represent the lectures given under the same title at the University of California, Berkeley, in the fall of 1982. The Preface, notes, and two appendices have been added; apart from these, material changes have been slight.

Opinions on the value of Pausanias' work still diverge. To some, he seems muddleheaded; to others, a most reliable guide. The strongest accusations against him have for some time been satisfactorily answered and are no longer a real issue. There is, nonetheless, still much current prejudice against him and also, among literary critics, a tendency to neglect him.[1] A low esteem for postclassical authors in general may have contributed more to this neglect than the assessment of

[1] Ed. Norden, in his monumental *Antike Kunstprosa*, has no room for a discussion of Pausanias; he gives him just one sentence (which does not even mention his name): "Ein Grieche registriert die Monumente der Vorzeit weniger aus künstlerischem als aus antiquarischem Interesse: er ist dadurch eine unserer wichtigsten Quellen für Religionsaltertümer geworden" (vol. 1, 3d ed. [Leipzig and Berlin 1915], 345). M. P. Nilsson, where he discusses Greek religion as reflected in the literature of the empire, has sections on Babrius, Lucian, Aristides, Philostratus, Aelianus, Heliodorus, and Nonnus, but nothing on Pausanias (*Geschichte der griechischen Religion*, vol. 2 [Munich 1950], 535–46; 3d ed. [1974], 558–69). In their introduction to a volume devoted to Greek literature written under the empire the editors especially regret the absence of essays "on Nonnus . . . or his many successors; . . . on Philostratus, the eminent sophists, Aelian, Quintus of Smyrna, the other novelists, the literary criticism of philosophers, Plutarch, Oppian, and many others who well deserve to be read . . ." (J. J. Winkler and G. Williams, *YCS* 27 [1982]: vii–viii)—again no mention of Pausanias, who could easily compete with most of those named. Finally, the recent collection *Ancient Writers: Greece and Rome*, edited by T. Luce (2 vols. [New York 1982]), has, among some fifty authors, no corner for Pausanias.

Pausanias' individual ability as a writer. If it is true of all these writers
that "the greatest need . . . is for sustained analyses of the fundamental
quality of literature written in the shadow of a . . . classical past,"[2]
Pausanias most definitely deserves a fresh study. The most pressing
need, it has been stated long ago, is for an interpretation of Pausanias'
work that does not lose sight of the whole for the sake of the particu-
lars.[3] The present volume is meant to be a modest contribution toward
this goal.

The English quotations from Pausanias' text are taken from James G.
Frazer's translation of 1898, whose literary quality far outweighs anything that might seem out of fashion in expression or in spelling of
ancient names. References with Roman numerals always refer to the
books of Pausanias.

My obligations are numerous and deeply felt. For the generous invitation to do these lectures I am obliged to the members of the Depart-
ment of Classics at the University of California, Berkeley, and to them
and their chairman, Charles Murgia, as well as to many colleagues in
other departments, for their kindness, assistance, and hospitality. They
all made our stay in the Bay Area a delightful and unforgettable
experience.

In the preparation of the book my greatest debt is to Dr. Alfred S.
Bradford, Jr., for many good suggestions and for a very thorough revi-
sion of my English draft. I am also most grateful to Mrs. Sandra S.
Lafferty of the Institute for Advanced Study for her meticulous prepa-
ration of the typescript and to Mrs. Doris Kretschmer and her staff at
the Press for all the care they provided during the editorial process.
Finally, I wish to acknowledge with gratitude the kindness of all those
who authorized me to reproduce photographs, maps, or drawings:
American School of Classical Studies, Athens (figs. 25, 26, 30); Ar-
chaiologike Hetaireia, Athens (figs. 8a, 9–11, 13, 14, 16, 23); A. S.
Bradford (fig. 8b); Deutsches Archäologisches Institut, Abteilung
Athen (figs. 15, 17–19, 28, 29, 31); Deutsches Archäologisches In-
stitut, Abteilung Istanbul (figs. 12, 20); Ecole Française d'Archéologie,
Athens (fig. 1); Alison Frantz (fig. 22); Pantos Pantos (figs. 3–5);
R. Schoder, SJ (figs. 6, 7); A. F. Stewart (fig. 34).

Ch. H.
Princeton, New Jersey, 1985

---

[2] Winkler and Williams (above, n. 1), p. viii.
[3] Regenbogen, p. 1095: "Was für das gesamte Werk des P. am dringendsten vonnöten,
aber nicht immer leicht ist, ist die Interpretation auch des Einzelnen aus dem Ganzen
heraus. Es ist fraglich, ob in unserer Zeit das noch einmal geleistet werden wird."

PREFACE TO THE PAPERBACK EDITION

The Sather Classical Lectures on Pausanias have long been out of print, as has the German edition of the book. I am therefore most grateful for the initiative of the Press in making them available again. I take the opportunity to review selectively recent scholarship and to make some corrections and additions prompted by it. For the production of the book, my thanks go to Mary Lamprech and Suzanne Samuel.

Interest in Pausanias, both the man and his work, long dormant, has skyrocketed over the past twenty years and led to a flood of books and articles. I would like to think that my Sather Classical Lectures, reprinted here, contributed to this boom; in fact, in the Preface to *Pausanias Historien* (*Entretiens* 41, 1996), the editor states that these lectures triggered the conference at Geneva. Among important scholarship since 1985, I would mention the reissue of the edition by H. Rocha-Pereira, 1989–1990. Bilingual editions with introduction and commentary are appearing in Italy[1] and have begun to appear in France.[2] A complete German translation of Pausanias with notes was published in 1986–1989,[3] and a Japanese translation in 1991.[4] A wider audience is targeted by J. Lacarrière's book *Als die Säulen noch standen: Spaziergänge mit Pausanias in Griechenland.*[5]

Major studies on individual regions treated by Pausanias have appeared for Attica (book I),[6] Corinth (II),[7] Sparta (III),[8] Messene (IV),[9] and Olympia (V–VI).[10] Other works analyze Pausanias' reports on

Achaia (VII),[11] Arcadia (VIII),[12] and Delphi (X).[13] Pausanias' use of
and approach to history continue to be widely discussed,[14] and the
same holds both for his standing as a Greek in a Roman world and
for his views on Rome and the Romans.[15] Art, artists, and architecture of the past and of the writer's own time form a major part of a
recent book and are the object of a recent article.[16]

The following pages will review in the light of recent scholarship
specific topics discussed in the book.

Chapter 1 (The Man and His Work): For what audience did Pausanias write? That question continues to be discussed, and also the question of what kind of book he wanted to write: a guide for tourists, a
literary work to be read at home, or an attempt (as I have argued) to
combine both aims. These days, most scholars hold that he had,
above all, if not exclusively, readers in mind, not people who would
want to use the book as a guide on tour. In this sense, see Ø. Andersen and D. Knoepfler in *Entretiens* 41 and other scholars quoted
therein.[17] F. Chamoux, on the other hand, argues that Pausanias
thought equally of both groups.[18] It is ironic that Wilamowitz, who
in fact set out to follow him in the field, got lost—through his own,
not Pausanias', fault.[19]

Chapter 2 (Pausanias as a Guide): The story of the burnt archive at
Kallipolis (pp. 34–35), for which I relied on the excavator's report
(P. Themelis), needs to be revised, after the archive's thorough publication by P. A. Pantos.[20] The results show that this was not the city's
archive but rather that of one of the leading and well-known families
of Aetolia. The documents were not burned in 279 B.C., but about a
century later, perhaps during the course of civic riots. The *strategos*
Charixenus, whose seal is shown (fig. 5), is, consequently, not Charixenus I, but his son Charixenus II, three-time federal *strategos* in the
240s and 230s. The archive from Delos (p. 34 and n. 24) has now
been published.[21]

Messene (pp. 36–63): New excavations are under way.[22] Important
new evidence for Damophon (pp. 38–57) has been found near the
Asklepieion on an inscribed column. It contained decrees of seven
states honoring Damophon. Most interesting is the one of Lycosura
(*SEG* 41.332). From the fact that it mentions tetradrachms as valid
currency, Themelis concludes that since they were no longer minted
in the Peloponnese after 190 B.C., this year was the *terminus ante*

quem for the inscription. He then argues that Damophon's career culminated between 223 and 190 or some forty to fifty years earlier than hitherto assumed. The fallacy of this argument is that tetradrachms continued to circulate long after minting had stopped (whenever that was).[23] There seems to be no good reason to abandon the traditional chronology that has Damophon active between ca. 180 and 150. If he in fact, as Themelis argues, was instrumental in the planning of the temple, the same will then be true for the temple's chronology.

The date of the important Messeniam inscription cited on p. 61 and n. 88 continues to be controversial; see now L. Migeotte, "La date de l'*oktôbolos eisphora* de Messène," *Topoi* 7 (1997), 51–61, who opts for a date between 70 and 30 B.C.

Chapter 3 (Pausanias and the Evidence of Inscriptions): Increased attention has recently been given to Pausanias' use of inscriptions.[24] For the three dedications at Delphi discussed on pp. 74–76 (nn. 39, 42, 46), my comments depended on Vatin's readings. These have since been questioned by other French scholars who were unable to read what he reported to have read.[25]

The invasion of Greece by the Celts (pp. 84–86) is told by Pausanias twice, in book I and in book X. He says (X.19.5) that he had planned it so from the beginning. His assertion has been questioned by Ameling, who holds that his interest was rekindled, long after he wrote book I, by the invasion of the Costoboci in A.D. 170 (see p. 9), and that this event prompted him to tell the story again, and in more detail.[26] There is general agreement that this event was very important to him, on the level of the Trojan and Persian wars. Furthermore, the view that Hieronymus of Cardia was his main source for it seems to gain ground.[27] Two important details can now be added: the Boeotian commander Lysandros, mentioned by Pausanias (X.20.3) is now epigraphically attested,[28] and for Archandros, the son of the Athenian general Kallippos (I.3.5; 3.4; X.20.5), an important decree was found at the Athenian fortress of Rhamnus, dating to the 240s.[29] This evidence further corroborates the quality of Pausanias' source and of his own factual report.

The inscription from Xanthus mentioning Tlepolemus (p. 88 and n. 89) has been published.[30]

For the Athenian statesman Cephisodorus (pp. 92–94), new evidence suggests two modifications: the mover of the decree of 229/8 is different from the politician honored in the early second century, and the date of this decree (fig. 30) is 184/3 rather than 196/5.[31]

Chapter 4 (Pausanias on the History of Greece): Little has been said recently about Pausanias' use of previous historians. An important borrowing (I.26.4) from Herodotus (I.5.3) has been observed by D. Musti and discussed by him and others.[32] There is a recent reaction against the traditional view that Pausanias made substantial use of Thucydides.[33] Whether or not he used Philistos, the historian of the Greek West, and Diodorus, the historian of the known universe, is a matter of controversy,[34] as is the extent of his use of the geographer Strabo.[35]

Chapter 5 (The Roman World of Pausanias): My interpretation (p. 121) of Pausanias' verdict concerning Sulla's cruelty (or savagery) in I.20.7 has been criticized by E. L. Bowie as going too far.[36] In support of his own view he adduces another passage (IX.33.6): "Sulla's treatment of the Athenians was also uncivilised and alien to the Roman character." I welcome this reference and accept his criticism as valid.

In connection with Hadrian's characterization as the benefactor of Athens (p. 124 and n. 29), a discussion has recently begun about what (if anything) this emperor's Panhellenion meant for Pausanias. D. Musti thinks that Pausanias' work reflects the *spirit* of the Panhellenion. Similarly, according to Arafat, Pausanias wrote "against the background of the creation of the Panhellenion," and, referring to an unpublished paper by A. Spawforth, Arafat states: "Pausanias' readers were, effectively, the delegates to the Panhellenion."[37] Contrary to this, Ameling holds that the author was probably critical in his opinion of the Panhellenion which, according to him, only feigned a nonexistent unity of the Greeks, whereas Bowie doubts "that the Panhellenion could have reflected Pausanias' conception or elicited his enthusiasm."[38] There is an unreal element in this discussion, insofar as Pausanias never mentions the Panhellenion and there is no evidence that he ever found readers (p. 1).

Concerning Pausanias' criticism that the Athenians altered the names on the statues of Miltiades and Themistocles into those of a Roman and a Thracian (p. 137, n. 79), I should have referred the reader to the ingenious suggestion of J. and L. Robert that the places of the famous Athenians were taken, respectively, by the Thracian king Rhoemetalces III, Athenian archon in A.D. 36/7, and by Iulius Nicanor of Hierapolis in Syria, acclaimed in Athens as the "new Themistocles" (and the "new Homer") at about the same time.[39]

Chapter 6 (A Profile of Pausanias): For the Roman emperors initiated into the Eleusinian mysteries (p. 156 and n. 6), see K. Clinton, "The Eleusinian Mysteries: Roman Initiates and Benefactors, Second Century B.C. to A.D. 267," *ANRW* II 18.2 (1989): 1499–1539.

Concerning the head of Aegira (fig. 34; Pausanias VII.26.4): Walter's identification of it as that of Zeus and as a work of Euclidas (p. 159, n. 80) is disputed by B. Madigan,[40] who opts for Dionysus. His assertion that Euclidas "must be a sculptor active in the middle of the 4th century B.C.,"[41] however, is arbitrary: Euclidas could very well have worked in the second century, as Damophon did.

Appendix One (Pausanias and His Critics): See also my paper "An Ancient Baedeker and His Critics: Pausanias' Guide to Greece," *Proceedings of the American Philosophical Society* 129 (1985): 220–224.

Christian Habicht
Princeton, New Jersey
March 1998

NOTES

[1] Pausanias, *Guida della Grecia*, ed. by various scholars; so far 5 vols., 1982–1995, Milan. Also R. Salvatore, *Pausania, Viaggio in Grecia: guida antiquaria e artistica*, vol. 1: *Attica e Megaride*, introduction, translation, and notes, Milan 1991.

[2] Pausanias, *Description de la Grèce*, vol. 1, ed. M. Casevitz et al., Paris 1992.

[3] Pausanias, *Reisen in Griechenland*, trans. E. Meyer and F. Eckstein, 3 vols., Zurich 1986–1989.

[4] Pausanias' *Description of Greece*, trans. Iio K., Tokyo 1991.

[5] Frankfurt 1991, originally *Promenades dans la Grèce antique*, Paris 1978.

[6] R. Garland, *The Piraeus*, London 1987. K.-V. von Eickstedt, *Beiträge zur Topographie des antiken Piraeus*, Athens 1991. D. Knoepfler, "Sur une interprétation historique de Pausanias dans sa description du Dêmosion Sêma Athénien," *Entretiens* 41: 277–311.

[7] D. Engels, *Roman Corinth: An Alternative Model of the Classical City*, Chicago 1990.

[8] C. M. Stibbe, "Beobachtungen zur Topographie des antiken Sparta," *Bulletin Antieke Beschaving* 64 (1989): 61–99. A. R. Meadows, "Pausanias and the Historiography of Classical Sparta," *Classical Quarterly* 89 (1995): 92–113.

[9] P. Themelis, "Damophon von Messene—sein Werk im Lichte der neuen Ausgrabungen," *AntK* 36 (1993): 24–40. J. Auberger, "Pausanias et les Messéniens: une histoire d'amour," *REA* 94 (1992): 187–97. P. Sineux, "A propos de l'Asclépieion de Messène: Asclépios Poliade et Guérisseur," *REG* 110 (1997): 1–24.

[10] H.-V. Herrmann, "Die Siegerstatuen von Olympia," *Nikephoros* 1 (1988): 119–83.

[11] Y. Lafond, "Pausanias historien dans le livre VII de la *Periégèse*," *Journal des Savants* (1991): 27–45; A. D. Rizakis (ed.), *Achaia und Elis in der Antike*, Athens 1991; the same, *Achaie I: sources et histoire régionale*, Athens 1995. M. Moggi, "L'excursus di Pausania sulla Ionia,"*Entretiens* 41 (1996): 79–105.

[12] M. Jost, *Sanctuaires et cultes d'Arcadie*, Paris 1985. M. Moggi, "Processi di urbanizzazione nel libro di Pausania sull' Arcadia," *REG* 99 (1991): 46–62.

[13] L. Lacroix, "Pausanias et les origines mythiques de Delphes: éponymes, généalogies et spéculations étymologiques," *Kernos* 4 (1991): 265–76; the same, "A propos des offrandes à Apollon de Delphes et du témoignage de Pausanias: du réel à l'impression," *BCH* 116 (1992): 157–76. A. Jacquemin, "Delphes au IIe siècle ap. J.-C.: un lieu de la mémoire grecque," in S. Saïd (ed.), Ἑλληνισμός: *quelques jalons pour une histoire de l'identité grecque*, Leiden 1991, 217–31.

[14] F. Chamoux, "Pausania historien," *Mélanges Tuilier*, Paris 1988, 37–45. U. Bultrighini, *Pausania e le traduzioni democratiche: Argo et Elide*, Padua 1990. C. Bearzot, *Storia e storiografia ellenistica in Pausania il Periegeta*, Venice 1992. *Pausanias Historien (Entretiens* 41), passim.

[15] J. Elsner, "Pausanias: A Greek Pilgrim in the Roman World," *Parola del Passato* 135 (1992): 3–29. S. Alcock, *Graecia capta: The Landscape of Roman Greece*, Cambridge 1993. Y. Lafond, "Pausanias et l'histoire du Péloponnèse depuis la conquête romaine," *Entretiens* 41 (1996): 167–98. K. W. Arafat, *Pausanias' Greece: Ancient Artists and Roman Rulers*, Cambridge 1996, 80–190 (Mummius, Sulla, Roman emperors).

[16] Arafat (n. 15), 36–79. U. Kreilinger, "Τὰ ἀξιολογώτατα τοῦ Παυσανίου. Die Kunstauswahlkriterien des Pausanias," *Hermes* 125 (1997): 470–91.

[17] Andersen, pp. 73–74; Knoepfler, p. 308, who quotes various other scholars as arguing in this vein.

[18] Ibid., pp. 48 and 74.

[19] The full story is told in Appendix One (pp. 165–74, esp. 170) and, in somewhat different terms, *Proceedings of the American Philosophical Society* 129 (1985): 220–24.

[20] Τὰ σφραγίσματα τῆς Αἰτωλικῆς Καλλιπόλεως, Athens 1985.

[21] M.-F. Boussac, *Les sceaux de Délos*, vol. 1, Athens 1992.

[22] P. Themelis reports on them annually in *Praktika*, so far 1986–1994 (1997). See also the works cited in n. 9 and Themelis in O. Palagia and W. Coulson, *Sculptors from Arcadia and Laconia*, Oxford 1993, 99–109.

[23] D. Knoepfler, *Museum Helveticum* 46 (1989): 212–13 and *Topoi* 7 (1997): 46–47.

[24] J. Tsifopoulos, *Pausanias as a στηλοκόπας. An epigraphical commentary of Pausanias' ΗΛΙΑΚΩΝ A and B*, Ph.D. diss. Ohio State University, 1991 (microfilm). H. Whittaker, "Pausanias and His Use of Inscriptions," *Symbolae Osloenses* 66 (1991): 171–86. A systematic study of the topic is now under way at Siena and Geneva (*Entretiens* 41 [1996]: 319).

[25] J. Bousquet, *Bull. épigr.* 1988, 644 (cf. 643) and *Bull. épigr.* 1994, 349, pp. 531–34, signed by five scholars. See also *SEG* 31.546.

[26] W. Ameling, *Entretiens* 41 (1996): 145–58.

[27] Ameling, ibid. 150, n. 163.

[28] D. Knoepfler, ibid., 166.

[29] *Ergon* 1993, 7.

[30] J. Bousquet, *REG* 101 (1988): 193–201; see also F. W. Walbank, *ZPE* 76 (1989): 184–96.

[31] A. P. Matthaiou, *Horos* 6 (1988): 13–18. D. M. Lewis, ibid., 19–20.

[32] *Entretiens* 41 (1996): 10–11; 35–39; 40–42. Arafat (n. 15), 9.

[33] T. Eide, "Pausanias and Thucydides," *Symbolae Osloenses* 67 (1992): 124–37.

[34] *Entretiens* 41 (1996): 303, 312, 317 (Philistos), 65, 72–73 (Diodorus).

[35] *Entretiens* 41 (1996): 87–92, 114–15.

[36] *Entretiens* 41 (1996): 218.

[37] Musti, ibid. 161. Arafat (n. 15), 13, 35.

[38] Ameling, ibid., 157. Bowie, ibid., 162 and 224.

[39] *Bull. épigr.* 1962, 137 (p. 155) and 1984, 183. For Iulius Nicanor see C. Habicht, *ZPE* 111 (1996): 79–87.

[40] B. Madigan, "A Transposed Head," *Hesperia* 60 (1991): 503–510.

[41] Madigan, 504.

LIST OF ABBREVIATIONS

For ancient authors see the *Oxford Classical Dictionary*, 2d ed., pp. ix–xxii; for works cited by the name(s) of the author(s) only see the Bibliography.

AA *Archäologischer Anzeiger.*
AAA *Athens Annals of Archaeology.*
AbhAkLeipzig *Abhandlungen der sächsischen Akademie, Leipzig.*
AJA *American Journal of Archaeology.*
AJP *American Journal of Philology.*
AnnPisa *Annali della R. Scuola Normale Superiore di Pisa, Sezione di Lettere.*
ANRW *Aufstieg und Niedergang der Römischen Welt.*
Antcl *L'Antiquité classique.*
AntK *Antike Kunst.*
ArtB *Art Bulletin.*
AthMitt *Mitteilungen des Deutschen Archäologischen Instituts, Athenische Abteilung.*
AZ *Archäologische Zeitung.*
BCH *Bulletin de correspondance hellénique.*
BPEC *Bollettino del Comitato per la preparazione dell'edizione nazionale dei classici greci e latini* (Accadèmia nazionale dei Lincei).
BPW *Berliner Philologische Wochenschrift.*
BSA *Annual of the British School at Athens.*
Bull. épigr. J. and L. Robert. *Bulletin épigraphique.* (In *Revue des études grecques.*)

CAH	*The Cambridge Ancient History.*
CIL	*Corpus Inscriptionum Latinarum.*
CJ	*Classical Journal.*
CR	*Classical Review.*
CRAI	*Comptes rendus de l'Académie des inscriptions et belles-lettres.*
CW	*Classical Weekly.*
Deltion	*Archaiologikon Deltion.*
FD	*Fouilles de Delphes.*
FGrHist	F. Jacoby. *Die Fragmente der griechischen Historiker.* Berlin and Leiden 1923–58.
GGA	*Göttingische Gelehrte Anzeigen.*
GRBS	*Greek, Roman and Byzantine Studies.*
IDélos	*Inscriptions de Délos.*
IEphesos	*Die Inschriften von Ephesos.*
IG	*Inscriptiones Graecae.*
ILS	H. Dessau. *Inscriptiones Latinae Selectae.* 1892–1916.
IMagnesia	O. Kern. *Die Inschriften von Magnesia am Mäander.* 1900.
IOlympia	W. Dittenberger and K. Purgold. *Die Inschriften von Olympia.* 1896.
IPergamon	M. Fränkel. *Die Inschriften von Pergamon.* 2 vols. 1890, 1895.
IPriene	F. Hiller von Gaertringen. *Inschriften von Priene.* 1906.
IstMitt	*Mitteilungen des Deutschen Archäologischen Instituts, Abteilung Istanbul.*
JdI	*Jahrbuch des Deutschen Archäologischen Instituts.*
JfNG	*Jahrbuch für Numismatik und Geldgeschichte.*
JHS	*Journal of Hellenic Studies.*
JRS	*Journal of Roman Studies.*
KlSchr	*Kleine Schriften.*
MdI	*Mitteilungen des Deutschen Archäologischen Instituts* (1948–53).
Moretti, ISE	L. Moretti. *Iscrizioni storiche ellenistiche.* 2 vols. Florence 1967, 1975.
NSc	*Notizie degli scavi di antichità.*
ÖJh	*Jahreshefte des österreichischen archäologischen Instituts.*

Olympiabericht Bericht über die Ausgrabungen in Olympia (vols.
1 – 3: Jahrbuch des Deutschen Archäologischen
Instituts, vols. 52, 53, 56; vol. 4ff.: Berlin 1944 –).
PBSR Papers of the British School at Rome.
PCPS Proceedings of the Cambridge Philological Society.
PIR Prosopographia Imperii Romani.
POxy B. P. Grenfell and A. S. Hunt, eds. Oxyrhynchus
Papyri. 1898 – .
Praktika Praktika tes en Athenais Archaiologikes
Hetaireias.
RA Revue Archéologique.
RE A. Pauly and G. Wissowa. Realencyclopädie der
classischen Altertumswissenschaft. 1893 – 1980.
REA Revue des études anciennes.
REG Revue des études grecques.
RendPontAcc Atti della Pontificia Accademia Romana di
Archeologia, Rendiconti.
RevPhil Revue de philologie, de littérature et d'histoire
anciennes.
RHist Revue historique.
RhM Rheinisches Museum.
RivFC Rivista di Filologia e d'Istruzione Classica.
RN Revue numismatique.
SBWien Sitzungsberichte der Akademie, Wien.
SEG Supplementum Epigraphicum Graecum.
SIG W. Dittenberger. Sylloge Inscriptionum
Graecarum. 1915 – 24.
Staatsverträge H. Bengtson. Die Staatsverträge des Altertums.
Munich 1962 – .
TAPA Transactions of the American Philological
Association.
WS Wiener Studien.
YCS Yale Classical Studies.
ZPE Zeitschrift für Papyrologie und Epigraphik.

I

THE MAN AND HIS WORK

Pausanias, the man whose work and personality will be discussed on the following pages, has not fared well with posterity. In his own time he missed the audience for whom he wrote his ambitious book (almost nine hundred printed pages in the Teubner text). The first sign that it had been read comes only some 350 years after the author's death,[1] and the reader, Stephanus of Byzantium (in the time of the emperor Justinian), did not read it for pleasure or entertainment. No, Stephanus exploited it for a limited scholarly purpose: to extract from it the names of Greek cities and their ethnics. He hardly seems to be a member of the audience the author had hoped to attract. It has even been claimed, and with strong reason, that before Stephanus there was perhaps not a single copy of the work except that in the writer's own hand, deposited in one of antiquity's famous libraries.[2]

After Stephanus, there is once more no sign of any interest in our

[1] It may seem that Pausanias' younger contemporary Aelianus (*VH* 12.61) is quoting Pausanias VIII.27.14, but already in the seventeenth century the passage had been deleted; it is in all probability an interpolation, as A. Diller has demonstrated (*TAPA* 87 [1956]: 88). K. Hanell has assumed ("Phaidryntes," in *RE* [1938], 1560) that Poll. 7.37 is a quotation from Pausanias V.14.5. The possibility cannot be excluded, since E. Bethe, an authority on the subject, states that Pollux added to the materials of his sources more from his own reading ("Iulius" [Pollux], in *RE* [1918], 778). But Hanell's suggestion is far from being certain.
[2] J. H. C. Schubart, *Zeitschrift für die Altertumswissenschaft* 20 (1853): 385–410, as quoted by A. Diller, *TAPA* 88 (1957): 169ff. (cf. idem, *TAPA* 87 [1956]: 84), who shares and develops the same opinion.

author or his work for several centuries. Only with the rise of modern scholarship did Pausanias finally receive attention. Unfortunately, those who now came to read him were scholars only, and most of them were more interested in pointing out his shortcomings than in acknowledging his merits.[3] On top of all this misfortune is heaped poor preservation of the text: the manuscripts are late and defective (the earliest one, from which all others are derived, is fifteenth-century).[4] Posterity has not smiled on our author. He has had to wait for the twentieth century and the age of tourism to attract attention and win the esteem he deserves.

Pausanias, often called "the Periegete" or "the Guide," wrote a description of Greece as it appeared on his extended journeys during the second century A.D. The first epithet is derived from the word περιηγέομαι (periegeomai), "to show around." In fact, the title of Pausanias' book seems to have been Περιήγησις Ἑλλάδος (Periegesis Hellados), "Description of Greece," that is, a book that conducts its reader around a certain area, large or small, in just the same way that local guides show tourists around a spot.[5]

The genre of periegetic literature, though of comparatively late origin (beginning only in the third century B.C.), was well established when Pausanias wrote. The matters usually discussed include topography, monuments, their history (or what is said to be their history),

---

[3] See app. 1.

[4] Fundamental are the two papers by A. Diller "Pausanias in the Middle Ages," TAPA 87 (1956): 84–97, and "The Manuscripts of Pausanias," TAPA 88 (1957): 169–88 (both reprinted in Studies in Greek Manuscript Tradition [Amsterdam 1983], 149–62, 163–82). Diller's main conclusions seem to have won universal approval: P. Vidal-Naquet, RHist 238 (1967): 286; Rocha-Pereira 1:v ff.; H.-W. Nörenberg, Gnomon 49 (1977): 132–34; W. K. Pritchett, Studies in Ancient Greek Topography, pt. 4 (Berkeley 1982), 73 n. 17.

[5] With the verb περιηγέομαι Menippus requests the tour around the underworld from Aeacus in Lucian's satire: περιήγησαί μοι τὰ ἐν ᾅδου πάντα (Dial. Mort. 20.1). The substantive περιήγησις is used by Lucian in the same sense: καί μοι δείξας αὐτὸ ἐντελῆ ἔσῃ τὴν περιήγησιν πεποιημένος, "You will have given me the complete tour" (Charon 22). Both the verb and the substantive occur in documents describing settlements of boundary disputes by judges of a neutral state; these judges are first given a tour at the spot, with explanations and pleading from both parties: "Arriving at the spot and shown around by both parties [περιαγησαμένων ἑκατέρων] we gave our verdict" (SIG³ 638.14–15; cf. FD III.1.362, col. I.16); "Arriving at the disputed area, we judged, according to the description given by both parties" (ἐπὶ τοὺς διαμφισβητουμένους τόπους ἐπελθόντες, κατὰ τὴν γενομένην περιήγησιν ὑφ' ἑκατέρων ἐκρίναμεν) (Moretti, ISE 43.10ff.).

works of art, votive offerings, anthropological features, and so on.[6] Its boundaries in relation to other branches of literature, such as geography, local history, or mythology, are flexible. Models like the first four books of Herodotus' *Histories*, with their descriptions of regions and peoples unfamiliar to most Greeks, certainly contributed to the origin of this literary type,[7] as did the descriptions of coastlines (the *Periploi*, or "Circumnavigations") written for the practical needs of sailors.[8] Except for Pausanias, nothing from a once large periegetic literature has survived but fragments in the form of quotations, names of various authors, and a number of titles.

The most famous periegetic writer was Polemo of Troy (in the first half of the second century B.C.);[9] others are Heliodorus the Athenian and, in Pausanias' own time, Telephus from Pergamum.[10] Typical titles are "Description of the Athenian Acropolis," "Description of Troy," "Description of Syracuse," "Description of the Painted Colonnade in Sicyon," "Description of the Treasuries in Delphi," and "Description of the Augusteum in Pergamum."[11] Most of these works, as their titles show, were monographs on restricted topics—a single city, a prominent quarter of a town, or even a single monument.

Pausanias "towers above them"—the whole of Greece is his topic.[12] This fact is important because it is a major obstacle to the theory put forward more than a century ago by U. von Wilamowitz-Moellendorff that Pausanias was largely dependent on earlier periegetic writers, especially Polemo.[13] Comparison of Pausanias' narrative and the frag-

---

[6] A good summary can be found in H. Bischoff, "Perieget," in *RE* (1937), 725–42.

[7] "Die Kunstform der Periegetik ist die Kunstform der altionischen Geographie und Historiographie, die des Hekataios und des Herodot" (Pasquali, p. 187). See H.-W. Nörenberg, *Hermes* 101 (1973): 238; F. Chamoux, in *Mélanges Dion*, ed. R. Chevallier (Paris 1974), 83–84. Pausanias is in fact as close to, and as fond of, Herodotus as the separation of some six hundred years allows. His frequent imitation of Herodotus is notorious.

[8] Ath. 7.278D sees the writers of one and the other as the same kind of people: οἱ τὰς περιηγήσεις καὶ τοὺς περίπλους ποιησάμενοι.

[9] Polemo was honored by the city of Delphi in 177/176 B.C. (*SIG*³ 585.114) and is thereby exactly dated.

[10] For authors and titles, see Bischoff (above, n. 6). For Heliodorus see also *FGrHist* 373.

[11] This is the provincial temple for the cult of Augustus and Roma.

[12] "Though Pausanias owes the idea of a guidebook to these various predecessors, he towers above them as a mountain above a plain. They had written monographs on single places, even single monuments; he had the grandiose notion of compiling a guidebook for all the memorable places and monuments throughout the whole of Greece" (L. Casson, *Travel in the Ancient World* [London 1974], 294–95).

[13] See app. 1.

ments of earlier periegetic literature, added to the evidence of excavations in numerous places, has proven conclusively that Pausanias, as he
claims, wrote from personal observation.[14]

In each of the ten books Pausanias describes sites, monuments (both
sacred and profane), and works of art. There are numerous digressions
into mythology, religion, and history. The ten books are: book I,
Athens, Attica, Megara, and the Megarid;[15] book II, the land of
Corinth[16] and the Argolid,[17] including the island of Aegina; books
III–VIII, the rest of the Peloponnese (III, Laconia;[18] IV, Messenia;[19] V
and VI, Elis [two books because Olympia is treated at great length];[20]
VII, Achaea; VIII, Arcadia);[21] book IX, Boeotia (in central Greece);[22]
book X, Phocis,[23] especially Delphi,[24] and parts of Locris.[25]

The work obviously does not cover all the areas inhabited by Greeks.
Pausanias undoubtedly used the term *Hellas* (Greece) in the restricted
(and proper) sense of the Greek homeland in the Balkan Peninsula;
he would therefore have excluded the Greek lands overseas: Sicily,
Greater Greece, Asia Minor, the Black Sea, Cyrenaica, and the rest.
Nor is it especially surprising that he did not include the Greek islands,
either those along the coast of Asia Minor and Thrace (for instance,

---

[14] Gurlitt, passim; Frazer, p. lxviii; K. Deichgräber, "Polemon," in *RE* (1952), 1294.

[15] The chapters on Megara and its territory (I.40–44) have recently been studied by A.
Muller in a series of papers called "Megarika": *BCH* 104 (1980): 83–92; 105 (1981):
203–25; 106 (1982): 379–407; 107 (1983): 157–79; 108 (1984): 249–66.

[16] There is the thorough commentary of G. Roux, *Pausanias en Corinthie (II 1–15)*
(Paris 1958).

[17] See M. Piérart, "Deux notes sur l'itinéraire argien de Pausanias," *BCH* 106 (1982):
139–52.

[18] See F. Bölte, "Sparta," in *RE* (1929), 1265–1373, esp. 1360–62: "Die Periegese des
Pausanias."

[19] See E. Meyer, "Messene," in *RE*, suppl. 15 (1978), 136–55, and "Messenien," in *RE*,
suppl. 15 (1978), 155–289, and the discussion in chap. 2, pp. 36–63.

[20] See A. Trendelenburg, *Pausanias in Olympia* (Berlin 1914); A. Mallwitz, *Olympia und
seine Bauten* (Munich 1972); H.-V. Herrmann, *Olympia: Heiligtum und Wettkampfstätte* (Munich 1972). The description of Olympia (V.7.1–VI.21.3) takes up one-eighth
(13 percent) of the entire work, whereas that of Delphi comes to only 7.75 percent; see
below, pp. 6–7.

[21] See M. Jost, "Pausanias en Mégalopolitide," *REA* 75 (1973): 241–67; "Sur les traces
de Pausanias en Arcadie," *RA*, 1974–75: 39–46.

[22] See P. Roesch, *Etudes béotiennes* (Paris 1982).

[23] See F. Schober, "Phokis," in *RE* (1941), 474–96.

[24] See G. Daux, *Pausanias à Delphes* (Paris 1936). Still of interest is H. Pomtow, "Delphoi," in *RE*, suppl. 4 (1924), 1189–1432, and the continuation in *RE*, suppl. 5 (1931),
61–152, by Pomtow and F. Schober.

[25] See W. Oldfather, "Lokris," in *RE* (1926), 1135–1288.

Rhodes, Cos, Samos, Chios, Lesbos, Samothrace, and Thasos) or those of the central Aegean (such as Crete and Delos). It might seem less natural that those close to mainland Greece, with the exception of Aegina, are also missing: Euboea, Andros, and others. On the other hand, Macedonia and Thrace are missing, but Pausanias certainly would not have considered them parts of Greece.

None of these omissions is troubling, but what does give rise to a serious problem is the fact that not even all of Greece proper is discussed. Parts of Locris are missing, and all of Aetolia, Acarnania, Epirus, and Thessaly (and its smaller borderlands).[26] To judge from Pausanias' work, the northern boundary of Greece would run from Thermopylae to Naupactus.[27]

Was his work really inscribed "Description of Greece" (Περιήγησις Ἑλλάδος)? Pausanias himself never cites a title. The traditional title is the one Stephanus of Byzantium uses occasionally (not more than three times, however, among the eighty quotations from the book; twice he just says "Description," and seventy-five times he only gives the name of the author).[28] But we do have, once, the author's own testimony that he indeed had the *whole of Greece* in mind. At a very early stage, when he is discussing the Athenian acropolis, he mentions an altar of the goddess Artemis, dedicated by the sons of Themistocles, and adds that this particular Artemis (Artemis Leukophryene) was at home in Magnesia on the Maeander, the city given to Themistocles by the Persian king. The observation is important since it explains why this altar was dedicated by the kin of the famous Athenian. Even so, Pausanias admonishes himself for this digression: "But I must pro-

---

[26] From VII.21.2 Meyer (p. 19f.) wants to deduce that Pausanias expressly excludes Aetolia and Acarnania from Greece. Pausanias narrates that the Calydonians in Aetolia applied to the oracle at Dodona in Epirus, "for the people who inhabited that part of the continent, to wit, the Aetolians and their neighbors the Acarnanians and Epirots, thought that. . . ." I fail to see how this could prove that these people were not Greeks in the eyes of the author.

[27] It is roughly the province of Achaea in Pausanias' time, which, however, also included Aetolia. Speaking of "Hellas" (Greece) in V.15.2, Pausanias actually means the province of Achaea. See also his explanation in VII.16.10 of why the Romans call the province "Achaea" instead of "Greece."

[28] In A. Meineke's edition p. 50, line 5, Παυσανίας ὀγδόῳ περιηγήσεως Ἑλλάδος; p. 108, line 16, δευτέρῳ περιηγήσεως Ἑλλάδος; p. 594, line 23, ἐν τρίτῳ περιηγήσεως Ἑλλάδος. Cf. p. 6, line 5, ἕκτῃ περιηγήσεως; p. 705, line 5, ὀγδόη περιηγήσεως. Heer (p. 11) rightly states that the title is uncertain, Gurlitt (p. 34) thought of Ἐξήγησις Ἑλλάδος (which would be only a trifle different from the usually accepted title), whereas Regenbogen (p. 1010) thinks the traditional title, Περιήγησις Ἑλλάδος, the most probable.

ceed, for I have to describe the whole of Greece." This is Frazer's translation, and it is accurate, though free; "all the Greek matters" would be closer to the actual wording, πάντα τὰ Ἑλληνικά.[29] Pausanias clearly intended to describe Greece in its entirety.

Two questions arise: Did Pausanias write more and is the remainder of the work lost? Or, alternatively, did he intend to write more, but not persevere or live long enough to carry out his intention? Either of these hypotheses would account for the fact that there is no epilogue (the work ends rather abruptly),[30] but the absence of an epilogue does not prove that the work is unfinished or incomplete, because, after all, there is no prooemium either.

Indeed, a few scholars think that there was an eleventh book, dedicated to Euboea, and Carl Robert, in 1909, even postulated three more books beyond that—XII–XIV—and went so far as to divine what they contained.[31] His speculations have not convinced others, for reasons that will soon appear, and they do not require further comment. However, the matter is different for the alleged book XI, since Stephanus does (or seems to) cite "Pausanias Book Eleven" in his article "Tamyna," a city of Euboea. This is the only reference to a book number higher than ten, and the only indication that there might once have been an eleventh book. The reference, however, has been explained, convincingly, as a mistake for "Book One" (IΑ' instead of Α') and in fact pertains not to Tamyna but to Tanagra, mentioned in Pausanias' first book.[32]

Pausanias, then, did not write more than ten books, but book X may be incomplete or its end lost, for a promise given in IX.23.7 (referring to a later treatment of Locris) seems not to have been fulfilled by what is said in X.38.1, the final chapter of the work as we have it.[33] The region in question, Opuntian Locris, was included in Pausanias' plan,

---

[29] I.26.4. Frazer, p. xxv: "the whole of Greece, or, more literally, all things Greek." The text runs Δεῖ δέ με ἀφικέσθαι τοῦ λόγου πρόσω, πάντα ὁμοίως ἐπεξιόντα τὰ Ἑλληνικά.

[30] Regenbogen, p. 1057, who considers the possibility that this may be intentional and another imitation of Herodotus. Nörenberg (above, n. 7) takes up this suggestion and elaborates on it.

[31] Robert, pp. 26, 61–64.

[32] A. Meineke, on p. 600 of his edition of Stephanus, where the entry "Tanagra" is the second next after "Tamyna." Meineke's opinion is approved by Gurlitt, p. 68 n. 13, and (with additional arguments) Regenbogen, p. 1011. See, however, A. Diller, TAPA 86 (1955): 274–75. The reference would be to I.34.1.

[33] Gurlitt, p. 2; Frazer, p. xxii; Heberdey, p. 107; Meyer, p. 20f. See also Regenbogen, p. 1046.

but the coverage is not thorough,[34] nor, moreover, is the description of Delphi, at least in comparison with the other descriptions in the work.[35] Pausanias either became tired or died before he could put the finishing touches to his work, but in any event only a very few pages can be missing.

A test of the completeness of the work is provided by the large number of cross-references—more than 100: 66 referring the reader back to earlier parts of the narrative, and some 35 anticipating matters and books still to come. All of them match existing passages[36] (with the one possible exception of the supposed "Book Eleven"). Most important seems the fact that there are many references in earlier books to books VIII–X, while not a single passage refers to any book beyond X.[37] And book X never refers to matters to be treated later, not even within the same book. In writing book X Pausanias saw the end of his job at hand.

Therefore the conclusion may be drawn that Pausanias did not write more than ten books and never intended to write more. The cross-references also prove that he planned in detail from the very beginning the outline of the whole work and the contents of the books: in the first book he is already referring the reader to matters that will eventually come only in books VIII and IX.[38] As scholars discerned long ago, Pausanias wrote the books, one after the other, in the order in which we have them,[39] and divided as we have them.[40]

Many scholars have argued that book I was published separately, long before the rest of the work.[41] Two reasons for this conclusion are given. First, in later books there are addenda to book I (which could

---

[34] Pritchett (above, n. 4), p. 147.

[35] Heberdey, pp. 96, 110; Daux (above, n. 24), p. 181; Heer, p. 46.

[36] This has always been observed. The fullest list of these references (although with some errors) can be found in S. Settis, *AnnPisa*, ser. 2, 37 (1968): 61–63: "Tavola delle citazioni interne di Pausania."

[37] References to book X: V.27.9; VI.12.9; VIII.37.1, 48.2; IX.2.4, 23.7; to book IX: I.24.5; II.19.8; IX.24.3, 32.5; to book VIII: I.41.2; IV.29.12; V.15.4; VI.2.4; VII.7.4, 8.6; VIII.5.9, 9.2, 47.3.

[38] I.24.5 cites IX.26.2; I.41.2 cites VIII.5.1.

[39] Gurlitt, p. 1; all others agree.

[40] A different opinion still in Meyer, p. 22, but see Pasquali, p. 221 ("Ich muss bekennen, dass ein nachalexandrinisches, nicht in Bücher eingeteiltes Werk für mich in den Bereich des schlechthin Unvorstellbaren gehört"), and Regenbogen, p. 1009.

[41] Gurlitt, pp. 2–3; Hitzig and Blümner, vol. 1, pt. 1 (1896), 115–16; Frazer, pp. xvii–xviii; Heberdey, p. 96; Robert, p. 217ff.; Meyer, p. 18. Against this assumption, Pasquali, p. 221f.; Regenbogen, p. 1010; A. Lesky, *Geschichte der griechischen Literatur*, 2d ed. (Bern and Munich 1963), 911.

have been inserted in their proper place had book I not already been made public). Second, some passages, occurring as early as in Book III, seem to be (in Frazer's view) Pausanias' response to criticism (so book I must have been known to critics).

One of the passages in question reads, "This seems to me a more probable account than the one I gave formerly," and is therefore not only an addition but also a correction.[42] It is, however, a very casual correction, and there is no cogent reason why Pausanias should have inserted this and similar additions to book I between the lines or in the margins of that book rather than in the later books (especially if the work was not copied during his lifetime). It does not warrant the conclusion that the first book had already been published when the passage was written. Furthermore, criticism does not presuppose publication: Pausanias may have given recitals, as Herodotus seems to have done; such recitals were a common practice also in Pausanias' day.[43] Moreover, it is far from certain that these passages are really meant to answer critics. The references in book I to material in books VIII and IX certainly do not support the assumption that this, and only this, book was published separately.[44]

So much can be deduced about the book, but what about the author? Who was Pausanias? And what do we know of his circumstances? The answer is that we know no more than he himself cares to tell us, and that is extremely little. From all of classical antiquity, during his lifetime and later, not a single note about him is preserved. And the same holds true for the Byzantine period, when so many learned men (the patriarch Photius, for instance) were interested in classical authors—not a whisper about Pausanias.

Since, however, Pausanias' date—in the second half of the second century A.D.—is known, numerous attempts have been made to identify him with one or another writer of the same period and the same name. For some time the suggestion that he was, in fact, none other than Pausanias of Damascus found favor,[45] but it is not worthwhile to

---

[42] This is VIII.5.1, referring to I.41.2.

[43] As Pausanias himself reports about Elis (VI.23.7): "In this gymnasium is also the Council House of the Eleans. Here are held exhibitions of extemporaneous eloquence and recitations of written works of every kind" (ἐπιδείξεις ἐνταῦθα λόγων αὐτοσχεδίων καὶ συγγραμμάτων παντοίων). See also Pliny *Ep.* 5.3.7–11, 8.21.2–4, 9.34.1.

[44] So Regenbogen, p. 1010; Nörenberg (above, n. 7), p. 240. Against the view that Pausanias was reacting to criticism, already Robert, p. 219.

[45] Kalkmann, p. 11; Robert, pp. 271–73; Pasquali, p. 222; O. Kern, *Die Religion der Griechen*, vol. 3 (Berlin 1938), 186; and, though reluctantly, Petersen, pp. 485–86

speculate how much would be gained if this identification were true, since Aubrey Diller has convincingly shown that the Damascene Pausanias was, in fact, much earlier; he wrote in the last quarter of the second century B.C. and composed the versified description of the ancient coastal regions that is commonly known as the work of Pseudo-Scymnus.[46] Diller has also demonstrated that our Pausanias cannot be identified with any other known writer of that name.[47] The "Description of Greece" itself is our only source of information about its author.

There is, alas, neither prooemium nor epilogue; the writer never mentions his name or his father's name or his city of birth. It is Stephanus alone who says the author's name is Pausanias, and we can only hope that Stephanus got this right. It has recently been said that Pausanias probably was a doctor, but the basis for such an assumption is extremely fragile.[48] Fortunately, however, Pausanias' time can be determined. In the fifth book, a passage (V.1.2) fixes a date: 217 years after Julius Caesar refounded the city of Corinth (which had been destroyed in 146 B.C.) as a Roman colony. Since the date of Corinth's revival is known to be 44 B.C., the passage was written in A.D. 174, during the reign of Marcus Aurelius. A slightly later date is provided by VIII.43.6, where Pausanias records this emperor's victory over the Germans (the Marcommani and Quadi in Bohemia) and Sarmatians. The victory can be dated to A.D. 175.[49] This passage is the latest within the work that can be verifiably dated; it may, of course, have been written a few years later, but hardly later than A.D. 180, since Marcus Aurelius, who died in that year, is the last emperor mentioned by Pausanias. (He mentions all of the emperors from A.D. 98 onward.) He also refers to the invasion of Greece by the barbaric tribe of the Costoboci, in either A.D. 170 or 171.[50] The conclusion is that Pausanias was still writing in

---

("Grieche, meinetwegen syrischer Grieche"). Against this view, Meyer, p. 14f.; Regenbogen, pp. 1012–13.

[46] A. Diller, "The Authors Named Pausanias," *TAPA* 86 (1955): 268–79, esp. 276ff.

[47] This was already Gurlitt's opinion (pp. 64–67).

[48] Levi 1:2: "Pausanias seems to have been a doctor; he was interested in questions of anatomy and personally devoted to the healing-god Asklepios." It is, however, not easy to see where Pausanias shows any substantial interest in anatomical matters; and there were certainly many more patients than doctors among those deeply devoted to Asclepius.

[49] P. Kneissl, *Die Siegestitulatur der römischen Kaiser* (Göttingen 1969), 107: late summer to fall of 175.

[50] X.34.5. For the invasion of the Costoboci see A. von Premerstein, "Kostoboken," in *RE* (1922), 1504–7; for the chronology, W. Zwikker, *Studien zur Markussäule* (Amster-

the later 170s, and that he probably finished writing sometime between 175 and 180.

It is not so clear when he began to write. A reference (II.27.6) to
Antoninus, Roman senator and benefactor of the shrine of Asclepius in
Epidaurus, was long believed to refer to Antoninus Pius before his ac-
cession to the throne in A.D. 138. If so, this passage must have been
written in the 130s.[51] The most recent commentator, Peter Levi, and
the most recent editor, Maria Helena Rocha-Pereira, are still uncertain
about this[52]—for no good reason, since it has long been clear from
Epicaurian inscriptions that the senator was, in fact, Sextus Julius
Maior Antoninus Pythodorus, whose floruit belongs to the 160s.[53]

In the same book (II.26.9), Pausanias says that a shrine and a temple
for Asclepius were built in Smyrna (Izmir) in his time, and he repeats
this information in VII.5.9. We know from the speeches of Aelius
Aristides that this Asclepieium was under construction in A.D. 151
and was completed in or before 166.[54] In another passage (on the
monuments of Patras) Pausanias praises the Music Hall, built in the
third century B.C., as the finest in Greece, except for the one in Athens,
which he describes as superior in size and construction: "It was built
by the Athenian Herodes in memory of his deceased wife" (VII.20.6).

---

dam 1941), 166–73; A. Birley, *Marcus Aurelius* (Boston 1966), 225, 229; A. Garzetti,
From Tiberius to the Antonines: A History of the Roman Empire A.D. 14–192 (London 1974), 491. See also below, pp. 176–80.
[51] Gurlitt, p. 61 n. 7, p. 442; Frazer, p. xvi.
[52] Levi 1:195 n. 161; Rocha-Pereira 3:197. B. Forte, too, thinks that the senator might
be the future emperor (*Rome and the Romans As the Greeks Saw Them* [Rome 1972],
331).
[53] Ch. Habicht, *Die Inschriften des Asklepieions*, Altertümer von Pergamon, vol. 8, pt. 3
(Berlin 1969), 63–66, no. 23; H. Halfmann, *Die Senatoren aus dem östlichen Teil des
Imperium Romanum bis zum Ende des 2. Jh. n. Chr.* (Göttingen 1979), 171–72, no. 89.
He was the descendant of a man whom King Mithridates Eupator hunted because of his
sympathies and support for Rome; this was Chairemon from Nysa, whose father was
likewise named Pythodorus (C. B. Welles, *Royal Correspondence in the Hellenistic Period* [New Haven 1934], nos. 73, 74). He was also related to King Cotys of Thrace (see
the stemma in *IG* IV.1², p. xxxiv). This connection explains why he also restored the
"Colonnade of Cotys" in Epidaurus, as reported by Pausanias, II.27.6. The correct identification in, for instance, Meyer, p. 578, and Roux (above, n. 16), p. 27.
[54] Ael. Aristides *or.* 50.102 (2:450 Keil), 47.17 (2:380 K.). For the chronology of the
events in question see A. Boulanger, *Aelius Aristide et la Sophistique dans la province
d'Asie au deuxième siècle de notre ère* (Paris 1923), 137–43; G. W. Bowersock, *Greek
Sophists in the Roman Empire* (Oxford 1969), 36–40; G. Alföldy, *Konsulat und Sena-
torenstand unter den Antoninen* (Bonn 1977), 214–17; R. Syme, *ZPE* 51 (1983):
278–79.

He is, of course, speaking of the magnificent building known as the Theater of Herodes Atticus, on the southern slope of the Acropolis, nowadays again the scene of musical and dramatic events. Pausanias continues: "In my book on Attica this Music Hall is not mentioned, because my description of Attica was finished before Herodes began to build the hall." Now, since Herodes' wife, Regilla, died in A.D. 160 or 161,[55] it is clear that Pausanias had already finished book I by that time. He must therefore have begun to write not later than, let us say, A.D. 155, and since he was still writing after A.D. 175, he must have spent at least twenty years on his work, writing, reading, traveling, and writing again.

Another indication, it may be noted, shows him at work after A.D. 165. After he has told the story of a heavyweight who won an Olympic crown but who, when he discovered, as he grew older, that his strength was diminishing, burned himself to death, Pausanias then adds, "In my opinion such deeds, whether they have been done in the past or shall be done hereafter, ought to be set down to the score of madness rather than courage." Since the incident in question belonged to the fifth century B.C., the sentence undoubtedly alludes to a more recent event, which can only be a famous incident during the Olympic games of A.D. 165, when the Cynic philosopher Peregrinus Proteus did what he had publicly announced: he lit a fire and flung himself onto the burning pyre in view of the festive crowd, which—in anticipation of the event—was even larger than usual.[56]

Book I was written first—all the other books contain references to it, invariably in the past tense.[57] And by the time Pausanias wrote it, he had already seen a good deal of the world, not only most of western Asia Minor and a good part of Egypt but also most of Greece, includ-

[55] A. Stein, *PIR* A².720; Halfmann (above, n. 53), p. 158. See also A. Diller, *TAPA* 86 (1955): 268; S. Follet, *REG* 90 (1977): 49.

[56] VI.8.4. It has more than once been assumed that this alludes to the end of Peregrinus Proteus: Gurlitt, p. 83 n. 40; Settis (above, n. 36), pp. 43–48. Furthermore, Frazer (p. xli) wanted to connect Pausanias' story about Chinese silk and the silkworm (VI. 26.6–9) with imperial ambassadors who seem to have arrived in China in October 166; see also M. P. Charlesworth, *Trade Route and Commerce of the Roman Empire* (Cambridge 1972), 72, 107–9. A. Dihle, however, disputes the connection, since Pausanias has a very unclear notion of where China is located—he wants to have it in the neighborhood of Ethiopia (*Antike und Orient: Gesammelte Aufsätze* [Heidelberg 1984], 204; cf. also 212–13, 83).

[57] They are to be found in II.19.8, 21.4, 23.6, 32.3; III.11.1, 17.3; IV.28.3, 35.4; V.10.4; VI.14.9, 20.14, 26.2; VII.3.4, 7.7, 20.6; VIII.5.1, 9.8 (cf. I.3.4); IX.6.5, 19.2, 19.4, 27.3; X.19.5, 20.5.

ing regions not treated in his work, such as Epirus and Thessaly. He must have been a fully grown man when he began to write. This accords well with his testimony (VIII.9.7) that he never saw Hadrian's favorite, Antinous, in the flesh, but only in paintings and statues, lasting testimonies of the emperor's emotional attachment to the boy, whom he even had deified. Antinous drowned in the Nile on October 30, 130. Pausanias seems to imply that he himself was already old enough, by the time of Antinous' death, to have seen him alive and to have been able to remember him. It is on the basis of this evidence, combined with the other indications already discussed, that Pausanias is commonly assumed to have been born around A.D. 115.[58] He must have written his work, then, between the ages (approximately) of forty and sixty-five.

Pausanias was thus the contemporary of some well-known writers: slightly younger than the famous sophist and lord of Athens Herodes Atticus, born in A.D. 101, millionaire and benefactor of many Greek cities, member of the Roman senate and consul in 143;[59] about the same age as the astronomer and geographer Claudius Ptolemy of Alexandria in Egypt, who, unlike Pausanias, was read and studied both in antiquity and during the Middle Ages. Pausanias was, it seems, a few years older than the satirist Lucian of Samosata on the Euphrates, the most brilliant writer of his century, and certainly the one who, next to the considerably older Plutarch, was to have the greatest impact on the literature of later centuries. And Pausanias was some fifteen years older than Galen of Pergamum, whose work was the culmination of ancient medicine; Galen was appointed the physician of the imperial family. In addition to these men there were numerous Greek sophists, celebrities in their own day, who will be discussed later;[60] for the moment, may it be said that it seems an irony of history that so much is known about these ambitious, influential, and arrogant but nonetheless shallow characters, while next to nothing is known about a substantial and sober man like Pausanias. A man much more serious than these sophists

[58] Meyer, p. 18; Regenbogen, p. 1010. Not later than A.D. 115 according to Robert, p. 270. Heer, who thinks (p. 12) that he was born in A.D. 125, seems to have misunderstood Diller (*TAPA* 86 [1955]: 269), to whom she is referring: "He had been born by then." I.5.5 indicates that Pausanias had been born when the tribe Hadrianis was created in Athens. Unfortunately, it is still an open question whether this was in A.D. 121/22 or 124/25 (S..Follet, *Athènes au II* siècle [Paris 1976], 116ff.).

[59] P. Graindor, *Un Milliardaire antique: Hérode Atticus et sa famille* (Cairo 1930); *PIR*[2] C. 802; Halfmann (above, n. 53), pp. 155–60; W. Ameling, *Herodes Atticus*, 2 vols. (Hildesheim 1983).

[60] See below, pp. 124–40.

was another contemporary of Pausanias, Julius Pollux from Naucratis in Egypt, a scholar like Ptolemy, and author of a learned, if controversial, lexicon of Attic words, terms, and institutions, whom the emperor Commodus, sometime after A.D. 180, appointed to the chair of rhetoric in Athens.

There are, in the second century A.D., far fewer equivalent figures in Latin literature, the outstanding one being Apuleius, a slightly younger contemporary of Pausanias (born ca. 125 in African Numidia), and author of the delightful work *The Golden Ass.*

Most of the figures mentioned are neither from Greece (Herodes being the only exception) nor from Rome or even Italy, but from the outlying provinces of the empire: from Asia, Egypt, Numidia, or, as in the case of Lucian, even farther away. A good many others could be named to give additional force to the statement that literature in the second century was mostly an affair of the provinces and Greek literature mostly an affair of the Greeks overseas.

This, then, is the moment to ask, where did Pausanias—this man who chose the Greek motherland as his subject—come from? Once the unfortunate identification with Pausanias of Damascus has been abandoned, there is no longer any need to dispute the clear indications pointing to Lydia in Asia Minor, in particular the region of Mount Sipylus. It is this region where, in 190 B.C., the Roman army, led by the brothers Scipio, destroyed the army of King Antiochus the Great.

Mount Sipylus, rising to some four and a half thousand feet southeast of Magnesia, was, in antiquity, the realm of King Tantalus and his children, Pelops and Niobe, all rather unfortunate individuals. Tantalus, in the well-known story, invited the gods to dinner and served them the butchered flesh of his own son, Pelops, to test whether they could tell what they were eating. They could, and he was punished with everlasting suffering. Niobe, who had been boasting to Leto about the number of her children, had to watch them all being killed by Leto's two children, Apollo and Artemis. Pelops, however, was revived by the gods and went on to win the hand of Hippodameia of Elis and to become the eponym of the Peloponnese.

This region, rich in old Anatolian and Greek myths, has been movingly depicted by Carl Humann, the man who discovered the Pergamum Altar.[61] Pausanias mentions Mount Sipylus time and again, and in such ways that there can be little doubt that he was brought up there. Since he must have been raised in a city with educational facili-

[61] *AthMitt* 13 (1888): 22–41.

ties, everything points to Magnesia on the Sipylus as his place of origin. Some scholars had already come to this conclusion in the early nineteenth century,[62] whereas others preferred Pergamum or some other place in Asia Minor. But Pergamum, a city of Mysia, is unlikely, since Pausanias knows Lydia best. IX.22.4 seems significant: Pausanias mentions blackbirds he has seen at Tanagra in Boeotia and adds, "These blackbirds are of the size of the Lydian birds." The place that comes to mind so easily and naturally for an incidental comparison must be home.

Within Lydia the indications point to the region of Mount Sipylus. In V.13.7, Pausanias says, "In my country there are still left signs that Pelops and Tantalus once dwelt in it. For there is a notable grave of Tantalus, and there is a lake called after him. Further, there is a throne of Pelops, on a peak of mount Sipylus, above the sanctuary of Mother Plastene. . . ." The lake has been identified as Lake Saloe, three miles east of Magnesia (VII.24.13; Pliny *HN* 5.31). Some four hundred yards above it is the throne of Pelops,[63] and the sanctuary of Mater Plastene was found nearby and identified in 1887 from dedications to the goddess.[64] Pausanias' description is as specific as it is accurate . . . and he calls the area *his own*. Some scholars have tried to deny the obvious sense of the passage and interpreted it as saying no more than that Pausanias lived there for some time.[65] No. He has told us that this is his home. And he simply knows too much about the region for it not to be home. Three times he has seen large swarms of locusts disappear from Mount Sipylus: "Once they were swept away by a storm that broke over them: once they were destroyed by intense heat following after rain; and once they were caught in a sudden cold and perished. All this I have seen happen to them" (I.24.8). Since such a disaster hardly befell the locusts every year, the implication is that Pausanias lived close to the mountain for a long time and visited it often.

[62] This conclusion was reached by C. G. Siebelis in 1819 (*Quaestio de Pausaniae periegetae patria et aetate*, Programm Bautzen [*non vidi*]) and by A. Boeckh in 1824 (now *KlSchr*, vol. 4 [Leipzig 1874], 209 n. 4, in which Boeckh is referring to Siebelis).

[63] VII.24.13; Pliny *HN* 5.31. As for the "grave of Tantalus," various suggestions have been made, but no certain identification seems possible (J. Keil, "Lydia," in *RE* [1927], 2166–67).

[64] *AthMitt* 12 (1887): 253, no. 17, and 271–74; *BCH* 11 (1887): 300, no. 8. All conjectures about the name of the goddess have been proven wrong by the epigraphic evidence (Πλακιανή, Πλαιζηνή, Μοστηνή); Pausanias is right. See also J. and L. Robert, *Bull. épigr.*, 1979: 360.

[65] So Kalkmann, pp. 11, 276; Robert, p. 271; A. Diller, *TAPA* 86 (1955): 270.

In ten passages,[66] Pausanias describes rivers, monuments, and birds he has seen in the region, and people performing an epichorial dance. As Frazer once remarked, "It is fair to surmise that Pausanias was born and bred not far from the mountains which he seems to have known and loved so well."[67] In an overlooked passage in his book on Athens, Pausanias speaks of the First Mithridatic War (88–84 B.C.), in which the Athenians defected to the Pontic king. The Roman commander Sulla encircled both the city and the Piraeus, which was defended by a large Pontic army under Archelaus, the most able of Mithridates' generals. Archelaus is a famous man; Pausanias, however, introduces him with the following sentence: "He was a general of Mithridates whom the people of Magnesia on the Sipylus wounded, when he attacked them, and they killed most of the barbarians" (I.20.5).

The main point is certainly true, since Appian, in his history of the war, describes how the king overran all of Roman Asia and many important cities joined him, including Magnesia on the Maeander; Appian adds that only a very few resisted and Mithridates sent his generals to reduce them. One of these cities is "Magnesia," which must be the city by Mount Sipylus.[68] Why does Pausanias introduce Archelaus with the story of the heroic resistance of Magnesia rather than one of Archelaus' major victories? Pausanias was a patriot: the men resisting the mighty king were his fellow citizens from the past, worth remembering after 250 years. We may safely conclude that Pausanias was a citizen of Magnesia on Mount Sipylus.[69]

[66] I.21.3; II.22.3; III.22.4; VI.22.1; VII.24.13, 27.12; VIII.2.7, 17.3, 38.10; X.4.6.

[67] Frazer, p. xix.

[68] App. *Mith.* 82 (cf. 250). Other testimonies are collected in Th. Ihnken, *Die Inschriften von Magnesia am Sipylos* (Bonn 1978), 161–62, T 19–22. An interesting document of Archelaus from a private collection has recently been published (*BCH* 105 [1981]: 566, no. 7, and fig. 48). It is an inscription on a silver bracelet (fig. 1): "In Piraeus. The general Archelaus gives this to Apollonius, son of Apollonius, a Syrian, as a reward for braveness" ('Εν Πειραιεῖ· 'Αρχέλαος στρατοπεδάρχης 'Απολλωνίωι 'Απολλωνίου Σύρωι ἀριστεῖον). This dates from 86 B.C., when Sulla was besieging Archelaus in the Piraeus.

[69] This had also once been Wilamowitz' view, if for the wrong reason. He thought that Pausanias had transferred a deed of Magnesia on the Maeander to the town on Mount Sipylus ("Dass Pausanias diese Ruhmestat auf Magnesia am Sipylos überträgt, spricht dafür, dass er wirklich diesem angehörte": *KlSchr*, vol. 5, pt. 2 [Berlin 1937], 363). See, however, Th. Reinach, *Mithridates Eupator*, German edition translated by A. Götz (Leipzig 1895), 122 n. 2; W. Ruge, "Magnesia," in *RE* (1928), 473; F. Geyer, "Mithridates," in *RE* (1932), 2170; D. Magie, *Roman Rule in Asia Minor* (Princeton 1950), 1102–3; R. Bernhardt, "Imperium und Eleutheria" (diss., Hamburg 1971), 132 n. 224: all agree that Pausanias is right. Wilamowitz, perhaps realizing that he had made a mis-

Fig. 1. Silver bracelet, 86 B.C.

Men like Pausanias came from affluent families that could afford to provide their sons with a solid education. They belonged to the municipal aristocracy, and in the province of Asia in the time of Pausanias they were more likely than not to have become Roman citizens.[70] The amount of traveling he did, both before and after he began to write, could not have been undertaken by a poor man. He has visited almost all of western Asia Minor and substantial parts of central Asia Minor, that is to say, the Troad, Mysia (he knows Pergamum well), Ionia (Ephesus is familiar territory), Caria, Phrygia, Galatia, and Lycia. He has been east to the Euphrates, and through Syria and Palestine, of which he speaks as an eyewitness.

He says that he never saw Babylon or Susa, but he did visit Egypt and see the Pyramids, the oasis of Ammon at Siwa, and the famous colossus of Memnon near Thebes. In the North he has seen Byzantium and the island of Thasos; in the Aegean he has seen Rhodes, Delos, Andros, and Aegina and in the West Rome, Campania (including Capua, Cumae, and Puteoli), and Metapontum (in southern Italy). He may also have been to Sardinia, and has probably been to the Liparian Islands north of Sicily, though perhaps not to Sicily itself.[71] Such travels were immensely expensive; his contemporary Apuleius, who studied in Athens and then did a tour, spent most of his inherited fortune on his travels—no less than one million sesterces.[72] Pausanias traveled even more than Apuleius and undoubtedly spent even more money.

In such wide travels and visits to important centers of cultural and social life, like Pergamum, Ephesus, Smyrna, Athens, Alexandria, and Rome, all of which were thriving metropolises in his time, he was bound to meet high officials of the imperial administration, members of the social elite (as it was in the different provinces and cities),[73] writ-

take, or withdrawing his former opinion, or forgetful of it, later wrote that it was still an open question where Pausanias came from (*Der Glaube der Hellenen*, vol. 2 [Berlin 1932], 508). For Siebelis and Boeckh, see above, n. 62. The following also declare themselves in favor of Magnesia on Mount Sipylus as Pausanias' place of origin: Gurlitt, p. 130; Frazer, p. xix; Meyer, p. 15; Levi, 1:295 n. 133; L. Robert, *RN*, ser. 6, 18 (1976): 28–29.
[70] The suggestion that Pausanias probably lacked Roman citizenship (Forte [above, n. 52], pp. 418–19) is unfounded—we do not know, but the odds are that he possessed it.
[71] References in Frazer, pp. xx–xxii. Heberdey's book restricts itself, as the title indicates, to Pausanias' journeys in Greece.
[72] *Apol.* 23; *Met.* 11.27–28.
[73] See F. Millar, *JRS* 71 (1981): 69: "A network of relationships connects the local aristocrats of different Greek cities."

ers, scholars as they worked (as he must have so often) in one of the great libraries,[74] and famous artists and athletes. Pausanias does, indeed, refer to a few identifiable contemporaries: the emperors Hadrian, Antoninus Pius, and Marcus Aurelius, two Roman senators of Greek origin, Herodes Atticus and Antoninus Pythodorus, and another such senator's father, Claudius Saethida.[75] He also mentions a Roman senator of his own time who won an Olympic victory, but he does not give his name;[76] he does name two other Olympic victors of his time, Granianus of Sicyon and Mnesibulus of Elatea.[77] These few names exhaust the list of his identifiable contemporaries. The list is strangely brief, and, what is even stranger, Pausanias never refers to any relative or friend or, it seems, any contemporary writer, and only two or three times to a casual personal acquaintance of his.[78]

From his reserved attitude toward the celebrities of his day it may be concluded that Pausanias was modest and discreet. He had a purpose; boasting about famous friends and connections would not contribute to that purpose; and he had no desire to enhance his own image, or, indeed, to use his work to gain influence with an influential man. In his time, writers commonly would dedicate their work, poor as it might be, to a famous person—to a Roman senator or the reigning emperor. Marcus Aurelius, for instance, was the recipient of a collection of stratagems written by the undistinguished Macedonian Polyaenus, of Oppian's poem on fishing (*Halieutica*), and of Herodian's *General Prosody*.[79] Pausanias' work, it is true, may once have had just such a dedication, but, considering the style of the man and the character of his work, to make such an assumption would be extremely hazardous.

---

[74] Several passages in the work reflect serious studies in libraries on specific questions, for instance IV.2.2; V.23.3; VI.3.5, 3.11, 4.4, 9.1.

[75] Hadrian is often mentioned (see Rocha-Pereira 3:190, in the "Index historicus"); Antoninus Pius is mentioned in VIII.43.1–6, Marcus Aurelius in VIII.43.6; Herodes Atticus occurs in I.19.6, II.1.7, VI.21.2, VII.20.6, and X.32.1, Antoninus Pythodorus in II.27.6, the Messenians Claudius Saethida, father and son, in IV.32.2 (see further Halfmann [above, n. 53], 174, no. 93a; 196, no. 127).

[76] V.20.8. For the disputed question of his identity see app. 2.

[77] For Granianus see II.11.8 and L. Moretti, *Olympionikai* (Rome 1957), 163, no. 848. For Mnesibulus see X.34.5. Mnesibulus was victorious in the short race and in the race of armed men in A.D. 161, and lost his life while fighting against the Costoboci (above, p. 9) ten years later, as Pausanias says. His son erected a statue in his honor in Elatea (*SIG*³ 871).

[78] See below, pp. 144f.

[79] Polyaenus *Strat.* 1.1: ἱερώτατοι βασιλεῖς Ἀντωνῖνε καὶ Οὐῆρε; Oppian *Halieut.* 1.3: γαίης ὕπατον κράτος, Ἀντωνῖνε.

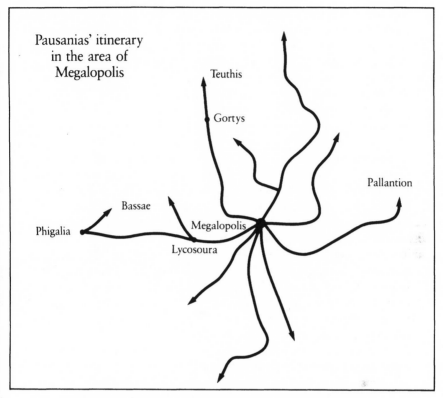

Pausanias' itinerary
in the area of
Megalopolis

Teuthis

Gortys

Pallantion

Bassae

Phigalia

Megalopolis

Lycosoura

Fig. 2. Route of Pausanias in the area of Megalopolis.

Pausanias spent at least twenty years and a substantial fortune to write his book, but what kind of a book is it?

The guiding principle is geographic: one district of Greece is treated and then another. Except for the first book (Attica), the arrangement of each book is strictly topographical. Pausanias, as all scholars admit, was still experimenting when he wrote the first book, and had not yet fully developed a standard procedure.[80] From the beginning of book II, however, his methodology is established. Pausanias moves from the

[80] Gurlitt, pp. 12–13, with the interesting observation that only in book I are all the stories that are taken from written sources (λόγοι) connected with one or another of the monuments described (θεωρήματα); idem, p. 274: "Das erste Buch ist eben ungeschickter gearbeitet als die folgenden"; Heberdey, p. 96: "eine gewisse Unerfahrenheit des Autors in der Behandlung seiner Aufgabe"; "unvollständige Ausbildung schriftstellerischer Eigentümlichkeiten"; Frazer, p. xxiii; Meyer, p. 18. See, however, the evaluation of book I in Regenbogen, pp. 1014–17.

border by the shortest route to the capital, describes what is to be seen there, takes another road to the border, describing what seems worth recording, and then, returning to the capital and taking another road, continues until he finally crosses the border to another district, where again he goes straight to its center [81] (as with Corinth, Argos, Sparta, Mantinea, Megalopolis, Tegea, and Thebes).[82]

The organization of his book makes patent his intention: the book was meant to be a guide for travelers who he hoped would follow the same route from point to point. His organization and intention are most obvious at a site with plenty to see (like the Athenian agora, Olympia, or Delphi); the author's aim of providing a guide very much like our Baedeker or Blue Guide is undeniable.

There is, however, another side to the coin. A Greek district is not an artificial creation but a region with a past, in myth as well as history, and with a distinct ethnic element, often with a particular dialect, different from its neighbors', and specific forms of religion, cult, and patterns of life. Pausanias always (book I being the exception) begins a book with a general introduction to the myths, heroes, migrations, and history of the district, and often introduces single cities in the same way. Historical passages are also inserted to explain a given monument. These passages are usually called "digressions" if they occur outside the introduction at the beginning of a book, but they are integral parts of the whole, meant to be of no less importance than the actual descriptions of buildings, monuments, or works of art. Myth and history play an important part in the work. Pausanias tells us this himself: "Such are, in my opinion, the most famous of the Athenian

---

[81] This was first observed by G. Hirschfeld (*AZ* 40 [1882]: 122), who was followed by Gurlitt (p. 21), Frazer (pp. xxiii–xxiv), and others. The method is nicely illustrated in the map of the region of Megalopolis (see fig. 2, p. 19 this work) in M. Jost, "Pausanias en Mégalopolitide," *REA* 75 (1973): 241–67, opposite p. 242.

[82] Frazer (4:91) remarks in this context, "It is worthy of note how often Pausanias carries his itinerary of a route up to the border of the province he is describing, then drops it, but only to resume and continue it across the border when he comes to deal with the next province." After a reference to various examples of Pausanias' procedure, Frazer concludes, "This piecing together of the routes, this picking up the thread of description exactly at the point where the plan of his book had compelled him to drop it shows how carefully Pausanias planned and edited his work." See also Heberdey, p. 74. The remarkable thing about Frazer's words is where he chooses to insert them: the occasion is VI.21.3, not the first example of Pausanias' method, where they could have been inserted, but the very paragraph that in 1873 irritated Wilamowitz so much and caused his contempt for Pausanias (see app. 1, pp. 165–75; cf. Wilamowitz' own testimony, p. 170 nn. 30, 31).

traditions [λόγοι] and sights [θεωρήματα]; from the mass of materials I have aimed from the outset at selecting the really notable."[83]

His aim was to record the most memorable features on two levels: λόγοι and θεωρήματα. The first term means "words," whether spoken or written; the second refers to what you can *see*. The *logoi* are not subordinate to the *theoremata*, not digressions but an integral part of the descriptions of what can be seen. Now, whereas Pausanias is a *witness* to everything that can be seen (and consequently can be checked by anyone who passes by the objects as long as they are still there and still intact), for the oral or written tradition he is dependent on sources, be these works of literature, the tales of citizens, or the explanations of guides, and he is only a *transmittor*.[84]

This distinction is fundamental to understanding his work. Sometimes the *logoi* predominate over the *theoremata*. Messenia, the subject of book IV, was a region of Greece that for centuries had been subject to Sparta and, consequently, had no history of its own and only a small number of important sites and monuments. The description of the long struggle between the Messenians and the Spartans fills most of the book (IV.4–27). This case is exceptional, but it shows, as do the other passages on mythology or history, that Pausanias wanted his book to be read at home for pleasure and edification. Pausanias has taken great pains to make it an interesting book to read; he has made every effort to provide variety in substance as well as in style, in order to hold the interest of his audience.[85]

Pausanias wanted to kill two birds with one stone: he wanted to provide a reliable guide for travelers and to produce a literary piece that would entertain as it informed.[86] He worked hard to achieve both

---

[83] I.39.3. The distinction between the two has, of course, always been noticed. See especially Robert, pp. 8–38, 39–68. That the two have equal rank has correctly been observed by Nörenberg (above, n. 7), pp. 238–39. The passage quoted is the only instance where Pausanias uses the word θεώρημα. The same juxtaposition occurs in Dem. De Cor. 68: the Athenians see every day the memorials of their forefathers' virtues ἐν πᾶσι καὶ λόγοις καὶ θεωρήμασι, "in allem was ihr hört und seht" (Blass). The meaning of λόγοι there is different, but the meaning of θεώρημα is exactly the same as in the passage from Pausanias.

[84] For the role of guides in Pausanias' work, see below, p. 145.

[85] See A. Engeli, *Die oratio variata bei Pausanias* (Berlin 1907), and Robert, Pasquali, and Strid. Robert remarks, "Es ist vielleicht das Charakteristischste an dem Stil dieses Autors, dass er bis zum höchsten Grad der Manieriertheit die Gleichförmigkeit vermeiden und den Leser durch unerwartete Wendungen überraschen will" (p. 210).

[86] It is for this reason that opinions of scholars differ as to what Pausanias intended his work primarily to be: a guidebook according to some (Gurlitt in his Preface, and passim;

ends, but his efforts were bound to fail because of his ambivalence of purpose. The audience he had in mind did not exist. The literary parts increased the book's length and weight and made it hard to use on the road. (Imagine handling the stack of bookrolls in the heat of a summer day in Arcadia and trying to find the passage describing, let us say, the temple of Apollo at Bassae.) On the other hand, those who wanted to read about the Messenian wars would not want to have to read eighteen pages of the description of every detail of the paintings with which Polygnotus had decorated a building at Delphi (X.25–31). A person wanting information on the Olympic victors had easy access to complete lists of victors (such lists, from Pausanias' time, have been found, for instance, in the small Egyptian village of Oxyrhynchus),[87] and certainly had no use for Pausanias' painstaking description of the 203 most notable statues of victors standing in the sanctuary of Olympian Zeus (VI.1–18). Other reasons may have contributed to his failing to find the audience he had hoped for, but the main reason must have been his ambivalence of purpose.

Pausanias rarely indicates his aim, and never explicitly. He does repeatedly reaffirm that he is including only a select part of a mass of material, and once he adds that the choice is his own (II.34.11). He explains frequently that he wants to present "the things most worthy of mention,"[88] or (a few times) "the most memorable things,"[89] or (once only) "the things most worth seeing."[90] The fullest and clearest statement of his intentions is found in III.11.1, at the beginning of the description of Sparta:

To prevent misconceptions, I stated in my "Attica" that I had not described everything, but only a selection of the most remarkable objects. This principle I will now repeat before I describe Sparta. From the outset, I aimed at sifting

---

Frazer, p. xxiv; Petersen, p. 485ff.; Meyer, pp. 30–33; R. E. Wycherley, *GRBS* 2 [1959]: 28; 4 [1963]: 158; E. Gabba, *JRS* 71 [1981]: 60), a piece of literature for reading at home according to others (Wilamowitz in many instances throughout his life, among them *Der Glaube der Hellenen*, vol. 2 [Berlin 1932], 508; Kalkmann, passim; Robert, passim; Pasquali, p. 192).

[87] Pausanias often refers to official lists kept by the Eleans: III.21.1; V.21.9; VI.2.3, 4.2, 8.3, 13.10, 22.3; X.36.9 (private lists: VI.6.3, 8.1). The list from Oxyrhynchus is *POxy* 222 (bibliography in R. A. Pack, *The Greek and Latin Literary Texts from Greco-Roman Egypt*, 2d ed. [Ann Arbor 1965], 119, no. 2188).

[88] τὰ ἀξιολογώτατα or τὰ μάλιστα λόγου ἄξια: for instance, II.13.3, 14.4, 29.1; III.11.1; V.21.1; VI.17.1; X.9.1.

[89] τὰ μάλιστα ἄξια μνήμης: for instance, II.34.11; III.11.1; VI.17.1, 23.1; VIII.54.7.

[90] τὰ μάλιστα θέας ἄξια: VIII.10.1.

the most valuable traditions out of the mass of insignificant stories which are current among every people. My plan was adopted after mature deliberation, and I will not depart from it.

The author of a work that pretends to be a guide to sites such as Athens, Olympia, or Delphi perforce must be selective. The very process of selection provides an insight into the taste of the author. In general, Pausanias preferred the old to the new, the sacred to the profane.[91] In his description of the Athenian agora, for instance, he includes a number of modest old buildings but omits the large and magnificent Stoa of Attalus, built around the middle of the second century B.C.; in his descriptions of Olympia and Delphi, or, for that matter, in any other part of the book, Pausanias hardly mentions any building or work of art or artist later than the third century B.C.[92]

No recent artist is praised like the old masters. Pausanias makes it clear that the oldest works, such as the wooden statues, unpolished as they are, are, to him, the most venerable, and those of the late archaic and classical periods, that is to say, of the fifth century B.C., are the most perfect products of Greek art. A predilection for the old was, of course, common in his time, in literature as well as in art. Pausanias shared this preference.[93]

Distinctly personal, on the other hand, is Pausanias' predilection for the sacred as opposed to the profane. He prefers sanctuaries, shrines, and the images of gods and goddesses to public buildings or secular statues. He grows warmer when he describes objects belonging to the gods and to the dead. His long account of the Kerameikos, the Athenian burial ground where the heroes of the glorious past lay in state (I.29), is one of the few passages in his work where his feelings really show in a moving way, which is the more remarkable in view of the fact that the latest of the graves he mentions date back to some 450 years before his own time.[94] This chapter has been called "the memo-

---

[91] This has often been recognized. See, for instance, Frazer, p. xxxiii: "The monuments described are generally ancient, not modern; . . . they are for the most part religious, not profane"; F. H. Sandbach, in CAH, vol. 11 (1936), 689: "He was much more interested in religious than in civic monuments"; Daux (above, n. 24), p. 177: "Il a le goût de vieilles choses"; Meyer, p. 46; Regenbogen, p. 1090; R. E. Wycherley, GRBS 2 (1959): 24: "His interests are mainly religious and antiquarian"; Casson (above, n. 12), p. 296: "It is when he gets to the sanctuaries and temples that he lets himself go"; Heer, p. 110.
[92] For Olympia see Gurlitt, p. 341ff., for Delphi Daux (above, n. 24), p. 173.
[93] More on this below, pp. 130–37.
[94] I.29.10, 13; both graves are from the eighties of the third century B.C.

rial plaque of Athenian victories and defeats, full of ethical spirit."[95]

Pausanias was selective and he had his preferences, but he still intended to be as complete as possible and to include all the sites in any
given area of Greece. Had he decided to describe only the most remarkable and the richest sites—Athens, Corinth, Argos, Mycenae,
Epidaurus, Tegea, Megalopolis, Sparta, Bassae, Olympia, Oropus,
Thebes, Orchomenus, and Delphi—he would still have performed a
great service, but he wanted to provide an exhaustive guide, which
would cover every place that had anything memorable to show.[96]

He discusses small, insignificant, remote, and barely accessible sites
if they had at least one object worth seeing: "The plan of my work
requires of me to describe Pallantium, if there is anything notable
there" (VIII.43.1). He made every effort to reach places where he
thought something of interest was to be seen, whether he had read
about it or been told about it, and no matter whether the sites were
deserted, or whether he had to climb several thousand feet or endure
hardship to get there.

He did not always reap the rewards of his efforts, and sometimes,
when a promising site has turned out to be in ruins, his disappoint-
ment shows. But how many sites that were once important but fell into
obscurity would be unknown, would never have been found and excavated, would not have yielded their works of art, their important inscriptions, or their remains of famous buildings, had he not endured,
had he not gone there and recorded their locations and what had once
been there! And how many artifacts and finds would not have been
understood without his narrative!

If through the centuries Pausanias was never read, nevertheless the
question still remains whom he expected to read him. Nowhere does
he state this explicitly. Scholarly guesses have differed: "not necessarily
Greeks" (Hermann Hitzig and Hugo Blümner); "primarily Greeks of
Asia Minor" (Otto Regenbogen); "Roman philhellenes" (Peter Levi).
Joyce Heer maintains that he addressed, above all, the public of the
eastern Mediterranean, not so much the inhabitants of Greece proper,
and also the Romans, whereas Glen Bowersock says, "The audience
for which Pausanias wrote was almost certainly Greek rather than Ro-

[95] Regenbogen, p. 1010: "die Ehrentafel athenischer Siege und Niederlagen, keineswegs
ohne Ethos."
[96] Heberdey, p. 112; Meyer, p. 30: "In der Nennung der Ortschaften, Städte und Heilig-
tümer ist ausserhalb Attikas ganz offensichtlich auch annähernde Vollständigkeit beab-
sichtigt und im ganzen auch erreicht."

man. . . . It is not unreasonable to suppose that his work was explicitly designed to introduce the literate peoples of Greater Hellas—Greece and Asia Minor—to their fatherland and its treasures."[97]

One point is immediately apparent: Pausanias expected his readers to understand Greek. And since nobody could claim to be educated who could not read Greek, such readers would be found all over the empire. Therefore, the answer to the question just asked could well be that Pausanias had all these in mind (Greeks wherever they lived as well as Romans), provided they had a real interest in the heritage and treasures of Greece.

His frequent use of the expression "the Greeks" (οἱ ῞Ελληνες) has been taken as an indication that he envisages an audience that does not include the inhabitants of Greece proper; some twenty times he speaks of "the Greeks" as though he were dissociating himself from them and explaining their manners to foreigners,[98] as "the Greeks" have a certain proverb, certain customs, certain myths, or "the Greeks" use certain expressions or admire foreign marvels more than their own.[99] Several scholars have concluded that such expressions suit an author who thinks his readers may not be Greek and does not count himself among the Greeks.[100] This conclusion seems extreme.

First, in a good many of the instances in which Pausanias speaks of "the Greeks" he ought to be understood to mean "*we* the Greeks." This is a well-known and long-standing figure of speech, the most famous example of which occurs in the Milesian Hecataeus' "The stories of the Greeks are numerous and seem to me ludicrous"[101] (echoed faintly by Pausanias, VIII.53.5: "The stories of the Greeks are mostly at variance, and not the least in the matter of genealogy").[102] Both authors are referring to traditional stories told wherever Greeks lived; obviously they do not dissociate themselves from the Greeks. Similarly,

---

[97] Hitzig and Blümner, vol. 1, pt. 2, pp. 553–54; Regenbogen, pp. 1013, 1032, 1048, 1093; Levi 1:1; Heer, p. 27; G. W. Bowersock, "Pausanias," in *Greek Literature*, vol. 1 of *The Cambridge History of Classical Literature*, ed. P. E. Easterling and E. J. Kenney (forthcoming).

[98] Hitzig and Blümner, vol. 1, pt. 2, pp. 553–54; Heer, p. 27.

[99] Proverbs: IX.30.1, X.1.7; customs: V.27.10, VII.17.7; foreign marvels: IX.36.5.

[100] So, in addition to others already cited, Heberdey, p. 115f.

[101] *FGrHist* 1 F 1: οἱ γὰρ ῾Ελλήνων λόγοι πολλοί τε καὶ γελοῖοι, ὡς ἐμοὶ φαίνονται, εἰσίν.

[102] οἱ μὲν δὴ ῾Ελλήνων λόγοι διάφορα τὰ πλέονα καὶ οὐχ ἥκιστα ἐπὶ τοῖς γένεσίν εἰσι. Similarly IX.16.7: διάφορα δὲ καὶ τὰ λοιπὰ ὡς τὸ πολὺ ἀλλήλοις λέγουσιν ῞Ελληνες, "Indeed, Greek traditions are generally discrepant."

in Pausanias' time the provincial assembly of Asia called itself (as it had for two hundred years) "the Greeks in Asia"[103]—Greeks like those of the motherland, but living apart from them.

The strongest proof that Pausanias regarded himself as Greek is provided by VII.23.7–8, in a dialogue between himself and a Phoenician from Sidon. The Sidonian tried to persuade Pausanias that the Phoenicians had a better understanding of the gods than the Greeks; Pausanias cut him short with the statement that Greeks had always known what the Phoenician was trying to teach him.[104] Pausanias speaks here as a Greek, responding to foreign arrogance with Greek arrogance.

But when Pausanias states that Greeks have certain expressions for certain things or a certain title for a poem of Hesiod, he clearly intends these explanations for foreigners, since in these instances Pausanias is drawing on and explaining what is common to all Greeks wherever they may live.[105] He therefore also had non-Greeks in mind as part of his audience, probably above all Romans.

He also wrote specifically for Greeks, as is clear from his lengthy digression on Sardinia: "My reason for introducing this account of Sardinia into my description of Phocis is that the island is but little known to the Greeks" (X.17.13). Pausanias wants to improve the knowledge of Greeks. The passage also seems to justify the assumption that he wrote primarily for Greeks, as does the following passage: "That Perseus was the founder of Mycenae is known to every Greek, but I will narrate the cause of its foundation" (II.15.4). He is obviously attempting to increase the common knowledge of Greeks; he is directing this account to their, not to any foreigner's, attention.

Greeks within Greece proper and abroad as well as Greek-speaking foreigners were all part of the audience for which Pausanias wrote, but he seems to have failed with all of them. The work, published around A.D. 180, came too late. The tide of philhellenism was already ebbing.[106] We are all the more fortunate that our author persisted in completing his task and that his manuscript survived. Notwithstanding his weaknesses and shortcomings (some of which will be exposed in due

---

[103] οἱ ἐπὶ τῆς Ἀσίας Ἕλληνες. See J. Deininger, *Die Provinziallandtage der römischen Kaiserzeit von Augustus bis zum Ende des dritten Jahrhunderts n. Chr.* (Munich 1965), 36–60.

[104] The decisive words are ἐγὼ δὲ ἀποδέχεσθαι μὲν τὰ εἰρημένα, οὐδὲν ⟨δὲ⟩ τι Φοινίκων μᾶλλον ἢ καὶ Ἑλλήνων ἔφην τὸν λόγον. More on this episode below, p. 157ff.

[105] Expressions: V.17.6, on the archaic fashion of writing βουστροφηδόν. Title: II.16.4, IX.36.7, referring to the epic that the Greeks call the "Great Eoeae."

[106] Regenbogen, p. 1093.

course), there can be no doubt that F. H. Sandbach (speaking of Greek literature under the Romans, which was dominated by rhetoric often without content) makes a valid point: "Pausanias . . . may serve to remind us that there was still conventional ability working with honest diligence." [107]

It is indeed a blessing that what this loner achieved can still be read today.

[107] Sandbach (above, n. 91), p. 689.

II

PAUSANIAS AS A GUIDE

In writing his book, Pausanias had two goals: to provide a reliable guide for tourists and to produce a work of literature. On both counts he missed the audience he aimed at. His book was not read in antiquity, for the very reason that its purpose was ambiguous (pp. 21f.). Widespread interest came only in modern times, first from classical scholars who used the information Pausanias has to offer about sites, monuments, works of art, mythography, history, cults, religion, and the like, and then from participants in sight-seeing tours of Greece once they became fashionable.[1] Most modern readers are interested primarily in his descriptions of sites. They consult mainly those parts of the work in which Pausanias speaks as an eyewitness, and less his stories about the myths, gods, and history of Greece. Since our author is generally consulted in this way and is at his best when he reports what he himself has seen, we should consider him first as a witness or guide.

Pausanias describes several hundred sites. Sometimes, when the sites are small towns, or shrines in ruins, or otherwise unremarkable, his account is brief—a single sentence or paragraph suffices—but there are many other sites, like the city of Athens or the sanctuary of Apollo at Delphi, that contain a multitude of important buildings and monuments. Pausanias spends more than sixty pages on each of these and

[1] The English translation of Pausanias by Peter Levi in two volumes of the Penguin Books (1971) is meant as a companion for tourists, and it was concern for the supposed needs of travelers in Greece that made Levi alter the original order of the books.

still passes over some remarkable objects; his description of the shrine of Zeus at Olympia, the holiest of all holy places in Greece, runs to some 110 pages (V.7–VI.21).

A separate book (or more) would be required to follow Pausanias closely through any one of these sites. A single chapter cannot deal systematically with his account of them, but various remarks on Athens, Delphi, and Olympia will be discussed in various sections of this book. Fortunately, as these sites are the most famous in Greece, there are excellent guidebooks that assess the significance of Pausanias' remarks on them in detail.[2]

This chapter aims, rather, to convey a general impression of what Pausanias has to offer and to assess the value of his account through his descriptions of other familiar, or less familiar, sites. It will emphasize those sites that had not yet been excavated at the turn of the century, when the two major commentaries on Pausanias—by Sir James Frazer (in six volumes) and Hermann Hitzig and Hugo Blümner (in three volumes in six parts)—were published. It will also emphasize those sites that, although partially known, yielded their most important results only recently. A few words about a familiar site may serve as a prelude.

MYCENAE

In little more than one page (II.16), Pausanias describes the myths that are told about Mycenae's foundation, the destruction of the town by the Argives in 468 B.C., and the ruins as he saw them, beginning with the famous Lion Gate (II.16.3–7). This single page is the origin of what may be called professional archaeology.

Heinrich Schliemann, who was not a scholar by profession but who may well deserve the honor of being considered archaeology's founder,[3] simply read this passage with greater care than the professionals. Pausanias says that the graves of Atreus, Agamemnon, and those slain with Agamemnon are "inside the wall."[4] The professionals had understood the "wall" to be the outer wall of the town, but Schliemann recognized

---

[2] For Delphi, Olympia, and Corinth see above, p. 4 nn. 24, 20, and 16; for Athens, R. E. Wycherley, "Pausanias in the Agora of Athens," *GRBS* 2 (1959): 21–44; "Pausanias at Athens, II," *GRBS* 4 (1963): 157–75.

[3] W. M. Calder, III, calls him "the father of field archaeology" (*Philologus* 124 [1980]: 150).

[4] II.16.7: ἐντὸς τοῦ τείχους. See also II.16.6.

that since Pausanias states that the Lion Gate is "*in* the wall" (II.16.5), the "wall" must be the inner wall of the acropolis.[5]

Schliemann's contribution, however, is greater than careful reading. Even if the scholars of his day had interpreted the text correctly, they would still have dismissed it, because they ridiculed the whole tradition and regarded it as pure myth with no foundation in reality. Schliemann, on the other hand, accepted the tradition: "My firm faith in the tradition made me undertake my late excavations in the Acropolis, and led to the discovery of the five tombs with their immense treasures."[6]

What Pausanias himself actually saw cannot be determined—did he see the markers erected on top of the tombs or did he report local tradition and guides' stories? The answer does not matter, nor does it matter whether the individuals interred are really Homeric heroes. What matters, and is so astonishing, is that Pausanias could uncover and report such accurate and detailed information about the cultural center of a world that flourished some 1,700 years before his own time, that Schliemann had the sense to recognize the value of the information, and that in 1876, some 3,400 years after the burials, with Pausanias as his guide, he could discover the graves.[7]

Pausanias describes seven monuments (or groups of monuments) in Mycenae. Now that Mycenae has been thoroughly excavated by the Greeks and the English, Alan Wace could weigh his account (in 1954) and summarize it: "As a result of the most recent excavations . . . all the monuments mentioned by Pausanias at Mycenae are now recog-

---

[5] H. Schliemann, *Mykene* (Leipzig 1878), 65–68; *Mycenae* (English edition, New York 1878), 59–61. See Ch. Belger, "Schliemann als Interpret des Pausanias," *BPW* 19 (1899): 1180–83; cf. 1211–15.

[6] Schliemann (above, n. 5), p. 335 of the English edition. The German text runs as follows: "Mein fester Glaube an die Tradition veranlasste mich die Ausgrabungen in der Akropolis zu machen und führte zur Entdeckung der fünf Gräber mit ihren ungeheuern Schätzen" (pp. 383–84). Schliemann says, further, "Ich hatte festes Vertrauen zu der Angabe des Pausanias (II, 16, 6), dass die ermordeten Personen in der Akropolis begraben wären" (p. 383; English edition p. 335).

[7] There is no need to enter here into the recent discussion of Schliemann's character and personality. See W. M. Calder, III, *GRBS* 13 (1972): 335–53; W. Schindler, *Philologus* 120 (1976): 271–89; W. M. Calder, III, ibid. 124 (1980): 146–51; D. A. Traill, *CJ* 74 (1979): 348–51; 77 (1982): 336–42; H. Döhl, *Heinrich Schliemann: Mythos und Ärgernis* (Munich 1981); K. Zimmermann, "Heinrich Schliemann: Ein Leben zwischen Traum und Wirklichkeit," *Klio* 64 (1982): 513–32 (with bibliography, pp. 531–32); D. F. Easton, "The Schliemann Papers," *BSA* 77 (1982): 93–110; D. A. Traill, *Gnomon* 55 (1983): 149–52 (review of Döhl, above); "Schliemann's 'discovery' of 'Priam's Treasure,'" *Antiquity* 57 (1983): 181–86; more fully, *JHS* 104 (1984): 96–115; D. Easton, "Schliemann's Mendacity—A False Trail?" *Antiquity* 58 (1984): 197–204.

nized." [8] If just the one passage on Mycenae had survived from Pausanias' entire work, Pausanias could still claim a place in the annals of history.

TROEZEN

The southeastern Argolid was, in antiquity, the territory of the Doric city Troezen. It was famous as the locale where Phaedra fell in love with her stepson, Hippolytus; it was the mother city of Halicarnassus in Caria; and, together with Aegina, it was the city where Athenian women and children found shelter during Xerxes' invasion of Greece and the forced evacuation of Athens. The evacuation and subsequent campaign were planned, and in 1960 a purported copy of the plan adopted by the Athenians on the motion of Themistocles, the "Decree of Themistocles," was found at Troezen. [9] Troezen is a quite respectable Greek town. Unfortunately, the modern city is built on the site of the ancient town and major excavations are not possible.

In about five pages Pausanias describes the city, its myths, and some thirty major monuments within its walls, on the acropolis, and at two sites not far removed (II.31–32). In the 1890s the French scholar LeGrand conducted minor excavations and managed to establish a few points of reference, [10] but not until 1941, when Gabriel Welter published the results of his research, were the locations of most of the major monuments known—of several temples, the agora, the sanctuary of Demeter outside the wall, and the shrine of Asclepius. [11] Welter, in the main, was able to locate them because of the precision of Pausanias. For instance, once Welter identified the temple of the Muses (built in imperial times), that became a reference point from which the arrangement of the entire complex of the agora could be determined and

---

[8] A. J. B. Wace, "Pausanias and Mycenae," in *Neue Beiträge zur klassischen Altertumswissenschaft: Festschrift B. Schweitzer,* ed. R. Lullies (Stuttgart 1954), 19–26; the quotation is from p. 26. See also the discussion of G. E. Mylonas, *Ancient Mycenae* (Princeton 1957), 171–74.

[9] *Editio Princeps:* M. H. Jameson, *Hesperia* 29 (1960): 198. From the vast bibliography may be cited *Hermes* 89 (1961): 1–35, where the present writer's opinion can be found, and N. G. L. Hammond, *JHS* 102 (1982): 75–93, the last substantial paper (so far).

[10] *BCH* 21 (1897): 543ff.; 29 (1905): 269ff.; 30 (1906): 52ff. A thorough summary of what is known about the city has been given by E. Meyer, "Troizen," in *RE* (1939), 618–53.

[11] G. Welter, *Troizen und Kalauria* (Berlin 1941), whose findings are approved by F. Kolb, *Agora und Theater, Volks- und Festversammlung* (Berlin 1981), 83–85. See also E. Meyer, "Troizen," in *RE,* suppl. 11 (1968), 1268–69.

the buildings in the agora identified using Pausanias.[12] The belief that
in Schliemann's day had seemed naive was now established knowledge:
confidence could be placed in Pausanias whenever he spoke as an eyewitness, confidence in him down to the smallest detail. The Germans
proved this in Olympia,[13] the Greeks in the sanctuaries of Epidaurus[14]
and Lycosura,[15] the French at Delphi,[16] the British at Sparta,[17] the
Americans in the Athenian agora.[18] Pausanias, whom the philologists
and historians of the nineteenth century denigrated, has been vindicated by archaeologists and excavators.[19]

KALLIPOLIS

Where the main road from Delphi to Naupactus reaches the eastern
border of Aetolia, there rises an impressive hill, flanked by two rivers
(fig. 3). At the foot of the hill is the village Veluchovo and the remains

[12] Welter (above, n. 11), pp. 17–19.

[13] H.-V. Herrmann in a survey of the excavations in the seventies of the nineteenth century: "Die Beschreibung des Pausanias diente als Leitfaden zur Identifizierung und als
Wegweiser zum weiteren Vorgehen" (*Stadion* 6 [1980]: 50); E. Kunze, *Olympiabericht* 5
(1956): 150: "Der Perieget, dessen Zuverlässigkeit wieder einmal eine glänzende Be-
stätigung findet. . . ." The excavations have also provided ample evidence that there is
reality behind the tradition and location of "Phidias' workshop" (Pausanias V.15.1); see
A. Mallwitz and W. Schiering, *Die Werkstatt des Pheidias in Olympia*, Olympische Forschungen, vol. 5 (Berlin 1964). It is perhaps too much to hope that the irresponsible
rumor will die that insinuates that the inscription on the bottom of a cup of 440/430
B.C., found there in 1958, "I belong to Phidias" (Φειδίο εἰμί), is modern; see W.-D.
Heilmeyer, *AA*, 1981:447–48.

[14] See, for instance, E. Kirsten and W. Kraiker, *Griechenlandkunde*, 4th ed. (Heidelberg
1962), 359.

[15] E. Meyer, "Lykosura," in *RE* (1927), 2419, on Lycosura and the shrine of Despoina:
"Einzige antike Quelle für die Stadt und das Heiligtum ist Paus. . . . , dessen Angaben
die Ausgrabungen vollkommen bestätigt haben."

[16] G. Daux, *Pausanias à Delphes* (Paris 1936), 7: "Il y a des 'ciceroni' plus brillants et
plus savants que lui; je ne sais s'il y a eu de plus scrupuleux."

[17] F. Bölte, "Sparta," in *RE* (1929), 1362: "Pausanias' Beschreibung von Sparta gibt also
in der Hauptsache eine wirkliche Wanderung durch die Stadt wieder, die sich unter
Berücksichtigung des Geländes und der durch die Ausgrabungen festgelegten Punkte in
ihren Hauptzügen vollkommen deutlich nach Süden, Norden, Westen und Osten ver-
folgen lässt."

[18] H. A. Thompson and R. E. Wycherley, *The Agora of Athens* (Princeton 1972), 204:
"Pausanias' credibility, already well established, ranks even higher as a result of the
Agora excavations." Cf. R. E. Wycherley, *Hesperia*, suppl. 20 (1982): 188: "His testimony stands and carries great weight. Unlike those who contradict him, and one another (occasionally, themselves), he walked on firm ground, and in the light of day."

[19] See app. 1.

Fig. 3. Kallipolis, location.

of a Greek city with fortification walls about one and a half miles in circumference. The city was identified in 1900 by Wilhelm Dittenberger as the Aetolian Kallipolis (sometimes called Kallion), first mentioned by Thucydides (3.96.3) in the year 426 B.C. A dedication of 289 B.C. to King Pyrrhus, in which Dittenberger correctly restored the ethnic *Kallipolitan*, provided the clue.[20]

In 1977 Greek, American, and French scholars began to excavate different sectors of Kallipolis. One of the results of their excavations has been the discovery that Kallipolis had not yet been fortified when Thucydides mentioned it. The fortification wall and all the major buildings were constructed in the middle of the fourth century. Some seventy years later Kallipolis met its doom, a doom that can be compared to that of Pompeii and Herculaneum or Santorini, except that the catastrophe at Kallipolis was not natural.

---

[20] *SIG²* (1899) 919 and n. 2 (*SIG³* 369). The text can also be found in *IG* IX.1².154. See D. Kienast, "Pyrrhos," in *RE* (1963), 123. It is by mistake that credit for the identification is often given to G. Soteriades (*BCH* 31 [1907]: 310), who not only wrote after Dittenberger but in fact refers to him (G. Nachtergael, *Les Galates en Grèce et les Sôtéria de Delphes* [Brussels 1977], 146 n. 94; P. Amandry, *BCH* 102 [1978]: 571 n. 1; *SEG* 28.504).

In the winter of 279/278, during the Gallic invasion of Greece (to sack the treasuries of Delphi), a contingent of Gauls attacked Kallipolis from the rear (while its men were with the Aetolian levy at Thermopylae) and annihilated it. "The sack of Callium by Combutis and Orestorius," Pausanias says, "was the most atrocious and inhuman in history. They put the whole male sex to the sword: old men and babes at their mothers' breasts were butchered alike; and after killing the fattest of the sucklings, they even drank their blood and ate their flesh." [21] For this event Pausanias is our only source.

The recent excavations have uncovered evidence of that destruction in the early third century: [22] several buildings had been burned down. One of the buildings was the city archive, in which were found the remains of some papyrus documents. The documents originally were sealed, and more than six hundred clay casts of the seals, baked by the fire, and all in excellent condition, have been unearthed. The seal impressions represent a large number of cities and leagues of the Aegean world, and include some easily recognizable devices, such as the labyrinth of Cnossus in Crete (fig. 4). A great number of casts are well-executed portraits. From another seal comes a representation of the Aetolian lance with the name of the *strategos* (the highest executive officer of the Aetolians) inscribed (fig. 5); it is the name of Charixenus, who held office in 281/280, only two years before the catastrophe. [23]

Masses of seals from the public archives have recently been found at other places in the Mediterranean—at Delos, for instance, and at Paphos on Cyprus. [24] These seals, however, date from the second or first century B.C., and have not yet been published.

The results of the excavation at Kallipolis confirm what Pausanias says about the destruction and the date of the destruction. Without Pausanias the excavators would have been able to establish that the city had been destroyed and an approximate date for the destruction. Pausanias, however, provides the information needed to understand the cause of the fire, and, above all, to fix its exact date.

What the value of the findings will be once they are published can be anticipated from what Homer Thompson recently wrote regarding catastrophes in Athens: "The archaeologist, as we all know, likes nothing

---

[21] X.22.3; more in the following paragraph.

[22] P. Themelis, *AAA* 12 (1979): 245–79.

[23] *IG* IX.1².14. For his earlier tenure of the post in 288/287 see *IG* IX.1², p. xlix.

[24] For Delos see P. Amandry, *CRAI*, 1974: 505; for Paphos, I. Michaelidou-Nicolaou, in *Actes du VII' Congrès international d'épigraphie grecque et latine, Constantza 1977*, ed. D. M. Pippidi (Bucharest and Paris 1979), 415–16.

Fig. 4. (Left) Kallipolis, seal of Cnossus.   Fig. 5. (Right) Kallipolis, Aetolian
seal with the name of Charixenus.

better than a first-rate disaster: a sack, a fire, a volcanic eruption, an
earthquake. Any such happening may provide him with a sealed cap-
sule of valuable evidence." [25] Sack and fire did in fact seal the evidence
excavated at Kallipolis [26]—everything there, the many seals and fine
artworks, must have been produced earlier than 279 B.C. (just as
everything from Pompeii and Herculaneum antedates A.D. 79).

Incidentally, the excavations were a matter of emergency: a large res-
ervoir was under construction. It has now been completed, and the site
of Kallipolis is flooded and forever lost. Modern technology, in the
name of progress, has outdone the ancient barbarians.

ONCHESTUS

Onchestus is a site in Boeotia, a little south of Lake Copais. It appears in literature as early as the late seventh century, in the catalog of
ships: "sacred Onchestus, Poseidon's shining grove." [27] Its location has
long been known, but no remains from antiquity were ever found.
Onchestus had a sanctuary of Poseidon, as the poet indicates, but it
was never a town; it belonged to the city of Haliartus and its shrine
became one of the two federal shrines of the Boeotian League. A

[25] *Hesperia* 50 (1981): 343.

[26] There seems to have been a revival of the town in the second century B.C., since several
proxeny decrees of that time have been found, some exhibiting the ethnic of the city; see
R. Laffineur, *BCH* 103 (1979): 631–34.

[27] *Il.*2.506. For the date of the catalog of ships see A. Giovannini, *Etude historique sur les
origines du catalogue des vaisseaux* (Bern 1969), 7–50.

number of federal documents have been found there,[28] and the archon
of the league is often referred to as "the archon in Onchestus," an expression that alternates with "the archon of the League of the Boeotians."[29] Onchestus, therefore, was an important place while the Boeotian League flourished, which is to say, down to 170 B.C., when the
Romans dissolved the league and gave the territory of Haliartus, together with Onchestus, to Athens.

Pausanias could not have expected much from a visit there (more
than three centuries after its day of importance), but he went there for
two reasons: first, because Onchestus had once been famous; second,
because it was his rule not to omit any site from the regions he describes. He says, "Fifteen furlongs from this mountain [that of the
Sphinx] are the ruins of a city Onchestus; they say that Onchestus, a son
of Poseidon, dwelt here. In my time there remained a temple and image
of Onchestine Poseidon and the grove which Homer praised" (IX.26.5).

Not only the sanctuary but also a temple of Poseidon and the god's
image were still to be seen. Recently the temple has been excavated by
the Greek Archaeological Service under the direction of Th. G. Spyropoulos. In addition to the places Pausanias mentions, the remains of
a council house (bouleuterion) were found, that is to say, the meeting
place where the delegates from the various Boeotian cities conducted
the affairs of the league. Several inscriptions—dedications to Poseidon
as well as previously unknown documents of the Boeotian League—
also came to light. Both the temple and the council house were originally built at the end of the sixth century B.C.; the earliest dedication
comes from about that time, after a temple had been added to the Homeric grove.[30]

MESSENE

The remainder of this chapter will be devoted to a detailed comparison of Pausanias' description of the city of Messene and the results

---

[28] For instance, *SEG* 25.553; *Teiresias*, Appendix epigraphica 1 (1976): 10, no. 24. A
copy of the treaty, concluded early in the third century B.C., between the Aetolians and
the Boeotians was to be set up at Onchestus (*Staatsverträge* 463a5), and it was at
Onchestus that the Boeotian magistrates took the oath on the treaty with the Phocians
in the early second century B.C. (Moretti, *ISE* 83.11).

[29] Numerous references in E. Kirsten, "Onchestos," in *RE* (1939), 415; P. Roesch, *Etudes
béotiennes* (Paris 1982), 266–82.

[30] Th. G. Spyropoulos, *Deltion* 28 (1973 [1977]): Chron. 269–72; *AAA* 6 (1973):
379–81; *Teiresias* 3 (1973): 4. See also S. Lauffer, *Chiron* 10 (1980): 162, no. 2.

of the recent excavations carried out by the Greek Archaeological Society.[31] Messene, situated beside Mount Ithome in the southwestern Peloponnese, is the capital of the tribe of the Messenians. Messene is not one of the old Greek cities; in fact, it was founded, like Megalopolis (in the center of Arcadia), during the fourth century B.C., and for the same purpose: to serve as a stronghold in a ring of defense against Sparta.[32]

The Messenians had been subjugated by the Spartans in the protracted Messenian wars of the eighth and seventh centuries, and for more than three centuries before the founding of Messene had labored under the harsh rule of the Spartans. Not even their national hero, Aristomenes, had been able to prevent the catastrophe that enslaved them to their foes. Only after the great Theban political figure Epaminondas had crushed the Spartans at Leuctra in 371 B.C. did the Messenians, with the help of the victorious Thebans, recover their independence. Epaminondas can be regarded as the true founder of Messene. The city was fortified with massive walls that formed a circuit of some five miles.

The Messenians remained free for more than two centuries. In 191 B.C. they joined the Achaean League, which then, and until 146, united the entire Peloponnese. In 146 the Achaean League declared war on Rome and was defeated; the Messenians shared the fate of the other Peloponnesians and came under Roman domination.

It was three centuries after this catastrophe that Pausanias visited Messene, some 530 years after her foundation. The great days of the city's independence were long gone, but Messene, under the patronage of the enlightened emperors of Pausanias' day, was still an important civic and cultural center. Messene contained remarkable contemporary buildings and the magnificent remnants of a glorious past. Pausanias found much worth reporting.

Book IV, Messenia, is unique (see above, p. 21): twenty-nine of the thirty-six chapters are devoted to its history and only seven to the various sites, towns, and monuments. Nothing illustrates better the lasting effect of Spartan domination over Messenia than this ratio: seventeen pages of description to seventy of history. Five of the seventeen pages are taken up by the description of the city itself (IV.31.4–33.3). The

---

[31] See the excellent articles by E. Meyer "Messene," in *RE*, suppl. 15 (1978), 136–55, and "Messenien," in *RE*, suppl. 15 (1978), 155–289.
[32] H. Braunert and T. Petersen, "Megalopolis: Anspruch und Wirklichkeit," *Chiron* 2 (1972): 57–90.

following abridged translation retains only what Pausanias has to say about the actual remains of the city and omits all his historical and mythological explanations.

[31.5] Messene is surrounded by a wall, the whole circuit of which is built of stone, and there are towers and battlements on it. . . . [6] In the market-place . . . there is an image of Saviour Zeus and a water-basin called Arsinoe; . . . water flows underground into it from a spring called Clepsydra. There is a sanctuary of Poseidon and another of Aphrodite. Most noteworthy of all is an image of the Mother of the Gods, in Parian marble, a work of Damophon. . . . [7] Damophon also made the Laphria. . . .³³ [9] There is also a temple of Ilithyia at Messene with a stone image. Near it is a hall of the Curetes. . . . There is also a holy sanctuary of Demeter at Messene and images of the Dioscuri. . . . [10] But the images in the sanctuary of Aesculapius are at once the most numerous and the best woɪth seeing. For besides images of the god and his sons, and images of Apollo, the Muses, and Hercules, the sanctuary contains an image of the city of Thebes, a statue of Epaminondas, son of Cleommis, an image of Fortune, and one of Artemis, Bringer of Light. The marble images are the works of Damophon, the only Messenian sculptor of note that I know of. The statue of Epaminondas is of iron, and is the work of some other artist. [11] There is also a temple of Messene ³⁴ with an image of gold and Parian marble. At the back of the temple are paintings of the kings of Messene. . . . [12] There is also a painting of Aesculapius. . . . These paintings are by Omphalion, a pupil of Nicias, son of Nicomedes. . . . [32.1] What the Messenians name the Place of Sacrifice contains images of all the gods recognised by the Greeks. It contains also a bronze statue of Epaminondas and ancient tripods. . . . The images in the gymnasium are by Egyptians, and represent Hermes, Hercules, and Theseus. . . .³⁵ [3] There is also a tomb of Aristomenes here. . . .³⁶ [6] There is a bronze statue of Aristomenes in the stadium at Messene. Not far from the theatre is a sanctuary of Sarapis and Isis. [33.1] On the way to the summit of Ithome, where is the acropolis of Messene, there is a spring called Clepsydra. . . . Every day they carry water from the spring to the sanctuary of Zeus at Ithome. [2] The image of Zeus is a work of Ageladas. . . . They also celebrate an annual festival called Ithomaea. . . . [3] Following the Arcadian road that leads to Megalopolis, you see at the gate a Hermes of Attic work-

---

³³ A special form of Artemis.
³⁴ The eponymous goddess of the city.
³⁵ There follows a corrupt passage. It is clear, however, that the statue of a rich contemporaneous Messenian is mentioned—Aethidas in the manuscripts of Pausanias, but undoubtedly Ti. Claudius Saethida Caelianus, who appears in two inscriptions from Messene and in another from Sparta, and was father of the Roman senator Ti. Claudius Frontinus (see below, p. 58 and nn. 80, 81).
³⁶ The famous hero of the Messenian wars.

manship. For the use of square-shaped images of Hermes is Athenian and from Athens the usage has passed to the rest of the world.

This condensation of Pausanias sounds much drier than the original, in which numerous explanations and digressions prevent the reader from being bored, but it does emphasize that his report is circumstantial and substantial. Pausanias is systematic: he walks from the wall to the marketplace, from the marketplace to the sanctuary of Asclepius, from the sanctuary to the place of sacrifice, from the place of sacrifice to the gymnasium, from the gymnasium to the stadium, from the stadium to the theater, from the theater to the acropolis; then he leaves the city through the Arcadian gate, which sends the traveler on his way to Megalopolis. He lists what he sees in each area, beginning with the "towers and battlements" of the wall and including the city's shrines, temples, images of the gods, statues of famous men, paintings, and offerings (such as tripods), until he reaches the herm in the Arcadian gate. He also attributes the works he sees to their artists: the sculptor Hageladas (Ageladas) of Argos,[37] the painter Omphalion,[38] and, above all, Damophon of Messene. He usually derives this kind of information from the artists' signatures on their own works. Altogether, Pausanias' treatment of Messene is a good example of his methodology in a major city.

The location of Messene was never in doubt: it was known to be at Mount Ithome, and its walls are extremely well preserved.[39] The circuit wall, which dates from the fourth century B.C., was in Pausanias' view (IV.31.5) the most impressive wall in all of Greece, mightier even than the walls of Rhodes and Byzantium. These walls are the most famous fortifications in ancient Greece.

The known remains of Messene, apart from its walls, were scant indeed until the end of the fifties, partly because the much smaller modern village of Mavromati overlies a section of ancient Messene. The theater, the stadium, and the ruins of a large temple were just recognizable west and southwest of Mavromati. On the way to the summit, farther north, Philippe LeBas, in 1844, identified the foundations of a

---

[37] For Hageladas, of the fifth century, see G. Lippold, *Griechische Plastik* (Handbuch der Archäologie) (Munich 1950), 88–89.
[38] G. Lippold, "Omphalion," in *RE* (1939), 398–99. Omphalion belongs to the end of the fourth century.
[39] Discussed by F. E. Winter, *Greek Fortifications, Phoenix,* suppl. 9 (1971), and A. W. Lawrence, *Greek Aims in Fortification* (Oxford 1979), passim, both with illustrations.

Fig. 6. Messene, aerial view of the large square (courtesy R. Schoder, SJ).

temple of Artemis. And that was that, except for a monumental complex southwest of Mavromati; excavations in 1895, 1909, and 1925 had uncovered parts of a large square and a few adjacent buildings.[40] This square was identified as the agora mentioned by Pausanias.

Major excavations, begun at the complex in 1957 under the direction of Anastasios Orlandos and lasting into the seventies, changed everything.[41] Figure 6 shows an aerial view of the complex as it looked after the new excavations had been under way for several years. An almost perfect square (200 by 215 feet) with several adjacent buildings (the most notable of which is the small theater in the northeastern corner) can easily be recognized. The large square appears to be empty, but seems, nevertheless, better suited for an agora, the political center

[40] Th. Sophulis, *Praktika*, 1895: 27; G. P. Oikonomos, ibid., 1909: 201–5; 1925–26: 55–66.

[41] The reports by A. K. Orlandos in *Praktika* can be found in the following volumes: 1957: 121–25; 1958: 177–83; 1959: 162–73; 1960: 210–27; 1962: 99–112; 1963: 122–29; 1964: 96–101; 1969: 98–110; 1970: 125–41; 1971: 157–171; 1972: 127–38; 1973: 108–11; 1974: 102–9; 1975: 176–77. Orlandos has also given a summary in *Neue Forschungen in griechischen Heiligtümern* (Tübingen 1976), 9–38. See also F. Felten, *AntK* 26 (1983): 84–93.

of the city, than for anything else, and so this square was still assumed to be the agora, as it had been for some seventy years.

As excavations continued, however, scholars became puzzled. Pausanias said that the water basin of Arsinoe was in the agora, but the excavators found no trace of it; on the other hand, they did find substantial fragments of sculpture, including the larger-than-life head of a youthful god, Apollo, in a room in the northeastern corner close to the theater. They then unearthed statues and inscriptions that proved that a building on the northwestern corner was a temple of Artemis. Did Pausanias not tell us (IV.31.10) that statues of Apollo and Artemis (Damophon's work) were to be seen in the sanctuary of Asclepius? Scholars began to wonder whether the complex with the so-called agora might in fact be the Asclepieium.[42]

Proof came soon enough. A large inscription, found *in situ* at the monumental staircase in the middle of the northern side, contains the provision that it be erected next to the shrine of the emperor cult.[43] This shrine was tentatively identified as the elevated level to the left and right of the stairs.

Another inscription, which had been known for some time, furnished the decisive proof that this shrine was the sanctuary of the emperors and that the larger complex was the Asclepieium, for it mentions "the four stoas of the Asclepieium and the adjoining upper level for the Caesareum."[44] Other inscriptions were found: an inscription on the base of a statue of a victor in the games held in honor of Asclepius[45] and, on a single stone, a dedication to Asclepius and Hygieia, goddess of health and daughter of Asclepius (or, in another tradition, his wife), and a dedication "to the gods," no doubt the same two, Asclepius and Hygieia.[46]

More and more pieces of sculpture were found, some identifiable: priestesses of Artemis, Fortuna (Τύχη), which Pausanias attests (IV.31.10) was in the sanctuary, a large, semicircular base that could

---

[42] E. Kirsten, *AA*, 1964:908. Orlandos had already thought of this possibility (*Praktika*, 1960:210 n. 1).

[43] *Praktika*, 1959:169, fig. 10, and pl. 142; *SEG* 23.207.39: ἀναθείτω παρὰ τὸ Σεβαστεῖον.

[44] *IG* V.1.1462.2–3: τὰς στοὰς τὰς τέσσαρας τοῦ Ἀσκληπιείου καὶ τὰς ὑπερκειμένας παραστ[ά]δας κατὰ τὸ Καισαρῆον. See K. Tuchelt, "Zum Problem 'Kaisareion–Sebasteion,'" *IstMitt* 31 (1981): 167–86.

[45] *Praktika*, 1958:178 and fig. 139.

[46] *Praktika*, 1971:166, no. 6 (pl. 203γ).

Fig. 7. Messene, temple and altar of Asclepius (courtesy R. Schoder, SJ).

only be the base of the nine Muses that Pausanias also mentions,[47] and more. These discoveries left no doubt that this was the sanctuary of Asclepius, not the agora.

So far, however, the excavation had found no trace of a temple. Now, while it is perfectly true that a god's shrine does not necessarily have to have a temple of the god, a complex of this magnitude and splendor would have been a striking oddity if it did not have an adequate temple for its master. In 1969, Orlandos removed a deep layer of earth and finally uncovered a temple and, east of it, a monumental altar, in the middle of the large square. Both were of fine Hellenistic workmanship (fig. 7).

The plan of the entire complex has now been made clear (fig. 8). In the center of the complex is the open square with the temple of Asclepius (and probably Hygieia), in front (east) of the temple is the altar of Asclepius, around the square are several bases for offerings (represented by circles in the diagram), and in the northwestern corner is an altar for Artemis. The open square is completely surrounded by a covered colonnade. Outside and around the colonnade, beginning opposite (west of) the altar of Artemis, is the temple of Artemis; in the next room, directly south, is Fortuna, then two rooms, the Muses, and two more rooms; on the south of the complex is a structure that may

[47] *Praktika*, 1963: pl. 105α; Pausanias IV.31.10.

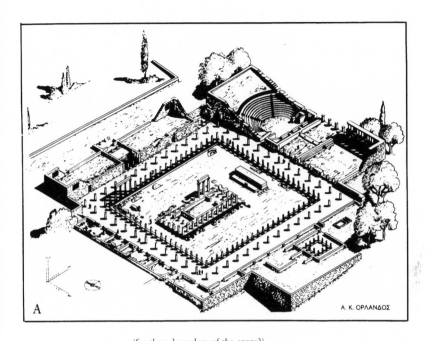

A

A. K. ΟΡΛΑΝΔΟΣ

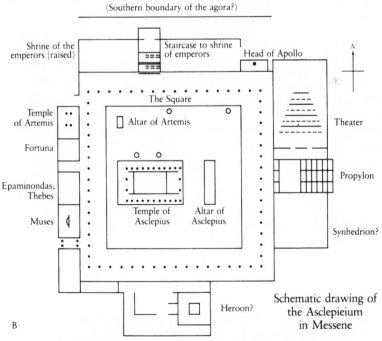

(Southern boundary of the agora?)

| Shrine of the emperors (raised) | | Staircase to shrine of emperors | Head of Apollo | | *N* |

The Square

Temple of Artemis

Altar of Artemis

Theater

Fortuna

Epaminondas, Thebes

Propylon

Muses

Temple of Asclepius

Altar of Asclepius

Synhedrion?

Heroon?

Schematic drawing of the Asclepieium in Messene

B

Fig. 8. Messene, reconstruction and schematic drawing of the Asclepieium (8b courtesy A. S. Bradford).

be a heroon. Turning the corner and proceeding north, one finds a large room (its purpose is disputed, but it is probably a synhedrion), the main gate (a propylon), and then the theater. Turning the corner again, one finds, on the northern side of the complex, the room in which the head of Apollo was found and then the monumental staircase and the shrine of the emperors.

Pausanias' description accords well with the excavated remains. Remember that he says that "besides images of the god and his sons, and images of Apollo, the Muses, and Hercules, the sanctuary contains an image of the city of Thebes, a statue of Epaminondas, son of Cleommis, an image of Fortune, and one of Artemis" (IV.31.10). The base for the Muses, Fortuna, and the temple of Artemis have been discovered *in situ* (see diagram) and in the order in which Pausanias mentions them. Obviously Pausanias went from room to room, south to north,[48] describing what he saw as he went. The images of Thebes and Epaminondas, therefore, must have been in the rooms between the Muses and Fortuna. (How the complex may have appeared in Pausanias' day can be seen from a plaster model: fig. 9. A photograph taken from a balloon may give a better idea of what is actually preserved: fig. 10. The latest plan of the entire complex is shown in fig. 11.)

The Messenian shrine of Asclepius bears a general resemblance to the sanctuary of Asclepius at Pergamum (fig. 12).[49] The latter has the same large square surrounded by halls with a theater attached to it, a propylon, and a temple of Asclepius, which is an exact, though smaller, copy of the Pantheon in Rome. All the major constructions in Pergamum date from the time of the emperor Hadrian,[50] but underneath them lies the earlier, Hellenistic sanctuary that has the temple of the god within the square as in Messene.

The Asclepieium of Messene was built during the Hellenistic period. The architecture of the temple, the theater, and the other buildings is an excellent example of the best Hellenistic style. If Damophon made the numerous large images for the major buildings at the time those buildings were erected, then the exact date of the constructions would depend on the exact date of Damophon. The shrine of the emperor cult is, of course, a later addition, but, as the inscription mentioned above (p. 41) showed, not later than the time of Augustus.

---

[48] As observed by G. Despinis, *AA* 81 (1966): 385.
[49] Kirsten and Kraiker (above, n. 14), pp. 426–27.
[50] Ch. Habicht, *Die Inschriften des Asklepieions*, Altertümer von Pergamon, vol. 8, pt. 3 (Berlin 1969), 10–11, against the assumption that they date from the reign of Hadrian's successor, Antoninus Pius.

Fig. 9. Messene, plaster model of the Asclepieium.

Fig. 10. Messene, the Asclepieium from a balloon.

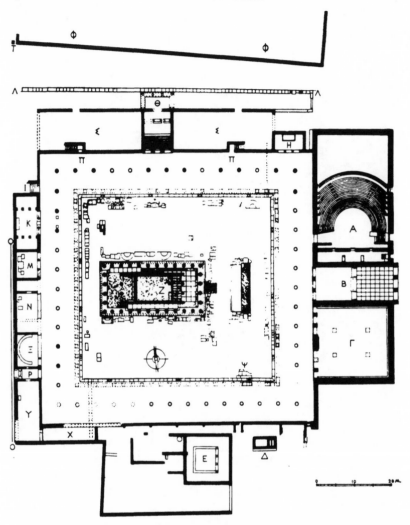

Fig. 11. Messene, map of the Asclepieium.

Among the large number of statues and fragments found are the following: a life-size, headless god (Apollo or Dionysus) dated to the early third century B.C. (fig. 13), several priestesses of Artemis, all from the goddess's temple and all dating from the second century A.D. (fig. 14), the head of Apollo already mentioned (fig. 15), a battered head of Asclepius (fig. 16), the foot of a seated goddess, in all likelihood Damophon's Fortuna of Messene, and fragments of Damophon's statues of Artemis and the Muses.

Fig. 12. Pergamum, Asclepieium (courtesy Deutsches Archäologisches Institut, Abteilung Istanbul).

Pausanias is the only ancient author who mentions Damophon of Messene. He refers to him several times. Damophon sculpted a group of Asclepius and Hygieia in Aegium, the capital of the Achaean League.[51] He made a Hermes and an Aphrodite in Megalopolis in Arcadia[52] and several cult images in the shrine of the Mistress (Despoina) in Lycosura, a sanctuary under the jurisdiction of Megalopolis (VIII.37.3ff.). Damophon fashioned the cult images of Despoina herself, Demeter, Artemis, and the Titan Anytus. The shrine was located by Edward Dodwell in 1819 with Pausanias' guidance, and excavated after 1889.[53] The four major statues of Despoina, Demeter (fig. 17), Artemis (fig. 18), and Anytus (fig. 19)[54] were found. They formed a group, which was carefully described by Pausanias (VIII.37.3–6) and also depicted

---

[51] Pausanias VII.23.7. (See also VII.23.6 for another work of Damophon in Aegium.)

[52] Pausanias VIII.31.6. (See also VIII.31.2 for another group that was probably also his.)

[53] A convenient survey can be found in Meyer (above, n. 15), pp. 2417–32.

[54] Very similar is a head found in the "Hallenstrasse" that leads to the sanctuary of Asclepius at Pergamum (fig. 20). It appeared in *AA* 81 (1966): 466–67 with figs. 41a–c, and Damophon's Anytus is mentioned for comparison. Erika Simon has argued that this head dates from the time of the Great Altar, and that it represents Asclepius, and is perhaps the famous image made by Phyromachus (*Pergamon und Hesiod* [Mainz 1975], 19–20).

Fig. 13. Messene, Apollo or Dionysus.

on a Megalopolitan coin of about A.D. 200.[55] The results of these excavations, as many scholars have duly noted, amply confirm Pausanias'
account (see above, n. 15). Pausanias errs, however, in saying that the
base for the four statues was formed from a single stone (VIII.37.3).

Damophon, despite the silence of other ancient authors, must have
been a highly respected artist, since it was to him that the Eleans en-
trusted the difficult repairs of Phidias' famous statue of Zeus, and

[55] G. Dickins, *BSA* 17 (1910–11): 81.

Fig. 14. Messene, priestesses of Artemis.

Fig. 15. Messene, head of Apollo.

Damophon was publicly honored by the Eleans for the excellent job he did (IV.31.6).

More than half a dozen large cult images attributed to Damophon with no possibility of error are now known; Damophon, indeed, may be said to be the Greek sculptor whose work modern scholarship knows best. His date, then, is crucial.

Scholars first postulated that he had worked in the period of the

Fig. 16. Messene, battered head of
Asclepius.

founding of Messene and Megalopolis, that is, around 370 B.C., but
they soon recognized that his sculptural style was not compatible with
that of the late classical period, but rather with a later style, and so
they lowered his date to the first half of the second century B.C., when
the Achaean League contained Megalopolis and Messene (from 191)
and had not yet suffered the catastrophe of 146. Damophon, then,
would be the contemporary of such prominent Achaean leaders as
Callicrates, Lycortas of Megalopolis, and his son, the historian Polybius. In fact, the famous relief depicting Polybius (fig. 21), found in
Arcadian Cleitor and dating from 145 B.C., was once thought to be the
work of Damophon, though doubts about this attribution have been
expressed in recent years.[56]

[56] P. C. Bol and F. Eckstein, "Die Polybios-Stele in Kleitor/Arkadien," *Antike Plastik*
(Berlin) 15 (1975): 83–93 and pl. 40b.

Fig. 17. Lycosura, Demeter of Damophon.

Fig. 18. Lycosura, Artemis of Damophon.

Fig. 19. Lycosura, Anytus of Damophon (courtesy Deutsches
Archäologisches Institut, Abteilung Athen, and A. F. Stewart).

Fig. 20. Pergamum, the "Wild Man"
(courtesy Deutsches Archäologisches
Institut, Abteilung Istanbul).

However that may be, Damophon's time seemed to have been established—between 180 and 160 B.C. Carl Robert, it is true, had argued for a date three hundred years later, in the time of Hadrian and the young Pausanias.[57] He based his argument partly on the fact that Pliny does not mention Damophon, which, if one believes that Pliny names all prominent artists up to his own time, would mean that Damophon lived after Pliny. Since the preface of Pliny's *Naturalis Historia* can be dated to A.D. 77, and since Pliny himself died in 79 (during the eruption of Mount Vesuvius), this argument establishes a firm *terminus*

[57]"Damophon," in *RE* (1901), 2078–79.

Fig. 21. Cleitor, Polybius.

post quem for Damophon. But Robert finally abandoned this argument and accepted the prevailing opinion.[58]

Recently, however, the argument for a Hadrianic date was reactivated by the French scholar Edmond Lévy. Lévy carried out fresh excavations at the base of Damophon's large group at Lycosura and found Hadrianic coins. He concluded that if the base rested on top of Hadrianic coins, then it and the statues that it supported could not be of an earlier date. He repeated Robert's argument from the silence of Pliny. Lévy's chronology was adopted by Guy Donnay, who in the pages immediately following Lévy's paper derided scholars who try to date works of art by subjective criteria, such as style, rather than by hard facts and indisputable evidence, such as coins, inscriptions, and the stratigraphic data of a dig.[59]

This vigorous attack on the accepted chronology of Damophon did not win much favor with archaeologists; several expressed their doubts about the validity of Lévy's arguments,[60] and a few years later Lévy himself retracted. He, and Jean Marcadé, an expert on Greek sculpture, studied the remains of Damophon in the museum of Lycosura and then wrote another paper. The two men had been able to join several new fragments to the main group of statues, but the principal result of their study was the discovery that the sculptures had been repaired in antiquity and that the base, therefore, had probably been shifted, which could very well account for the Hadrianic coins.[61]

And so once more there is general agreement that Damophon worked in the second century B.C., no earlier than the second quarter of that century, but opinion is still divided as to his exact date. Most scholars put his major period of productivity within the years 180–160, but others prefer 150–120, and one, Andreas Rumpf, prefers a still later time.[62] Scholars will never agree on an exact date as long as the arguments are based on internal style or comparisons with other artists and works (which themselves are insecurely dated) or vague impressions that his work was influenced by Pergamene sculpture of the second century or by an early classicist reaction to the Pergamene "baroque."

[58] See Meyer (above, n. 15), pp. 2429–30.
[59] Ed. Lévy, *BCH* 91 (1967): 518–45, esp. 532ff.; G. Donnay, *BCH* 91 (1967): 546–51.
[60] W. Fuchs, *Die Skulptur der Griechen* (Munich 1969), 595, no. 698; J. Frel, *AAA* 5 (1972): 73.
[61] Ed. Lévy and J. Marcadé, *BCH* 96 (1972): 986; E. Meyer, "Messenien," in *RE*, suppl. 15 (1978), 288.
[62] A. Rumpf, *Der kleine Pauly*, vol. 1 (Stuttgart 1964), 1377.

Epigraphy might one day give us the answer, but of eight inscriptions found so far that mention Damophon or members of his family—five from Messene,[63] one from Megalopolis,[64] and two from Lycosura[65]—none has been convincingly dated, and no family tree has been reconstructed.

The historical circumstances, however, make it rather unlikely that Damophon could have been commissioned to do major works in Megalopolis, Lycosura, Messene, and Aegium after 146 B.C., the year the great catastrophe befell the Achaean League and deeply and adversely affected each of these cities. Damophon must belong to the second quarter of the second century B.C. and must, therefore, have produced the sculptures for the sanctuary of Asclepius at Messene in this period.[66]

Nor is the silence of Pliny, if Damophon's period is 180–160, any longer surprising. Rather, it is exactly what would be expected, since Pliny explicitly states that between the 121st and 156th Olympiads, that is to say, between 296 and 156 B.C., there was no art worth mentioning.[67]

In 167, when Aemilius Paullus, the victor over Perseus, visited Olympia, he was overwhelmed by the majesty of the Zeus of Phidias.[68] It would be nice to think that he saw the famous statue in all its restored splendor,[69] after the large cracks in the ivory sections of the image had been repaired by Damophon.

---

[63] *IG* V.1.1443 (*BCH* 91 [1967]: 540, figs. 28, 29); *Praktika* 1962:111 (*BCH* 91 [1967]: 541, fig. 30); 1972:135 with pls. 114α.β and 138 with pl. 116 (cf. *Bull. épigr.*, 1973:199).

[64] *IG* V.2.454 (*BCH* 91 [1967]: 541, fig. 31).

[65] *IG* V.2.539, 540a,b (*BCH* 91 [1967]: 541, figs. 32–34).

[66] This agrees closely with the date assigned to Damophon by the following scholars: V. Müller, *ArtB* 20 (1938): 399–400; M. Bieber, *AJA* 45 (1941): 94–95; W. B. Dinsmoor, *AJA* 45 (1941): 422–27; L. Alscher, *Griechische Plastik* 4 (1957) 79; H.-V. Herrmann, *Olympia: Heiligtum und Wettkampfstätte* (Munich 1972), 253 n. 575; J. Onians, *Art and Thought in the Hellenistic Age* (London 1979), 140.

[67] Pliny *HN* 34.52: "cessavit deinde ars ac rursus . . . revixit." This, at least, is the explanation of F. Preisshofen, "Kunsttheorie und Kunstbetrachtung," in *Le Classicisme à Rome aux I^{ers} siècles avant et après J.-C.*, ed. H. Flashar (Geneva 1979), 269ff. See, however, the different interpretation of W. D. E. Coulson, *CW* 69 (1975–76): 361–62.

[68] Polyb. 30.10.6; Livy 45.28.4–5; Plut. *Aem.* 28.

[69] The same thought has occurred to Dinsmoor (above, n. 66), p. 424. However, Dinsmoor's suggestion that it was King Antiochus IV Epiphanes who commissioned Damophon to repair the Zeus and that the work can therefore be dated to the years 169–167 B.C. seems unwarranted. This was the Eleans' business, and it was the Eleans who honored Damophon for the quality job he had done (above, p. 48).

Damophon produced the sculptures for the Asclepieium in Messene in the period 180–160. If the Messenians did commission Damophon to make all the major cult statues to be set up in the shrine of Asclepius, and commissioned him to do this when the complex of buildings was under construction, then the Asclepieium was built in the first half of the second century B.C. Further study of the architecture will yield more precise evidence.

The complex of the Asclepieium was once thought to be the agora. Once the Asclepieium was recognized, the question arose again, where was the agora? Pausanias says the agora has a water basin called Arsinoe (IV.31.6). Ernst Meyer identified this as Mavromati, the source of water for the village Mavromati.[70] If he is right, the ancient agora is north of the Asclepieium and underneath the modern village.

The fields depicted in figure 6 lie between the Asclepieium and the village. Orlandos may already have discovered the southern boundary of the agora, immediately north of the shrine of the emperor cult in the Asclepieium. The large wall marked by the letters *phi* in figure 11 seems to be that boundary. Excavations in the fields might perhaps uncover the images of Zeus Savior and the Mother of the Gods, another work of Damophon (IV.31.6), or other evidence that this is the agora.

A base of an honorary statue for *Cnaeus Manlius Luci filius Agrippa, legatus* (that is to say, the second in command to the Roman governor of the province of Achaea) from the time of Augustus has been found in these fields. The statue was erected by the city as a token of gratitude for Agrippa's benefactions.[71] The obvious place for such a monument was the agora. The base, it is true, was found built into a wall, not *in situ*, but it may not have been moved very far, and it does add to the evidence that the fields cover part of the ancient agora.

Quite a number of Messenian inscriptions have been found that confirm other details of Pausanias' account. A dedication of imperial date to Zeus Savior must come from the agora where Pausanias saw the statue of the god.[72] An earlier dedication (from the second century B.C.) is addressed to Ilithyia (that is, the Artemis who assists women in labor); Pausanias states that she has a temple in Messene.[73] Pausanias mentions a temple to Demeter (IV.31.9). From the fourth or early third century B.C. comes a dedication to Demeter by her priestess,[74] and her

---

[70] "Messene," in *RE*, suppl. 15 (1978), 148.
[71] *Praktika*, 1969:115 and fig. 22.   [72] *IG* V.1.1440.
[73] *IG* V.1.1445; cf. Pausanias IV.31.9.   [74] *IG* V.1.1444A.

temple is also attested in the large Augustan inscription that was found close to the Sebasteum at the monumental staircase.[75]

This inscription lists the many public buildings that needed repairs and the wealthy citizens who contributed to the repairs and the amount that each citizen contributed. The inscription mentions buildings mentioned also by Pausanias, such as the gymnasium, and a temple of Hermes and Hercules (the gods usually associated with the gymnasia).[76] Pausanias says that Aristomenes was worshipped as a hero; the inscription specifies that he received a sacrifice of bulls.[77]

Pausanias speaks of Zeus Ithomatas on the summit of Mount Ithome; and inscriptions record that the priest of Zeus Ithomatas was the eponymous official of the city; public documents were dated with the name of the priest of each year. The annual festival in the god's honor, the Ithomaia, likewise appears in both Pausanias and inscriptions.[78] Pausanias left the city through the Arcadian gate (to this day a major tourist attraction). At the gate he saw a herm. This is lost, but an inscription from it survives and says that this herm was repaired in the time of Augustus by a certain Quintus Plotius Euphemion.[79]

Finally, Pausanias mentions a monument in honor of a very rich Messenian, Saethida, who, he says, was his older contemporary. The man is well known from Messenian inscriptions: an honorary base showing him on horseback was found in the small theater of the Asclepieium, and he himself set up a statue of the Caesar Marcus Aurelius sometime between 139 and 161. Saethida was a Roman citizen, with the nomen Claudius, and a high priest of the cult of the emperors.[80] His son was made a Roman senator by Hadrian and selected consul under Hadrian's successor; two grandsons were also senators, and one of them erected a statue of the emperor Lucius Verus in Messene in A.D. 164.[81] These men are the only Messenians known to have

---

[75] *Praktika*, 1959:169, fig. 10, and pl. 142; *SEG* 23.207.28: ναὸς τᾶς Δάματρος.

[76] Line 33 of the inscription quoted above, n. 75: a certain Domitius promises τὸν ναὸν ἐπισκευάσειν τοῦ Ἡρακλέος καὶ Ἑρμοῦ ἐν γυμνασίῳ.

[77] Pausanias IV.14.7 (cult of Aristomenes), 32.3 (his tomb); *SEG* 23.207.13: ἐναγισμὸς for Aristomenes, that is to say, the offerings appropriate for a hero.

[78] Pausanias IV.33.2–3; *IG* V.1.1468 and *Bull. épigr.*, 1970:286 (Zeus Ithomatas); *IG* V.1.1467–69 and *SEG* 23.208.22 (the festival).

[79] Pausanias IV.33.3; *IG* V.1.1460.

[80] Pausanias IV.32.2; *IG* V.1.1451, 1455a. From Sparta is *IG* V.1.512. See H. Halfmann, *Die Senatoren aus dem östlichen Teil des Imperium Romanum bis zum Ende des 2. Jh. n. Chr.* (Göttingen 1979), 174, no. 93a.

[81] For the son see Halfmann (above, n. 80), p. 174, no. 93; for the grandsons, p. 196, nos. 126, 127.

been elevated to the aristocracy of the empire, and the family is one of not more than five from all of Greece that acquired this status during the first two centuries of the empire.

Next to inscriptions, coins best confirm Pausanias' account; a detailed discussion of the evidence is not needed here, since Friedrich Imhoof-Blumer and Percy Gardner's *Numismatic Commentary on Pausanias* has been available for a century (and has been recently reproduced and enlarged).[82] Messenian coins depict most (at least nine or ten) of the gods whom Pausanias mentions. Some scholars even believed that the Messenian coin depicting the cult image of Zeus Ithomatas (a work of Hageladas of Argos, as Pausanias reports: IV.33.2) proved, because of their striking similarity, that the famous bronze statue of Zeus or Poseidon found underwater at Cape Artemisium and known as the "God from the Sea" (fig. 22; now in the National Museum of Athens) was Hageladas' statue of Zeus Ithomatas. Other scholars regard the "God from the Sea" as a work of the Aeginetan Onatas, the Athenian Myron, or the Boeotian Calamis. R. Wünsche, however, has recently pointed out that it is highly unlikely, given the enormous number of statues of Zeus from the time and the great number of active sculptors, that blind chance would have preserved the work of a celebrity.[83]

An assessment of Pausanias' description of the city of Messene as it was in his day must conclude that his account is full of substantial detail, that the detail has been amply confirmed by the remains of the excavated sites, works of art, inscriptions, and coins, and that the detail in turn has served as the key to important discoveries and conclusions. Without Pausanias the sculptor Damophon would be an unknown figure—the large number of major statues found in Messene (and Lycosura) could not be attributed to him or to any other artist.

Nor is Pausanias useful only for his description of physical remains. He paints a picture for us of the Greece of his time, which picture, it is true, can be misinterpreted. Ulrich Kahrstedt, in his book on the economic profile of Greece in imperial times (which aims to be a commentary on Pausanias), expressed the view that Pausanias depicts Messene

[82] F. Imhoof-Blumer and P. Gardner, *A Numismatic Commentary on Pausanias*, *JHS* 6 (1885): 50–101; 7 (1886): 57–113; 8 (1887): 6–63; new edition, edited and enlarged by Al. N. Oikonomides, published under the title *Ancient Coins Illustrating Lost Masterpieces of Greek Art: A Numismatic Commentary on Pausanias* (Chicago 1964).

[83] "Der 'Gott aus dem Meer,'" *JdI* 94 (1979): 77–111, where earlier bibliography can be found, including those scholars who ascribed the statue to Onatas, Myron, Hageladas, or Calamis.

Fig. 22. Cape Artemisium, the "God from the Sea"
(courtesy A. Frantz).

as a decaying city.[84] During the second century A.D., according to Kahrstedt's thesis, large parts of Greece had fallen into decay, or at least were deteriorating rapidly. Now the unbiased reader of Pausanias does not get such an impression of Messene; in fact, it takes what Louis Robert once called "Kahrstedtian logic" to extract anything of that sort from Pausanias.[85]

Kahrstedt did take into account the material remains—buildings, works of art, inscriptions, and so on—but not much of a search had been made for these by 1954, when Kahrstedt's book was published. Since then, Orlandos' excavations have provided ample evidence that by the time of Augustus and on into the first and second centuries A.D. Messene was flourishing: important imperial buildings, sculptures, dedications, and inscriptions have come to light, and have shown clearly that great care was taken to maintain the older buildings. Messene had the resources to make several dedications in Olympia during the second century.[86]

Kahrstedt says that the generous bourgeoisie found to exist, for instance, in Sparta and Argos was not to be found in Messene;[87] not only did he disregard Pausanias' testimony and the inscriptions of the rich senatorial family of Claudius Saethida and some other indications, but he also misdated the important Messenian inscription that testifies precisely to such a society of wealthy citizens in the early imperial period. This inscription, it is true, had been dated to ca. 100 B.C. by the great Adolf Wilhelm, and Kahrstedt did lower the date by one generation, but that was not enough. The correct date, ca. A.D. 40, was established just a few years ago by Adalberto Giovannini.[88]

During the last war of the Roman Republic, Messene, like almost all the rest of Greece, sided with the loser, Mark Antony, and Augustus

---

[84] U. Kahrstedt, *Das wirtschaftliche Gesicht Griechenlands in der Kaiserzeit* (Bern 1954), 9: "Das Buch will einen unter heutigen Gesichtspunkten abgefassten Kommentar zu Pausanias geben." On Messene pp. 220–22.

[85] *Bull. épigr.*, 1956:39: "raisonnement du type Kahrstedt." This comes apropos Kahrstedt's book in question.

[86] *IOlympia* 445–49, 465; Th. Schwertfeger, *Olympiabericht* 10 (1981): 249–55. From the third century *IOlympia* 486.

[87] Kahrstedt (above, n. 84), p. 222: "Ruinen wie Inschriften wollen eigentlich die spendenfreudige Bourgeoisie nicht zeigen, nach der wir fragen. Kein Vergleich mit Argos oder Sparta."

[88] *IG* V.1.1432–33; Ad. Wilhelm, *ÖJh* 17 (1914): 48ff.; Kahrstedt (above, n. 84), p. 220 and n. 6; A. Giovannini, *Rome et la circulation monétaire en Grèce au IIe siècle avant Jésus-Christ* (Basel 1978), 115–22.

Fig. 23. Messene, statue of the
fourth or fifth century A.D.

did punish the city in some way, as Pausanias himself says (IV.31.1−2).
Her alliance with Antony is reflected in the name of the citizen Marcus
Antonius Proculus, who certainly owed his Roman citizenship to the
triumvir Antony. He appears in a Messenian inscription from the time
of Augustus, but the same inscription also shows, as do others, that
the city was healthy and wealthy.[89] Messene continued to flourish at

---

[89] *Praktika*, 1959: 170, line 21 (*SEG* 23.207). He is, in all likelihood, none other than
the dedicant of *IOlympia* 428 (*SIG*³ 789), the Messenian M. Antonius Proculus.

least until Pausanias' time—the end of the second century A.D.—and probably beyond that. A major statue found in 1969 dates from the fourth or fifth century A.D. (fig. 23).

In his section on Messene Pausanias has done a careful and thorough job, but that is not surprising—he nearly always did. His faithfulness in reporting what he saw has, time and time again, been proven at a large number of sites and could easily be demonstrated at a good many others; but let us conclude this chapter by taking Pausanias as our guide up on the Athenian acropolis. Here, he says, is an image of the goddess Earth (Ge), and very close by (literally "there") are statues of Timotheus (the son) and Conon (the father).[90] We are a bit surprised that Pausanias mentions the son before the father. In 1870 H. Heydemann recognized an inscription, *Ge Karpophoros*, cut in the living rock, some ten yards north of the seventh column (counting from the west) of the Parthenon's northern side, so we know where the image of Earth stood.[91] At a distance of little more than one yard are the remains of the base that once bore the statues of Conon, the father, and Timotheus, the son.[92] Now we know why the son is mentioned first. As Heydemann has explained, Pausanias walked along and first saw Ge, then Timotheus, and finally Conon.[93] When Pausanias speaks as an eyewitness, he can be trusted.

[90] Pausanias I.24.3: "Here also [ἐνταῦθα καί] is a statue of Timotheus, son of Conon, and a statue of Conon himself."
[91] H. Heydemann, *Hermes* 4 (1870): 381–89. The inscription of Ge is now *IG* II².4758. See also the comments of G. P. Stevens, *Hesperia* 15 (1946): 1–4.
[92] The inscription on the base for Conon and Timotheus is now *IG* II².3774. See Stevens (above, n. 91), p. 4ff.
[93] Heydemann (above, n. 91), p. 388: "Wir ersehen aus diesem Beispiel, wie buchstäblich ein ἐνταῦθα und die Reihenfolge der Namen zu benutzen sind, und wie man sich auf seine Angaben verlassen kann."

III

PAUSANIAS AND

THE EVIDENCE OF

INSCRIPTIONS

Wherever Pausanias went, he was interested in learning whom the local inhabitants venerated: who were the principal deities, the lesser gods, the local heroes, and the nymphs. Since all Greek states depicted these figures on their coins, it was natural that numismatists were among the first to show a substantial interest in Pausanias. A numismatic commentary on Pausanias, by Friedrich Imhoof-Blumer and Percy Gardner, appeared in different volumes of the *Journal of Hellenic Studies* during the 1880s. The commentary was subsequently published as a book, of which a second edition appeared in 1964.[1]

In addition to deities, Greek coins often depict monuments or famous works of art. In a good many instances, we have both Pausanias' description of a masterpiece of Greek art and its reproduction on a coin, so that his description and the reproduction can be compared and studied. The numismatic commentary on Pausanias provided the indispensable basis for such studies.

In view of this, one wonders why there was never a similar attempt to collect the inscriptions relevant to Pausanias' text and why no epigraphic commentary on Pausanias was ever written. If it were true that "Pausanias seldom bothers to record inscriptions"[2] or that "for all of Athens [he] alludes only to a pair of inscriptions,"[3] there would be no need for it, but these statements, it must be said, strangely misrepre-

[1] See above, p. 59 n. 82.
[2] B. Forte, *Rome and the Romans As the Greeks Saw Them* (Rome 1972), 423–24.
[3] C. Gallavotti, *BPEC*, n.s., 26 (1978): 3: "In tutta Atene, se non erro, allude solo ad un paio di iscrizioni. . . ."

sent the facts. Pausanias has, indeed, transcribed numerous inscriptions, mainly epigrams, word for word, and he has summarized the content of hundreds of others (in book VI some two hundred just for Olympic victors).[4]

The use that Pausanias makes of inscriptions can be instructive. Whenever the text of an extant inscription can be compared with Pausanias' transcription or summary of the same inscription, the comparison will show how thorough—or careless—he was, what he thought to be important enough to include and what not, how he used evidence, and what his methodology was. For instance, after he mentions some bronze images at Sicyon, he says, "They say they are the daughters of Proetus, but the inscription refers to different women." His informants could hardly have been other than the "Sicyonian guides" whom he mentioned a line before; Pausanias uses evidence from the dedicatory inscriptions on the bases of the statues to prove them wrong.[5]

This chapter is divided into three sections devoted to mythology, archaeology, and history.[6] Some inscriptions will testify to Pausanias' accuracy; some, which, in order to be properly understood, require an explanation from another source, will be shown to receive it from Pausanias; and some, together with the evidence of Pausanias, will be shown to be our only source for the preservation of the memory of historical events and important persons.

MYTHOLOGY

Each region in Greece had its myths—had once been inhabited or visited by gods or heroes, goddesses or nymphs, giants or monsters, or famous men or women of so distant a past that they were part of a

---

[4] Actually 203, if H.-V. Herrmann, *Olympia: Heiligtum und Wettkampfstätte* (Munich 1972), is correct in his amusing n. 438 on p. 244. My own count, several times repeated, has shown that he is at least much closer to the truth than others who give figures of 188, 192, or 213 statues.

[5] Pausanias II.9.8. It does not necessarily follow that the guides were illiterate. See also I.2.4: "but the existing inscription assigns the statue, not to Poseidon, but to someone else."

[6] Under the title of this chapter I published a paper in *Classical Antiquity* 3 (1984): 40–56. That paper had the same purpose as this chapter, and the same division into three sections devoted to mythology, archaeology, and history; nevertheless, the topics discussed here are all different, as are, consequently, the passages of Pausanias cited. Taken together, the materials discussed here and there will strengthen the contention that Pausanias deserves an epigraphic commentary. Given the tremendous proportions of such an enterprise, any such commentary for part of the work—for instance, a single book—will be useful.

mythical age, not of history. Since Pausanias was always keen to include in his descriptions not only what could be seen at a spot but also what had been transmitted about its past through books or local tradition or the guides, he has much to say about those times when gods and heroes dwelt on earth. Greek mythology is, as everyone knows, a jungle of fascinating, loosely connected, and quite contradictory traditions,[7] which nonetheless had an impact throughout the whole of antiquity, including the most "enlightened" periods, and thus also play their part in inscriptions. More than once it is Pausanias who provides the clue for an understanding of such mythical allusions.

Endymion and Aetolus

Some sixty years ago, a decree of the Aetolian League, which dates from about 260 B.C. and contains certain grants of privilege for a city called Heraclea, was found in Delphi.[8] The question is, which Heraclea? There are at least fifteen ancient towns called "city of Heracles." Discussion was lively, and no less than six different cities were identified as the Heraclea addressed by the Aetolians.

Since, in the decree, the Aetolians promise to talk to King Ptolemy Philadelphus on behalf of Heraclea, the city was undoubtedly subject to him; furthermore, the Aetolians call the people of Heraclea their descendants (ἄποικοι).[9] This, as Louis Robert was able to show, settles the question in favor of Heraclea on Mount Latmus, close to Miletus in Ionia; this Heraclea, under the rule of Ptolemy by 260 B.C., had already been suggested by some scholars as the city in question.[10] They had not, however, been able to furnish proof. The proof is found in Pausanias V.1.2–5.

Heraclea on the Latmus was famous as the locale of Endymion. Endymion was the lover of Selene (the Moon) and Zeus granted him immortality. In the end he withdrew to the Latmus, founded the city of Heraclea, and then retreated to a grotto in the mountain to enjoy eternal sleep. His son was Aetolus, from whom the Aetolians were descended. The Aetolians therefore had ties of kinship with the Heracleans on the Latmus. The Aetolians were a mighty nation and, next to

---

[7] Very helpful is R. Graves, *The Greek Myths*, 2 vols. in the Penguin series, rev. ed. (London 1960), because of the way the ancient sources are presented.

[8] *Klio* 18 (1923): 297ff.; *FD* III. 3.444; *IG* IX.1².173; Moretti, *ISE* 77.

[9] G. Daux has remarked, "Il ne faut prendre au sérieux ni la συγγένειαν ni même le mot ἄποικοι" (*FD* III.3, p. 112).

[10] For instance, by K. J. Beloch, *Griechische Geschichte*², vol. 4, pt. 2 (Berlin 1927), 609; G. Klaffenbach in his commentary on *IG* IX.1².173.

Macedonia, the strongest power in Greece at the time of the decree, while Heraclea was just a little town. The myth and the mythical relationship served the people of Heraclea well in obtaining some favors from the Aetolians. Pausanias, by preserving the myth, made possible a secure identification of the city.[11]

Elatus and Stymphalus

Shortly after 200 B.C., the inhabitants of the Phocian city Elatea (northeast of Delphi) were expelled from home. Whether the Romans or their Aetolian allies were the cause of this misfortune is disputed, but that is immaterial here. The Elateans turned for help to a city far away, to the city of Stymphalus in Arcadia, where they were given shelter for several years. We learn this from an inscription found in Stymphalus and published in 1947.[12] It is a decree passed by the Elateans to express their gratitude to their Arcadian hosts, after the Roman consul Acilius had allowed them to return home in 191.

The text enumerates all that the Stymphalians had done for them: they had taken them into their own homes, and shared their grain with them and whatever else was needed to live; they had allowed them to participate in all religious ceremonies; and they had assigned them land from their own territory, tax-free for ten years. The Stymphalians also approached the authorities of the Achaean League, of which they were members, and the league, at their request, sent an embassy on behalf of the Elateans to the Roman consul and secured their return. But when the Elateans were to go home, there were no crops in their own territory to feed them—a problem with no easy solution, since there was, at the time, a shortage of grain, and the Achaean League had ordered that no grain be exported. The Stymphalians persuaded the central authorities to lift the ban and authorize the Elateans to take with them the grain that they had harvested on the land assigned to them by their hosts.

It is a moving story that illustrates how far solidarity among Greeks could go when a Greek city was in distress,[13] and yet we want to know, why did the Elateans turn to Stymphalus and not to their neighbors in

---

[11] L. Robert, *BCH* 102 (1978): 477–90.

[12] M. Mitsos, *REG* 59–60 (1946–47): 150–74; Moretti, *ISE* 55; G. Klaffenbach, *BCH* 92 (1968): 257–59; Y. Garlan, *BCH* 93 (1969): 159–60; *SEG* 25.445.

[13] See also IV.29.8, where Pausanias reports that the Arcadians of Megalopolis, when their city was occupied by Cleomenes of Sparta in 223 B.C., were given refuge in Messene, because the Arcadians had fought on the side of the Messenians against Sparta several centuries earlier.

Phocis, and why did the Stymphalians act with such generosity? We would expect to find the answers in the opening lines of the decree; but unfortunately these are lost, though enough is preserved to show that the Elateans and Stymphalians thought they were related.[14] In his description of Elatea Pausanias explains the basis of their kinship: "They claim to be of foreign race, and assert that they were Arcadians originally. For they say that . . . Elatus, son of Arcas, . . . settling with his army in Phocis founded Elatea" (X.34.2). Here he has explained why the Elateans could turn to Arcadia, but why did they choose Stymphalus in particular? Again Pausanias, this time in the book on Arcadia, provides the clue: as Elatus was a son of Arcas, so Stymphalus, the founder of Stymphalus, was a son of Elatus (VIII.4.5–6). Arcas, son of Zeus, from whom the Arcadians descended, and his son Elatus and Elatus' son Stymphalus are, to be sure, mythological figures. The myth, however, was not just some story that the Elateans invented to gain help from the Arcadians; it was a myth that both they and the Arcadians believed. Zeus, Callisto (the mother of Arcas), and Elatus are among the figures represented on an official Arcadian monument of 369/368 B.C. in Delphi, which is described by Pausanias (X.9.6ff.; the inscriptions are largely preserved: *FD* III.1.3–11). The same three names also appear on another dedication at Delphi.[15] Both monuments show that, long before the events discussed here, the Arcadians had been aware of these ties.

This incident clearly demonstrates the impact of myth as late as the second century B.C. The Elateans turned to their Arcadian brothers in time of need, and the Stymphalians shared what was theirs; half a century later, in 146 B.C., during the war between the Achaean League and Rome, it was Elatea's turn to be tested. Once more our witness is Pausanias. The Achaean army, in which the Stymphalians served, had been defeated by the proconsul of Macedonia, Metellus, at Scarphea in Locris. During the retreat, one thousand Arcadians asked to be admitted to Elatea. Pausanias says:

They were received into the city on the strength of some ancient tie of kinship, real or imaginary. But when the news came of the defeat of the Achaeans . . . , the Phocians ordered the Arcadians out of Elatea. . . . Metellus came upon them at Chaeronea. There and then, the gods of Greece took vengeance on the Arcadians, who were now slaughtered by the Romans on the very ground where they had left the Greeks to fight against Philip and the Macedonians. (VII.15.5–6)

[14] Line 2 of the decree.   [15] *FD* III.4.142–44.

This time the relationship worked the other way, to the benefit, at least initially, of the Arcadians at Elatea. This story, however, does not have the same happy ending. The fear of Rome was stronger than the ties of kinship, and led to the slaughter of the Arcadians, a disaster that had a moral significance for Pausanias because the Arcadians were slaughtered at Chaeronea, at the very spot where, in 338 B.C., they were absent from the ranks of those who fought against the Macedonian invader, and so failed to fulfill their duty to Greece.[16]

Anthas

An inscription said to have been found in Athens' Plaka is a dedication: Συνθύται οἱ κατασκευάσαντες τὸ γυ/μνάσιον Διὶ Κεραιῶι καὶ Ἄνθαι. It was transferred to the library of the British School at Athens and published by J. G. C. Anderson as an Attic inscription belonging to the "Roman period."[17] The text was republished in the Attic corpus by J. Kirchner in 1931 as *IG* II².2360. Kirchner tried to link the names of several men on the list to names of members of known Athenian families. Anderson himself, however, had already seen indications in the inscription that pointed to Boeotia: he was struck by the large number of Boeotian names, he knew that the cult of Zeus Ceraeus (or Caraeus) was attested in Boeotia, and he recognized that Anthas was the founder not only of Anthea, which later (together with Hyperea) became Troezen, but also of the Boeotian city Anthedon. He concluded, "It seems probable that the original nucleus of the Guild consisted not of native Athenians, but of foreigners resident in Athens; and that these foreigners were Boeotians."[18]

It was Adolf Wilhelm who recognized that the document must, in fact, have originated in a Boeotian town and later been carried to Athens. He stated correctly that there were too many Boeotians on the list for it to be admissible as an Athenian document.[19] He mentioned Thebes, Thespiae, and Tanagra as Boeotian cities where συνθύται were known, but he added that the mention of Anthas pointed to Anthedon.[20] This observation led M. Feyel to state categorically that the

---

[16] This will be discussed in a wider context in chap. 4, pp. 106–8.

[17] J. G. C. Anderson, *BSA* 3 (1896–97): 106–11. The list seems to have contained 104 names, all with patronymics, some 80 of which are preserved.

[18] Anderson (above, n. 17), p. 109.

[19] *ÖJh* 8 (1905): 278–79.

[20] See also A. Wilhelm, *SBWien* 179 (1915): 12–13. For συνθύται in Boeotia see now P. Roesch, *Etudes béotiennes* (Paris 1982), 119ff., nos. 1–10.

Anthas cult settled the question: the text originated at Anthedon.[21] His conclusion was then happily confirmed by a decree of the same guild of συνθύται, found at Anthedon, in honor of one of their members, Caphisias, son of Homoloichus, who also happened to figure in the list of names in Anderson's inscription (col. A.10).[22] Both the dedication and the decree are therefore from Anthedon and are contemporary[23] (not later than the second half of the second century B.C.).[24] The dedication has recently been republished and thoroughly discussed by P. Roesch.[25]

It was our knowledge of the hero cult of Anthas that enabled us to attribute Anderson's stone to Anthedon well before the second inscription was found at Anthedon itself. Anthas' role in the foundation of Troezen is mentioned by several authors,[26] but only Pausanias has the information that Anthas was the founder of Anthedon: "In Boeotia . . . is a Boeotian city, Anthedon. Some say that the city got its name from a nymph, Anthedon, while others say that one Anthas reigned here, a son of Poseidon and Alcyone, daughter of Atlas" (IX.22.5).

The conclusion is inescapable: Pausanias, and Pausanias alone, enables us to identify the origin of this dedication, said to have been found in Athens, but actually originating in Anthedon.

This is the third of three cases in which Pausanias was the only source for the information needed properly to understand the inscriptions. From his pages the Heraclea of the Aetolian decree can be iden-

---

[21] M. Feyel, *Contribution à l'épigraphie béotienne* (Le Puy 1942), 51–52.

[22] M. H. Jameson, "New Inscriptions from Anthedon," *AA* 83 (1968): 99, no. 3, and fig. 1. More complete edition: Roesch (above, n. 20), p. 91ff. and pl. 6. See also R. Etienne and D. Knoepfler, *Hyettos de Béotie et la chronologie des archontes fédéraux entre 250 et 171 av. J.-C., BCH*, suppl. 3 (1976): 163–66, 244.

[23] The decree orders in line 23 that Caphisias be crowned "in the gymnasium," obviously the one dedicated by the guild of Anderson's text (Jameson [above, n. 22], p. 102), which must therefore be a little earlier.

[24] Wilhelm (above, n. 19), p. 279; see also Etienne and Knoepfler (above, n. 22), p. 244. E. Bethe ("Anthas," in *RE*, suppl. 1 [1903], 88) and H. Schwabl ("Zeus," in *RE* [1972], 319) have erroneously taken Anderson's words "Roman period" to mean "kaiserzeitlich."

[25] Roesch (above, n. 20), pp. 112–17 and pl. 7; cf. pp. 91–112 for the decree of the guild.

[26] Strab. 8, p. 374 (cf. 14, p. 656); Steph. Byz., s.v. Ἀνθηδών; Pausanias II.30.8–9, 31.10; Plut. *Quaest. Graec.* 19 (*Mor.* 295E); Vgl. Toepffer, "Anthas," in *RE* (1894), 2357–58. An epigram of Troezen for her citizen Diomedes, dating from the first half of the third century B.C. and found at the Amphiareum of Oropus, calls Diomedes, who had liberated the town from a foreign garrison, the descendant of the famous hero: Ἄνθα ἀπ᾽ εὐσήμου κεκριμένον γενεᾶς (Moretti, *ISE* 62).

tified, the action taken by the people of Stymphalus on behalf of the Elateans made intelligible, and Anthedon in Boeotia identified as the home of an important (but wandering) inscription. These cases also remind us that Greeks considered myth a part of history—the earliest known part of their past—no matter what critics like Xenophanes or Thucydides might have said. A community could use tradition—even mythological tradition—to obtain rights or favors from communities supposed to be related to it or even from one of the enlightened Roman emperors.[27] In this respect, myth continued to play an important role in Greek political life down into imperial times, and Pausanias, perhaps more than any other writer, provides us with the information needed to assess myth's continuing impact.

ARCHAEOLOGY

More than eighty years have gone by since Frazer completed his commentary, more than seventy years since Hitzig and Blümner published the last volume of theirs. Since then, numerous sites described by Pausanias have been excavated, and numerous monuments mentioned by him have been found and identified. In most cases Pausanias has provided some sort of guidance, but sometimes the new archaeological evidence has seemed to contradict him. As will soon be demonstrated, however, though he does make mistakes, the odds, when there is a contradiction, are not that Pausanias is wrong but that modern scholars are.

Let us consider the sanctuary of Apollo at Delphi, Pausanias' description of it, and the modern scholarship devoted to it, in particular a recent paper by Claude Vatin.[28] Some of the most conspicuous monuments within the sanctuary stood near its entrance (fig. 24): the Bull of Corcyra (no. 3), an offering of the Tegeans (no. 4), and the monument of the Spartans and their allies for the victory of Lysander over the Athenians at Aegospotami in 405 B.C. (no. 5). This monument depicts Lysander, crowned by Poseidon, in the midst of six gods and surrounded by twenty-eight commanders of the fleet. Pausanias, in his book X, states: "On entering the precinct you see a bronze bull made by Theopropus, an Aeginetan, and dedicated by the Corcyraeans" (9.3). "Next are offerings of the Tegeans from booty taken from the

---

[27] See the case of Pallantium in Arcadia and Antoninus Pius as reported in Pausanias VIII.43.1–2.

[28] C. Vatin, *BCH* 105 (1981): 429–59.

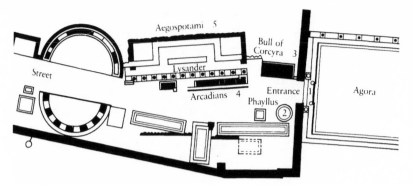

Fig. 24. Delphi, entrance to the sanctuary of Apollo.

Lacedaemonians" (9.5). "Opposite them are offerings of the Lacedaemonians from booty taken from the Athenians" (9.7).

Pausanias is clear: the first two monuments (nos. 3 and 4) were on the same side of the sacred street, the third monument on the other ("opposite them"). Plutarch, himself a priest at Delphi and thoroughly familiar with the sanctuary, agrees; he says that the Spartan victory monument (no. 5) comes first, as one enters the precinct.[29] True, Pausanias says it is third, but he has begun his description on the right side, whereas Plutarch starts on the left. Pausanias' first two monuments are first and second on the right; the third monument, which is opposite them, as he says, was, in fact, the first on the left side. In other words, the Spartan monument must have been to the left—and so the text was understood for a long time.

Things changed, however, with the excavations of the late nineteenth century. Hermann Pomtow claimed that the Spartan offering, too, must have been on the right side (because, otherwise, what could the large colonnade they found have been?).[30] For some fifteen years there were acrimonious debates, with Georg Karo as the most sensible opponent of the new theory,[31] but when the French excavators finally rallied to the opinion of their archfoe Pomtow in 1910, the case seemed settled,[32] and for some seventy years since scholars were almost unanimous in placing the three monuments side by side on one and the same (right) side of the street.

[29] Plut. *De Pyth. or.* 2 (*Mor.* 395B).
[30] *AA*, 1895:8; *AthMitt* 31 (1906): 492ff.
[31] *BCH* 33 (1909): 219–37; 34 (1910): 201–7.
[32] E. Bourguet, *FD* III.1, p. 24ff.

Some scholars did assert that Pausanias could not have been mistaken, since he was there and he reports what he *saw*. They concluded that the text must be corrupt: instead of "opposite" (ἀπαντικρύ) he had written "upward" or "higher up" (ἀναντικρύ).[33] They were not bothered by the awkwardness of such an expression for "next" (ἐφεξῆς) or by the fact that the word Pausanias was supposed to have used is not attested in Greek.

Other scholars preferred to accept the text, but to interpret it. "Opposite," in their view, was not meant to distinguish "opposite" sides of the street, but "opposite" experiences of the Spartans: victory over the Athenians as opposed to defeat by the Arcadians.[34] Others simply maintained that Pausanias was confused, but, one way or another, everybody agreed that the large building next to the Bull of Corcyra and the votive offerings of Tegea (or, as most scholars believed, of Arcadia) was the victory monument of Lysander, the Spartans, and the nauarchs. As if to confirm their interpretation, in 1947 the excavators moved all the remains and inscriptions from the actual Spartan monument (on the left, where all the Spartan remains had been found) to the large colonnade (supposedly the Spartan monument) on the right side of the street.

Now, Pausanias has painstakingly described the Spartan monument (X.9.7–10). He names all thirty-seven gods or commanders represented, and the city of each (twenty-two different ethnics). He also enumerates eight different sculptors and assigns to each the statues he made. Furthermore, he quotes from the epigrams inscribed on the monument. Large parts of these epigrams, two signatures of sculptors, and the inscribed names of twelve statues still exist.[35] All the evidence

[33] This was Pomtow's interpretation, which he still defended in his last discussion of the problem, "Delphoi," in *RE*, suppl. 4 (1924), 1209–14. There he went so far as to say (p. 1211) that most of the numerous contributions on the subject ought never to have been written, since they were based "on Pausanias' corrupt ἀπαντικρύ."

[34] G. Daux, *Pausanias à Delphes* (Paris 1936), 82: "Les deux bases . . . se font en quelque sorte face; Pausanias semble avoir compris la valeur de ce symbole et s'être efforcé de l'exprimer en opposant les Lacédémoniens vaincus . . . et les Lacédémoniens glorieux"; Meyer, p. 690 n. 2: "Der Ausdruck soll wohl besagen, dass das Arkaderdenkmal als Denkmal einer spartanischen Niederlage dem pompösen spartanischen Siegesdenkmal 'entgegen' gesetzt wurde." Good on all these efforts is Regenbogen, p. 1051: "Wenn es nun c. 9, 7 heisst ἀπαντικρύ, so darf man das weder weginterpretieren noch durch Konjektur ändern wollen: es kann nichts anderes heissen als 'auf der gegenüberliegenden Seite der Strasse', wozu man c. 10, 4/5 vergleichen mag" (ἀπαντικρύ δὲ αὐτῶν ἀνδριάντες εἰσὶν ἄλλοι). This is sound reasoning, and the more remarkable since Regenbogen had no solution to offer for the main problem.

[35] *FD* III.1.50–69 (*SIG*³ 115); J. Bousquet, *BCH* 90 (1966): 428ff.

testifies to the accuracy of Pausanias.[36] Could he really have been mistaken in assigning this monument, the largest and richest victory sculptures ever dedicated by a Greek state to Apollo in Delphi, to the wrong side of the street? Hardly.

Nonetheless, it was not until 1963 that the accepted interpretation was contested (for the first time since 1909). Georges Roux argued that there was no valid reason to doubt Pausanias' statement as is: the Spartan monument was on the left side of the street.[37] Roux, however, could not identify the large colonnade on the right side, and had to leave the question open.[38]

Claude Vatin now has proof that the large colonnade was a monumental offering of the city of Tegea,[39] as is, in fact, indicated by Pausanias in the same chapter: "Next are offerings of the Tegeans from booty taken from the Lacedaemonians. . . . [The statues and their artists are enumerated.] These offerings were sent by the Tegeans to Delphi after they had made prisoners of the Lacedaemonians when the latter marched against them" (X.9.5–6). Scholars had assumed that this passage referred only to the base in front (no. 4 in fig. 24), not to the large colonnade behind (no. 5), and, since the statues are those of Arcadian heroes, assumed that the base was dedicated by the whole of Arcadia, not by Tegea alone. Vatin has now read several inscriptions on the stylobate and the walls of the large colonnade, inscriptions that have been there ever since the excavations but have gone unnoticed. There are three dedications by the Arcadians of Tegea (Τεγεᾶται 'Αρκάδες) from booty taken from the Spartans in 370/369, and there is, as Vatin explains, all the likelihood in the world that the attached smaller base, too, was dedicated not by Arcadia but by Tegea.

The Spartan monument for Lysander's victory must then be elsewhere, just as Pausanias—and Plutarch—says it is: to the left, the first monument after the entrance. Pausanias, after all, is correct, and his text sound. And, at the same time, he has been cleared of two other

---

[36] It is only a minor inaccuracy that the herald attested by an inscribed block is missing in Pausanias' text (J.-F. Bommelaer, *Lysandre de Sparte* [Paris 1981], 15). On the other hand, it is not at all certain (despite Bommelaer, p. 113 n. 65) that Pausanias X.9.10 has the ethnic of Theopompus wrong. He was Μήλιος; Niccoli's manuscript of Pausanias had Μίδιος, probably a mechanical corruption.

[37] G. Roux, in J. Pouilloux and G. Roux, *Enigmes à Delphes* (Paris 1963), 16–36. Roux's main point was accepted by several scholars, for instance N. M. Kontoleon, *Gnomon* 39 (1967): 292–93; A. H. Borbein, *JdI* 88 (1973): 77; Th. Hölscher, *JdI* 89 (1974): 78 n. 23.

[38] Roux (above, n. 37), pp. 18–19.

[39] Vatin (above, n. 28), pp. 453–59.

charges: first, that he confused the city of Tegea with the whole of Arcadia and therefore erroneously mentioned a part instead of the whole; second, that he did not mention the large colonnade (if this, in fact, was not the Spartan monument).[40] Given the tremendous number of learned papers written on these problems, Vatin's study will have the effect of an archaeological earthquake.

Pausanias says in connection with the other offerings standing in the square in front of the temple, "There is an ox dedicated by the Plataeans at the time when, along with the rest of the Greeks, they defended themselves against Mardonius, son of Gobryas, in their own territory" (X.15.1). The reference is to the famous victory over the Persians at Plataea in 479 B.C. Pausanias does not identify the artist. In 1950 Pierre Amandry suggested that an inscribed base of the early fifth century with the signature of Theopropus of Aegina belonged to this dedication rather than to the Bull of Corcyra.[41] Vatin has now found proof that this suggestion is correct. On the upper face of the base he was able to read "The Plataeans dedicated this to Apollo in revenge, having seized it from the Medes."[42] The dedication must be from 479 B.C., which gives a new and precise date for Theopropus.

Theopropus was also the artist of the Bull of Corcyra, the first monument to the right as you enter the sacred precinct (no. 3). To repeat what Pausanias says, "On entering the precinct you see a bronze bull made by Theopropus, an Aeginetan, and dedicated by the Corcyraeans" (X.9.3). The huge base is still *in situ*;[43] however, the piece with the signature of Theopropus, which was assumed to belong to it, belongs in fact to the victory offering of the Plataeans (and was found where Pausanias puts this monument, close to the temple, but far from the Bull of Corcyra). The problem with the offering of Corcyra has been how to assess the story Pausanias tells about it, for, indeed, the story does sound ridiculous:

It is said that in Corcyra a bull used to leave the herd and the pasture and go down and bellow by the sea-shore. The same thing happened every day, till the herdsman went down to the shore and beheld a countless shoal of tunnies. He told the Corcyraeans in the city, and they, after laboring in vain to catch them, sent envoys to Delphi, and in consequence they sacrificed the bull to Poseidon,

---

[40] Daux (above, n. 34), pp. 79, 186.

[41] *BCH* 74 (1950): 10–21.

[42] Vatin (above, n. 28), pp. 450–53: Πλαταιὲς Ἀπόλλωνι ἁρπάξαντες Μέδον ποινάν.

[43] For this base, its date, and its remodeling in the fourth century B.C., see Roux (above, n. 37), p. 8ff.

and immediately after the sacrifice they caught the fish; and with the tithe of their take they dedicated the offerings at Olympia and Delphi. (X.9.3–4)

Pausanias had already mentioned the gift to Zeus in the book on Olympia (V.27.9), and there promised to tell the story in his book on Delphi—because it had been Apollo who advised the Corcyraeans to sacrifice the bull to Poseidon and, therefore, was responsible for their success.

Not surprisingly, the story has met with a good deal of skepticism. Georges Daux was very cautious on this point: "There remains the question whether the story is based on truth or whether it only represents some late reasoning: one can suspect but not prove the latter."[44] Ernst Meyer, on the other hand, is less reserved: "The story about the cause of the dedication sounds suspiciously like a tourist guide's fairy tale."[45]

The point is not whether the story as told is true but whether there was a connection between the tunnies and the dedicated bull. And there was. The upper part of the base long regarded as belonging to the Trojan horse (an offering of Argos) was, in fact, the upper part of the base for our bull. On the front side of this badly weathered stone are the remains of dedicatory inscriptions, cut at various times from the early fifth to the third century B.C. (Parts were redone several times when they tended to become illegible.) Vatin has read the inscriptions. The name of the Corcyraeans appears five times; there is the word *tithe* (δεκάτη) as found in Pausanias; there is the name Apollo, and the word *wealth* (εὐδαιμονία); there are, above all, the phrases "pursuit of tunnies" and "from the pursuit of tunnies" (ἀπὸ θηράων θύννων); and, finally, there is, clearly visible, the signature of Theopropus of Aegina, the artist attested by Pausanias. His date (ca. 480 B.C.) and the letter forms of the earliest inscriptions are in complete harmony.[46] This was the bull made by Theopropus in the early fifth century, and dedicated to Apollo by the Corcyraeans from the tithe of the wealth that tuna fish had brought to the city.

How does Pausanias come out of this? With flying colors. He saw the bull some six hundred years after it had been dedicated. He either was able to read the worn inscriptions, parts of which were in the difficult Corinthian alphabet, and so report the story (Vatin doubts this possibility), or sought out and reported a story that tradition had kept

[44] Daux (above, n. 34), p. 78 n. 2.
[45] Meyer, p. 689: "klingt bedenklich nach einem Fremdenführermärchen."
[46] Vatin (above, n. 28), pp. 440–49.

alive for centuries: the bull was dedicated by Corcyra and paid for by the tithe from recently acquired wealth, and the source of this wealth was tuna fish. The pattern recalls Mycenae, where Schliemann's firm belief in the local tradition (as reported by Pausanias), which had preserved the knowledge of where the royal tombs were located, led him to their discovery.[47]

The upshot of the foregoing discussion is this: when scholars condemn Pausanias, even when their verdict is unanimous against him, he may still be right, and all the ingenuity of his critics wrong.[48]

HISTORY

In the northern part of the Athenian agora, between the statue of "Hermes of the Market" (*Hermes Agoraios*) and the "Painted Colonnade" (*Stoa Poikile*), Pausanias says there is a gate, and "on this gate there is a trophy of a victory gained by the Athenian cavalry over Pleistarchus, who commanded the cavalry and the mercenary troops of his brother Cassander."[49] No other source mentions either the victory or the trophy.

Pausanias thus presents us with an otherwise unrecorded event, but when should it be dated? Scholars, following Johann Gustav Droysen, have dated it to 318 B.C., but, as has recently been pointed out by Stanley Burstein, this date is too early for Pleistarchus.[50] Pleistarchus appears for the first time in our sources in 312, and then pursues a remarkable, if varied, career down into the early third century.[51] The years 317–307 can be excluded, because Athens was then an ally of

---

[47] See above, pp. 29f.

[48] R. E. Wycherley, in a recent paper, "Pausanias and Praxiteles," *Hesperia*, suppl. 20 (1982): 182–91, says about Pausanias, "To challenge and disprove a statement by him one needs to be sure of one's own ground, to have clear, solid, ancient evidence and agreement about it" (p. 188). And his final advice is, "Stay with Pausanias" (p. 191).

[49] Pausanias I.15.1. The gate is shown on the plan in E. Vanderpool, *Hesperia* 18 (1949): 130, no. 27 (see fig. 25); it seems that its foundations were found in 1982 (T. L. Shear, Jr., ibid. 53 [1984]: 19–24 and pls. 4a,b and fig. 12). The most recent reconstruction of Pausanias' route in the Agora, from H. A. Thompson and R. E. Wycherley, *The Agora of Athens* (Princeton 1972), 206, is shown in fig. 26; for comparison, fig. 27 illustrates how, in 1909, Robert (p. 330) tried to reconstruct the Athenian agora from the text of Pausanias.

[50] *Classical World* 71 (1977): 128–29.

[51] L. Robert, *Le Sanctuaire de Sinuri près de Mylasa*, vol. 1 (Istanbul 1945), 55ff.; H. Schaefer, "Pleistarchos," in *RE* (1951), 196–99; K. Buraselis, *Das hellenistische Makedonien und die Ägäis* (Munich 1982), 22–23.

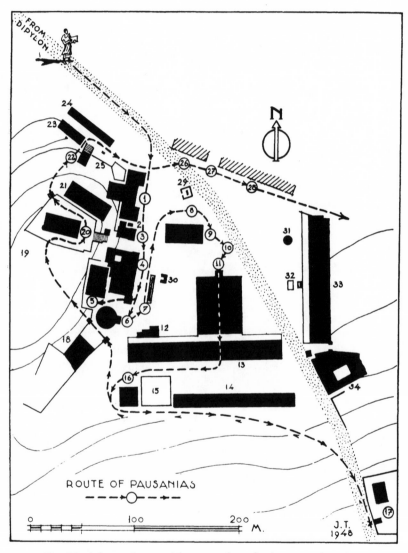

Fig. 25. Athens, Agora with gate and trophy (courtesy American
School of Classical Studies, Athens).

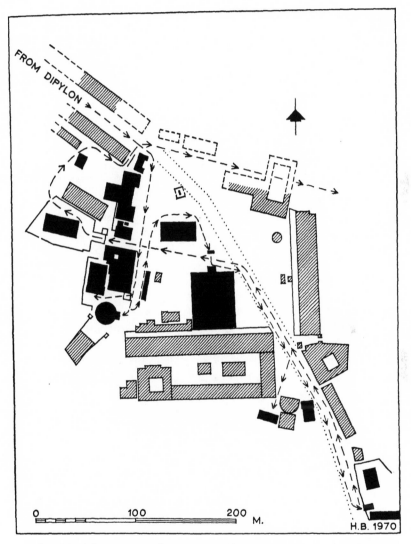

Fig. 26. Athens, route of Pausanias in the Agora (courtesy American
School of Classical Studies, Athens).

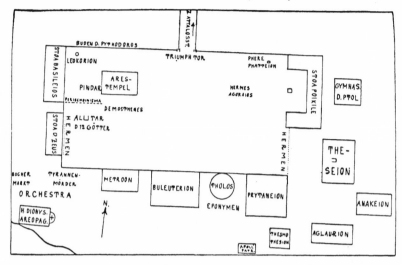

Fig. 27. Athens, the Agora according to C. Robert.

Cassander and under the rule of Cassander's creature Demetrius of Phaleron. Burstein prefers a year between 307 and 302, during which period Athens had to defend herself against Cassander, and specifically 303, but he was thinking of a victory of the Athenians over Pleistarchus somewhere in the Peloponnese.[52]

The word *trophy* comes from the Greek word *tropaion*, which is derived from *trepo*, "to turn back"; a victory monument, therefore, is erected on the very spot where the enemy was forced to retreat. This is the original, and in the fourth century B.C. still prevailing, meaning.[53] The engagement must have taken place at Athens.

The trophy, as described by Pausanias, was inside the walls, not far from the Dipylon gate. It may be that some attacking Macedonians climbed over the walls and were turned back by Athenian cavalry, or perhaps the engagement was fought just outside the walls, at the Dipylon, where Athens always seemed most vulnerable and was often at-

---

[52] On the role of Pleistarchus in the Peloponnesian campaign of 303 see the inscription from Argos published by Moretti, *ISE* 39, and the decree from the Athenian agora published by W. S. Ferguson, *Hesperia* 17 (1948): 114–36, and republished by Moretti, *ISE* 5. A new fragment was identified by A. G. Woodhead and published by him in *Ancient Macedonian Studies in Honor of Charles Edson*, ed. H. J. Dell (Thessaloniki 1981), 357ff. The new evidence indicates that the date is early 303 (not 302) and that the decree was voted by the Athenian assembly (not by the tribe Akamantis).

[53] W. K. Pritchett, *The Greek State at War*, pt. 2 (Berkeley 1974), 246–75. See also Y. Garlan, *War in the Ancient World* (London 1975), 62–64.

Fig. 28. Athens, lead tablet from the Kerameikos (courtesy Deutsches
Archäologisches Institut, Abteilung Athen).

tacked.[54] The trophy would, in this case, be several hundred yards away
from the actual spot of the engagement, perhaps in front of the cavalry
commander's office, which must have been close by.[55]

There the matter rested until an inscribed lead tablet found in a well
in the Kerameikos was published in 1970 (fig. 28). It contains the
names of Pleistarchus, Eupolemus, Cassander, and Demetrius of Phaleron.[56] (Eupolemus was appointed by Cassander as his commander
for the affairs of Greece in 312.)[57] The tablet has been identified by
David Jordan as a curse directed against the men whose names are inscribed: Cassander, his brother Pleistarchus, his Macedonian general
Eupolemus, and his Athenian follower Demetrius of Phaleron. According to Jordan, the tablet must have been prepared when all these men

[54] For instance, by Philip V in 200 B.C. (Livy 31.24) and by Sulla in 86 B.C. (Plut. *Sull.*
14; cf. App. *Mith.* 147–48).
[55] Ch. Habicht, *AthMitt* 76 (1961): 138, accepted by Thompson and Wycherley (above,
n. 49), p. 73 n. 199, and J. H. Kroll, *Hesperia* 46 (1977): 84.
[56] *AthMitt* 85 (1970): 197–98.
[57] Diod. 19.77.6. This is the same chapter in which Pleistarchus makes his first appearance. For the chronology, see R. M. Errington, *Hermes* 105 (1977): 498–99.

"were or were expected to be in or reasonably near Athens, within the ghost's striking distance." Jordan assumed a date when Demetrius was still in power and Pleistarchus already in command, that is to say, between 313 and 307.[58]

But this cannot be correct, because during these years Cassander was never near Athens. Moreover, since Pleistarchus is mentioned first on the tablet, even before Cassander, we can fairly assume that there is a close connection between the curse and the Athenian trophy celebrating Pleistarchus' defeat. Cassander did attack Athens with all his forces in 304, and came close to retaking the city.[59] Pleistarchus and Eupolemus were certainly with him, and perhaps also Demetrius of Phaleron, who may have hoped to regain control of Athens, just as the tyrant Hippias had once hoped to do with the aid of the Spartans and later the Persians.[60] Demetrius' name may, however, have been included, even though he was not present, out of a fear that he might be with Cassander and might return.

The case to which we now turn will show how Pausanias often sheds light on fresh epigraphic evidence. A recently published inscription from Ephesus is a dedication in honor of the emperor Nerva (A.D. 96–98) by the international athletic guild's president, Tiberius Claudius Artemidorus of Tralles (in western Asia Minor).[61] Artemidorus, as his name shows, had inherited or acquired Roman citizenship; he had also been granted honorary citizenship in Ephesus and Alexandria. His citizenship and the prominent post he held are positive indications that he himself must have been a renowned athlete in his earlier years. And so he was; he describes himself as a *pancratiast*, that is, a specialist in a contest combining wrestling and boxing. He also was a *periodonikes*[62] and a *paradoxonikes*.[63] A *periodonikes* has been victorious in all the major Panhellenic contests (there were six by this time: the Olympia, Pythia, Isthmia, and Nemea as of old and the two Ro-

[58] *AthMitt* 95 (1980): 229–36.
[59] The sources are conveniently collected and discussed by H. Hauben, *ZPE* 14 (1974): 10.
[60] Hdt. 5.91–93, 96; 6.102ff.
[61] H. Engelmann and D. Knibbe, *ÖJh* 52 (1978–80): 32, no. 34 (*IEphesos* 1124). The editors say on p. 33 that he is identical to the Artemidorus famous for his strength who is mentioned in Mart. 6.77.3. This is an error. Martial's athlete is Titus Flavius Artemidorus from Adana (*IG* XIV.746; L. Moretti, *Iscrizioni agonistiche greche* [Rome 1953], no. 67).
[62] H. C. Montgomery, Περιοδονίκης, in *RE* (1937), 813–16; Ch. Habicht, *Olympiabericht* 6 (1961): 222–23.
[63] K. Schneider, Παράδοξος = παραδοξονίκης, in *RE* (1949), 1166–67.

man additions, the Actia and Capitolia); a *paradoxonikes* (victor against the odds) has been victorious in two or more major contests on one and the same day.

Since his triumphs include an Olympic victory and Pausanias has so much to say about Olympionikai, there is a certain likelihood that Artemidorus will be found in Pausanias. And he is. Having just mentioned a memorable victory of a young man from Rhodes, Pausanias continues:

The feat of the Rhodian wrestler was surpassed, in my opinion, by Artemidorus of Tralles. Artemidorus failed, it is true, in the boys' pancratium at Olympia, the cause of his failure being his extreme youth. But when the time came for the games which the Ionians of Smyrna celebrate, his strength had grown so much that on one and the same day he vanquished in the pancratium his former boy antagonists from Olympia, and besides them the youths called beardless, and thirdly, the best of the men. He competed amongst the beardless youth in consequence of the encouragement of his trainer, and amongst the men in consequence of a taunt which one of the men had levelled at him. He gained an Olympic victory amongst the men in the two hundred and twelfth Olympiad. (VI.14.2–3)

Pausanias' account explains why Artemidorus can boast the title *paradoxonikes*: he had been victorious in three major contests on a single day.[64] More important, Pausanias states the year of Artemidorus' Olympic victory: the 212th Olympiad, or A.D. 69. It must have been a memorable event, since it came only two years after so many mock victories had been awarded to the emperor Nero, in 67, when the games were held two years earlier than scheduled just to allow Nero, who was in Greece at the time, to compete.[65] Not surprisingly, these games were expunged from the official record of the Eleans as soon as Nero died (A.D. 68). For this, once more, Pausanias is our only witness. In a quite different context, and without stating the reason, he simply interjects, "The two hundred and eleventh Olympiad . . . is the only Olympiad which is omitted in the Elean register" (X.36.9). The reason, however, is obvious.[66]

Another area in which Pausanias provides important historical information not found in any other writer is prosopography. A large number of individuals who were important in their own time and do

[64] Plutarch uses the term for Cimon, who had defeated the Persian army and navy in two battles at the river Eurymedon on one and the same day (*Comp. Cim. et Luc.* 2.1).

[65] On Nero's participation in the Olympic games see Suet. *Ner.* 23–24; Cass. Dio 63.14, 20–21.

[66] See, however, *FGrHist* 416 T 8, with Jacoby's comments.

appear in inscriptions are found in Pausanias, but have left no other trace (or almost none) in the extant literary tradition.

Hieron

At the beginning of the book on Achaea, Pausanias says that the Ionians originally lived in Achaea, but were driven out by the Achaeans and settled in western Asia Minor.[67] He continues with brief accounts of the twelve major Ionian cities.[68] Priene, he says, suffered under Persian domination and, thereafter, under a local tyrant, Hieron. No other ancient author mentions Hieron, but inscriptions from Priene and Ephesus show that he did rule Priene for three years at the very beginning of the third century B.C. He took advantage of the defeat of Antigonus and Demetrius at Ipsus in 301 and seized power. Many Prienians fled the city, seized a fortification called Carium, and eventually succeeded in overthrowing the tyrant. About a century later a dispute arose between Priene and Samos (the Samians owned land on the Continent) over Carium. The two parties pled their case before the Rhodians, who acted as arbiters, and the story of the tyrant Hieron played its role therein.[69] The Rhodians awarded Carium to Priene. We learn all this from an inscription set up in Priene to record the decision.

Cydias, Callippus, and Eurydamus

Three other persons not mentioned by any other author were involved in the Gallic invasion of Greece in 279 B.C., of which Pausanias gives, though not our only, by far our most substantial account.[70] The Gauls were finally stopped by a combined Greek force at Delphi. Among the Greeks, says Pausanias (X.21.5–6), the bravest was the young Athenian Cydias, who lost his life fighting against the barbarians. His shield was dedicated in Athens in the Hall of the Zeus of Freedom, and Pausanias quotes the epigram engraved on it, which, how-

---

[67] Pausanias VII.1.4; a similar statement already in Hdt. 1.145.
[68] Pausanias VII.2–5. Several passages of this are discussed in my paper in *Classical Antiquity* (above, n. 6), pp. 43–46.
[69] Pausanias VII.2.10; *IPriene* 11 and 12 (see L. Robert, *Opera minora selecta*, vol. 3 [Amsterdam 1969], 5–10), 37, 65ff., 76ff., 110ff.; *IEphesos* 2001; W. Otto, "Hieron," in *RE* (1913), 1513–15; H. Berve, *Die Tyrannis bei den Griechen* (Munich 1967), 1:423; 2:720; L. Robert, *Gnomon* 42 (1970): 602.
[70] Pausanias X.19.4–23.14. See M. Segre, *Historia* (Milan) 1 (1927): 18–42; G. Nachtergael, *Les Galates en Grèce et les Sôtéria de Delphes* (Brussels 1977), 3–205; Ch. Habicht, *Untersuchungen zur politischen Geschichte Athens im 3. Jahrhundert v. Chr.* (Munich 1979), 87–94.

ever, he had not seen for himself, because Roman soldiers destroyed the shield during the sack of Athens in 86 B.C. (just as they destroyed the shield of Leocritus, who had been the bravest man in the fighting that occurred when the Athenians expelled King Demetrius' garrison in 287 B.C.).[71] Pausanias, therefore, has taken the epigram for Cydias from a literary source, in all probability from the history of Hieronymus of Cardia.[72]

The young Athenian hero is not on record anywhere else, but a son comes to light in 246 B.C., when the Aetolians had decided to make the festival commemorating the events of 279 Panhellenic and to celebrate it every four years. The Aetolians sent emissaries to invite each Greek city to participate. The Athenian assembly accepted the invitation on the motion of Cybernis, son of Cydias, that is, not coincidentally, the son of the man who had distinguished himself against the barbarians some thirty years earlier.[73] The son is also the subject of an honorary decree at Delphi, and some other members of the family are mentioned in Athenian inscriptions.[74]

The Athenian contingent during the Gallic invasions was led, as we learn from Pausanias, by Callippus, son of Moirocles. He came from a well-known family (in Eleusis), which had been playing a significant role in Athenian public affairs for some time. Callippus himself was honored by the Athenians for his brilliant performance against the

---

[71] Pausanias I.26.2. These events have recently been illuminated in a dramatic fashion by the decree of Athens in honor of Callias of Sphettus published by T. L. Shear, Jr., *Hesperia*, suppl. 17 (1978). See also, for these events and their chronology, Habicht (above, n. 70), pp. 45–67; M. J. Osborne, *ZPE* 35 (1979): 181–94; Ph. Gauthier, *REG* 92 (1979): 348–99; H. Heinen, *GGA* 233 (1981): 189–94.

[72] The case for Hieronymus (*FGrHist* 154), made long ago by Droysen, has been made more recently by Segre (above, n. 70), pp. 28–29, and Habicht (above, n. 70), p. 89 n. 9. A different opinion is expressed by J. Hornblower, *Hieronymus of Cardia* (Oxford 1981), 72–74, who thinks it unlikely that Pausanias had direct knowledge of Hieronymus (the same skepticism is found in F. Jacoby, *FGrHist*, comments on 154, pp. 544–45, and Regenbogen, p. 1070), but admits, about the report on the Celtic invasion, that "some features do suggest Hieronymus" (p. 73). I am not at all convinced that Pausanias knew Hieronymus only at second hand; see in general below, p. 97.

[73] *IG* II².680.4–5 (*SIG*³ 408). For the date, under the archon Polyeuctus, see Habicht (above, n. 70), p. 133ff.; idem (below, n. 92), p. 28 n. 82, pp. 64–69. I do not think that the recently published new decree from Polyeuctus' year necessitates a different chronology (*Hesperia* 52 [1983]: 48–63, esp. 57).

[74] Decree of Delphi: *FD* III.2.159. Cybernis, demarch of Halimus, probably father of the hero of 279, ca. 325 B.C.: *SEG* 2.7. The latter's grandson Cydias: *AthMitt* 85 (1970): 221, nos. 311–14; Kroll (above, n. 55), p. 130, no. 77; p. 133, no. 84.

Gauls; they commissioned Olbiades, a famous artist, to do a portrait of him for the city hall.

No other writer mentions him, but we learn from inscriptions that some ten years later Callippus was sent to the Peloponnese as an ambassador to forge the coalition that allied Athens, Sparta, King Ptolemy of Egypt, and many other Greek states against King Antigonus and the Macedonians in the so-called Chremonidean War (268–262).[75]

Incidentally, one of Callippus' two colleagues on that mission was the famous Athenian Glauco, the brother of Chremonides, who moved acceptance of the alliance with Ptolemy and Sparta. Glauco himself was an Olympic victor (Pausanias mentions his statue; and the base with its inscription has been found in Olympia), and later Glauco became one of Ptolemy's counselors. A long decree in his honor was recently found in Boeotia.[76]

After a common council of the allies was established, Callippus was elected one of the two Athenian representatives.[77] A picture of Callippus emerges: he is an Athenian nationalist, a general, and a political figure, one of a handful of men predominant in Athenian politics in the 270s and 260s. But, despite his brilliant career, we would have sought in vain for him in the remains of ancient literature were it not for three short passages written four and a half centuries later and found in Pausanias.

The third man connected with the Gallic invasion is an Aetolian, Eurydamus. He was one of the Aetolian generals in command at the time the Gallic chieftain Brennus attacked Delphi. Pausanias relates that the Aetolians dedicated a statue of him in the Delphian shrine of Apollo after the victory, and also that the Boeotian city of Thespiae honored his son, Pleistaenus, with a statue in the sanctuary of Zeus in Olympia some thirty-five years later (X.16.4, VI.16.1). Neither father nor son is mentioned by any other extant writer, but we have a dedication found at Delphi and published in 1941, which reads as follows: "Pleistaenus, son of Eurydamus, the Aetolian, dedicated this to Apollo."[78] Pausanias, then, has preserved precise information, gleaned from an excellent contemporary source (probably Hieronymus).[79]

---

[75] For Callippus see Ch. Habicht, *Chiron* 6 (1976): 8–9; idem (above, n. 70), p. 88. See also C. Ampolo, *La Parola del Passato* 34 (1979): 176–78.

[76] For Glauco see Ch. Habicht, *Chiron* 6 (1976): 9 and bibliography. See also W. C. West, *GRBS* 18 (1977): 307–19; K. Buraselis, *Archaiologike Ephemeris* 1982 (1984): 136–60.

[77] *IG* II².686.32 (*SIG*³ 434.69; *Staatsverträge* 476).

[78] *BCH* 64–65 (1940–41): 65, no. 4.   [79] See above, p. 85 n. 72.

Dropion

We even find in Pausanias a third-century king not mentioned in any other literary source: Dropion, king of the Paeonians, northern neighbors of the Macedonians in the area of the upper Vardar.[80] Pausanias (X.13.1–3) saw a dedication at Delphi sent by Dropion, in the form of a bison's head (which prompts Pausanias to insert "a full and sober account of the method of capturing the bison": Frazer, p. xli). There is, in fact, another dedication of the king in Delphi, a statue of his grandfather, King Audoleon, set up by Dropion in faithful observance of an oracle,[81] and there is, in Olympia, the base of a statue of Dropion himself, set up by the Paeonians.[82] Incidentally, the monarchy seems to have ended with Dropion; his land was incorporated into Macedonia.

Aristolaus

Pausanias mentions, as among the monuments in the grove of Olympia, a statue of King Ptolemy II Philadelphus with an inscription on the base that says that it was erected by Aristolaus, a Macedonian (VI.17.3). A decree of Samos in honor of Aristolaus, son of Ameinias, has revealed the identity of this man. Aristolaus was Ptolemy's governor in Caria; he was a member of the ruling class of the Ptolemaic Empire.[83]

Tlepolemus

Tlepolemus, son of Artapates, of Xanthus in Lycia is another, even more eminent official of the same king and of his successor, Ptolemy III Euergetes. The Iranian name Artapates shows that the family belonged to the Persian nobility before it became hellenized. The Artapates who, in 279 B.C., made a dedication to Apollo at Delos, as recorded in Delian inscriptions, must be the father.[84] The son, Tlepolemus, appears in no other writer, but Pausanias says that Tlepolemus of Lycia won an Olympic victory in 254 B.C. in the race of colts, one of the prestigious hippic events (V.8.11). The same Tlepolemus, son of Artapates, is attested as the eponymous priest of Alexander the Great and the dei-

---

[80] I. L. Merker, "The Ancient Kingdom of the Paeonians," *Balkan Studies* 6 (1965): 35–54.

[81] Moretti, *ISE* 79.

[82] *IOlympia* 303 (*SIG*³ 394). His father's name was Leon, as both inscriptions show; "Deon" in Pausanias must be a copyist's error.

[83] Ch. Habicht, *AthMitt* 72 (1957): 218, no. 57, and pl. 133.

[84] *IG* XI.2.161.B.72; *IDélos* 1441 A, col. I.18: Ἀρταπάτου ἀνάθημα.

fied Ptolemaic rulers in two consecutive years, 247/246 and 246/245.[85] This priesthood was the most prestigious honor in the empire of the Ptolemies; the priest, officiating for one year, was mentioned in the preambles of all documents, just after the king. Tlepolemus must therefore have enjoyed the highest favor of the royal court at Alexandria.

Given the prominence of the family in his time it is no wonder that his grandson, Tlepolemos (son of Artapates), rose even higher: in 203 B.C. he was appointed tutor of the boy king Ptolemy V Epiphanes and chancellor of the Ptolemaic Empire.[86] He is also known at Delphi (in two inscriptions), where he was honored as a benefactor for his contributions of substantial gifts of money for the games held in honor of Apollo.[87] In Xanthus in Lycia, his hometown, he served as a priest under both Ptolemy IV (in the late third century B.C.)[88] and Antiochus III, the Seleucid king (in the fall of 196).[89] Tlepolemus, a high dignitary of Ptolemy VI in 169 B.C., was probably another member of the same family.[90]

This family, originally Persian, made its mark in southern Asia Minor, Delos, Delphi, Olympia, Alexandria, and the Ptolemaic Empire during the third and second centuries. Pausanias alone among ancient writers, and just by browsing through the Altis in Olympia more than four hundred years later, preserved an important highlight of its history, the Olympic victory of the elder Tlepolemus.

Besides a number of individuals who, were it not for Pausanias, would have left no trace in the extant literature of antiquity, there are others who are mentioned by Pausanias and one other ancient author.

Diogenes

Diogenes was rescued from oblivion by Ulrich Koehler in a paper published in *Hermes* in 1873.[91] In the 230s B.C., Diogenes was in com-

---

[85] *Prosopographia Ptolemaica*, vol. 9 (Louvain 1981), 40, no. 5288, superseding earlier discussions; W. Clarysse and G. van der Veken, *The Eponymous Priests of Ptolemaic Egypt*, Papyrologica Lugduno-Batava, vol. 24 (Leiden 1983), 8–10.

[86] Th. Lenschau, "Tlepolemos (6)," in *RE* (1937), 1618–19; H. Volkmann, "Ptolemaios," in *RE* (1959), 1693.

[87] G. Daux, *Delphes au IIe et au Ier siècle depuis l'abaissement de l'Etolie jusqu'à la paix romaine, 191–31 av. J.-C.* (Paris 1936), 517–18; *BCH*, suppl. 4 (1977): 127, line 54ff.: καὶ ἃ ἀνέθηκε Τληπόλεμος Ἀρταπάτου Λύκιος ἐν τὸ ἐλαιοχρίστιον.

[88] Unpublished inscription from Xanthus, discussed by J. and L. Robert, *Fouilles d'Amyzon en Carie*, vol. 1 (Paris 1983), 162ff.

[89] J. and L. Robert (above, n. 88), p. 154, no. 15B.

[90] Polyb. 28.19.6; *Prosopographia Ptolemaica*, vol. 6 (Louvain 1968), 51, no. 14787; E. Olshausen, "Tlepolemos (6a)," in *RE*, suppl. 14 (1974), 799.

[91] *Hermes* 7 (1873): 1–6: "Ein Verschollener."

mand of the Macedonian possessions in Greece, notably the Piraeus (the harbor of Athens), the island of Salamis, and several fortresses in Attica. After the death of King Demetrius in 229, Diogenes agreed to a treaty whereby, for the sum of 150 talents (to pay off his mercenary troops), he would evacuate the Piraeus and all of Attica. The Athenians could raise the 150 talents only with the help of other Greek states, notably cities in Boeotia, and some individuals, such as Aratus, the Achaean statesman, and possibly King Ptolemy of Egypt.[92] The bare facts are related by Plutarch (*Arat.* 34) and Pausanias (II.8.6), and the details are filled in by Athenian and Boeotian inscriptions, some of which were unknown to Koehler.[93] For the first time in sixty-five years, the whole territory of Attica was free of Macedonian posts. The Athenians therefore honored Diogenes as a public benefactor. They built a new gymnasium and named it after him (Διογένειον γυμνάσιον), and he was venerated in Attica for centuries to come as a hero.[94]

Philopoemen of Pergamum

Pausanias says that Philopoemen commanded the Pergamene soldiers sent by Attalus II to support the Romans in their war against the Achaeans (in 146 B.C.), and that when the Romans in their victory sacked Corinth, the consul, Mummius, sent the best works of art from there to Rome, but did allow Philopoemen some second-rate pieces. These, Pausanias remarks, could still be seen in Pergamum in his own time (VII.16.1, 8). Peter Levi recently said of Philopoemen that he was "apparently an unknown Pergamene general who has skipped through the net of Pauly-Wissowa and is not mentioned in any commentary on Pausanias, even by way of ignorance."[95]

Philopoemen appears in Plutarch's treatise "Whether an Old Man Should Run the Affairs of State." Speaking of Attalus, who was getting on in age, Plutarch says that Philopoemen, in fact, was running the kingdom, so that the Romans asked people returning from Asia, "Does the king have any influence with his minister?"[96]

---

[92] Comprehensive discussion in Ch. Habicht, *Studien zur Geschichte Athens in hellenistischer Zeit* (Göttingen 1982), 79–93: "Die Befreiung von der makedonischen Herrschaft."

[93] Above all, *IG* VII.2406 from Thebes, VII.1737, 1738 from Thespiae, well discussed by Feyel (above, n. 21), pp. 19–37.

[94] For the Διογένειον γυμνάσιον and for the other honors paid to Diogenes see Habicht (above, n. 92), pp. 83–84. See also L. Robert, *REG* 94 (1981): 359; Al. N. Oikonomides, *ZPE* 45 (1982): 118–20.

[95] Levi 1 : 265 n. 68.

[96] Plut. *An seni* 16 (*Mor.* 792AB). The puns in the Greek text cannot easily be translated.

Fig. 29. Samos, base of statue of Philopoemen (courtesy Deutsches
Archäologisches Institut, Abteilung Athen).

The base of a statue of Philopoemen, found in Samos and dedicated
to the goddess Hera, reads, "King Attalus, son of King Attalus, honors
Philopoemen, son of Andronicus, general, keeper of his seal, for his
virtue, bravery, and good will" (fig. 29).[97]

Olympiodorus

At the turn of the fourth century, the most daring and popular Athenian (as he would be for some thirty years) was Olympiodorus. Were it

[97] *AthMitt* 44 (1919): 30, no. 16.

not for Pausanias, nothing specific about him and his memorable career would be known except for two facts: he was archon in 293/292 (as attested by Dionysius of Halicarnassus and by three inscriptions dated "in the archonship of Olympiodorus")[98] and he was a general, ca. 280 B.C. (as attested in a letter of Epicurus preserved on a papyrus found in Herculaneum).[99] Pausanias alone, because of his interest in Athens' past, has enabled historians to recognize Olympiodorus as the leading statesman in this crucial period of her history. Pausanias speaks of him no less than three times in the first book and twice more in the tenth.[100]

What emerges is the profile of a man born at about the same time as Alexander the Great, but who rose to prominence only in his late forties, that is to say, after 307, when Demetrius Poliorcetes overthrew the government of Demetrius of Phaleron (who had ruled the city for ten years as Cassander's man). Poliorcetes returned the Piraeus (which a Macedonian garrison had occupied for fifteen years) to Athens and declared the city free. For six years Olympiodorus frustrated the desperate attempts of Cassander, first in 304, when he almost recaptured the city,[101] but was stopped by the armed intervention of the Aetolians, whom Olympiodorus had persuaded to come to Athens' rescue. Olympiodorus spoiled Cassander's efforts to recapture the Phocian city Elatea when it defected from the king (I.26.3; X.18.7, 34.3), and he defeated and thus stopped a Macedonian attempt on the Piraeus.[102]

In 294 Demetrius Poliorcetes became master of Athens once more; he suspended the constitution, and appointed Olympiodorus (whose worth he had recognized during the war with Cassander) archon for two consecutive years. This extended archonship in fact meant dictatorial power.[103] However, as soon as Lysimachus and Pyrrhus had wrested Macedonia from Demetrius and Athens had an opportunity to shake off his rule, Olympiodorus took the lead: with a party of daring Athenians he stormed the stronghold called Museion and expelled

[98] Dion. Hal. *De Dinarcho* 9; *IG* II².389, 649 (with W. B. Dinsmoor, *The Archons of Athens* [Cambridge, Mass., 1931], 7); *Hesperia* 7 (1938): 97, no. 17.
[99] *PHercul.* 1418, col. 32a, discussed in Habicht (above, n. 70), p. 99 and n. 28. See also for the text L. Spina, *Cronache Ercolanesi* 7 (1977): 64–65 (cf. 60, col. 27). Full bibliography in M. Gigante, ed., *Catalogo dei Papiri Ercolanesi* (Naples 1979), 312–14.
[100] I.25.2, 26.1–3, 29.13; X.18.7, 34.3.
[101] See above, p. 82 n. 59.
[102] Pausanias I.26.3, as discussed in Habicht (above, n. 70), pp. 102–7. See, however, U. Bultrighini, *Riv FC* 112 (1984): 54–62.
[103] Habicht (above, n. 70), pp. 22–33, esp. p. 28.

the Macedonian garrison.[104] The Athenian casualties were given a state funeral. Athens was free and was to remain free for one generation.

Olympiodorus was once again the hero of the day. He remained at the helm until his death (ca. 280). The honors he received were unique: a statue on the Acropolis, a monument in the Prytaneion, which held the common hearth of the city, and an officially commissioned painting in Eleusis (I.25.2, 26.3). The Elateans also honored him with a bronze statue and an image of a lion in gratitude for his services (I.26.3, X.18.7). Pausanias records all this; it is generally agreed that his source must have been a decree in honor of Olympiodorus standing alongside the statue on the Acropolis. Pausanias aptly summarizes Olympiodorus' impact: "Olympiodorus earned fame both by the greatness and the opportuneness of his exploits, for he infused courage into men whom a series of disasters had plunged into despair." [105]

Cephisodorus

Finally, another Athenian, Cephisodorus, a century later than Olympiodorus and, like him, the leading figure of his age, is known in the literary tradition apart from Pausanias only as Athenian ambassador to Rome in the winter of 198/197 (when the issue was whether peace with King Philip should be concluded).[106] Some scholars have thought that that is all we know: "We know nothing else about Kephisodoros, though Polybius mentions the embassy." [107] Fortunately, this is incorrect. It is true that Polybius does not say that Cephisodorus was the leading statesman of Athens at that time, nor could this be inferred from the decree adopted by the Athenian assembly on his motion in 229/228 B.C.[108] Just as for Olympiodorus, it is Pausanias alone who informs us that Cephisodorus was the foremost political figure in Athens during this critical period. Here, too, as with Olympiodorus, Pausanias was assumed—especially as the style of his account resembles that of Athenian decrees—to have drawn his information from a contemporary decree. Such a decree (fifty-six well-preserved lines in

---

[104] See the works cited above, p. 85 n. 71.

[105] I.25.2. See also J. K. Davies, *Athenian Propertied Families* (Oxford 1971), 164–65.

[106] Polyb. 18.10.11. For these negotiations, see the classic paper of M. Holleaux, *REG* 36 (1923): 115–71 (reprinted in *Etudes d'épigraphie et d'histoire grecques*, vol. 5 [Paris 1957], 29–79).

[107] Levi 1:103 n. 216.

[108] *IG* II².832.11 (with the comments of B. D. Meritt, *Hesperia* 5 [1936]: 420); L. Moretti, *ISE* I, p. 79 n. 11; M. J. Osborne, *ZPE* 41 (1981): 160–61.

Fig. 30. Athens, decree for Cephisodorus (courtesy American School
of Classical Studies, Athens).

length) came to light during the American excavations of the Athenian agora in 1934.[109]

Pausanias says that he saw a monument for Cephisodorus on his way from Athens to Eleusis (I.36.5–6). Cephisodorus, he says, was the leader of the people and a bitter enemy of Philip V. He made allies of Attalus and Ptolemy and also the Aetolians, the Rhodians, and the Cretans. He also went to Rome to ask for help against Philip and the Macedonians. The Romans listened, fought a war with Philip, and defeated him. The decree from the Agora says, among other things, that Cephisodorus was responsible for the acquisition of new friends, that he foresaw and forestalled attacks from the outside, that he concluded profitable alliances, and that he went on highly important embassies for the rescue of Attica. The inscription accords well with Pausanias, although it is phrased in such general terms that it cannot have been Pausanias' source. Probably more specific decrees from the years 200–198 once stood by Cephisodorus' monument and were seen and summarized by Pausanias.

Only a few selections from the vast amount of material available have been discussed in this chapter. As can be easily seen from these samples, an epigraphic commentary on Pausanias is urgently needed.

---

[109] *Hesperia* 5 (1936): 419–28; Moretti, *ISE* 33. See fig. 30.

IV

PAUSANIAS ON THE
HISTORY OF GREECE

Pausanias the Guide has already been discussed—the knowledgeable
authority who describes and explains to others less knowledgeable
what is worth seeing at each site. The Guide's accuracy was tested
through a comparison of his account with the evidence of modern excavations. Pausanias the Guide is highly trustworthy, but Pausanias
also relates events from the history of each region or city, usually
events in the distant past, that he has read about, not experienced, in
short, the *logoi*, not the *theoremata* (see above, p. 21). Pausanias the
Historian, then, except for a few instances, depends on the written
works of others.

The Historian complements the Guide,[1] but the two are not equal.
Pausanias wanted to produce both a guide for sightseers and a work of
literature. He may have intended the historical sections of the book
more for those readers who would never see the monuments he has
described, although the history would benefit those touring the sites as
well; but Pausanias does not write history for the sake of history, or
mythology for the sake of mythology. He is not, and does not intend to
be, a historian, and should not be judged by the standards applied to
historians.[2]

The history that Pausanias chooses to narrate always springs from a
site or monument and is to that extent predetermined, not the author's

[1] H. L. Ebeling, "Pausanias as an Historian," *CW* 7 (1913): 138–41, 146–50.
[2] "Pausanias . . . has treated his sources unhistorically—for which he should not altogether be blamed: he was not writing history—but not unintelligently, and the relevant
chapters contain scraps of information which seem to come directly from Pausanias'
own fund of general knowledge" (R. M. Errington, *Philopoemen* [Oxford 1969], 238).

choice—a truth that is crucial (and self-evident) but seldom stated. The history that Pausanias relates is often assessed as though it had been written by a professional historian for historical reasons.[3] Pausanias—it cannot be overemphasized—did not choose a historical subject, then read the sources, consult documents, compare accounts, and resolve contradictions. He did not seek ultimate causes of events.

Unlike his older contemporary Arrian, who, when he decided to write the history of Alexander the Great, could read all the available accounts, choose the two that seemed most trustworthy, "present matters on which they agree as true, and . . . select from those matters on which they conflict according to probability and interest,"[4] Pausanias had to deal with historical events scattered over a time span of almost a millennium.

Pausanias wanted to enliven his descriptions of regions, cities, and monuments with the historical facts; they might be, and usually were, already established by others, and more or less well known, though not, of course, known to all of his readers. He uses the historical passages to introduce a certain region or city, or to explain the historical context of a monument, which could be an honorific statue, a dedication to the gods, or a public memorial for those who fell in war. Pausanias gives the names of those honored and often expands on their role in history.

These individuals (and most of the sites and objects) came from a past ancient even to Pausanias. Pausanias had to depend on other historians. Consequently, Pausanias the Historian can be judged only after his sources have been judged, and the sources can be judged only after they have been identified; but it is rare that they can be securely identified, and even when they can they are usually no longer extant—only the name of the author is known—and so must be judged through Pausanias just as Pausanias is judged through them. In these cases, it is impossible to separate Pausanias from his source.

The search for his sources has not taken scholars very far in the analysis of Pausanias. A great battle (the last such) was fought in the thirties over the sources of his long account of the Messenian wars in the eighth and seventh centuries, and fought to no conclusion, even

---

[3] This tendency is obvious in many contributions, for instance in the pages of M. Holleaux cited below, n. 14.

[4] Arr. *Anab.*, *praef.* 1. The quotation is from Ph. A. Stadter, *Arrian of Nicomedia* (Chapel Hill 1980), 61. See also A. B. Bosworth, *A Historical Commentary on Arrian's History of Alexander*, vol. 1 (Oxford 1980), 16.

though, in this case, Pausanias himself names his two principal authorities, Rhianus and Myron.[5]

It is inappropriate to judge Pausanias by the standards applied to professional historians.[6] Pausanias cannot, and does not try to, compete with historians like Thucydides or Polybius. The work contains a good deal of solid historical information (probably still underestimated), but whereas Pausanias' descriptions have been proven time and again to be accurate and trustworthy, there are quite a number of errors and other shortcomings in his historical narrative. Scholars have been more inclined to point out the latter than to appreciate the former. Therefore, it is worthwhile to look more closely into his performance in the field of history and, more important, into his views on history.

Pausanias had read widely in history. He is familiar with Herodotus,[7] Thucydides, Xenophon, Hieronymus of Cardia (the main authority on the early Hellenistic period—that is, from the death of Alexander in 323 to the death of Pyrrhus in 272), Polybius, and a good many others.[8] His complete familiarity with Herodotus sometimes shows in offhand remarks; for instance, after he has described an offering in Olympia by Aenesidemus of Leontini, he adds, "This last is not, I suppose, the Aenesidemus who was tyrant of Leontini" (V.22.7)—a

[5] The main participants were J. Kroymann, *Sparta und Messenien* (Berlin 1937) and *Pausanias und Rhianos* (Berlin 1943), and Ed. Schwartz, "Die messenische Geschichte bei Pausanias," *Philologus* 92 (1937): 92ff. From the forties, F. Jacoby, commentary on Rhianos, *FGrHist* 265 F 38–46, pp. 109–95. The balance has been drawn by E. Meyer, "Messenien," in *RE*, suppl. 15 (1978), 240–53, who gives the copious bibliography. The fragments of Myron can be found in *FGrHist* 106.

[6] Modern historians seem not always to be aware of that, and for this reason are often inclined to criticize Pausanias severely, for instance M. Holleaux (see below, n. 14); W. K. Pritchett, *Studies in Ancient Greek Topography*, pt. 2 (Berkeley 1969), 62: "Pausanias' accuracy in topographical (in contrast with historical) matters"; J. and L. Robert, *Bull. épigr.*, 1978:58: "le périégète, dont on peut confirmer souvent la valeur, et l'historien, qui est déplorable, comme on le reconnaît généralement, et dont il s'agit dans l'article de M. Holleaux. . . ."

[7] See I. O. Pfundtner, "Pausanias Periegeta imitator Herodoti" (diss., Königsberg 1866); C. Wernicke, *De Pausaniae Periegetae studiis Herodoteis* (Berlin 1884); more recently, for instance M. Segre, *Historia* (Milan) 1 (1927): 26–28. Already in 1890 Gurlitt claimed (p. 106 n. 55) that in at least eighty-two passages where he is not named Herodotus was demonstrably used.

[8] For Thucydides and Xenophon see below, n. 30; for Hieronymus, above, p. 85 n. 72; for Polybius, Frazer, p. lxxiv; M. Segre, *Athenaeum*, n.s., 7 (1929): 483ff.; Regenbogen, p. 1075.

hidden reference to Herodotus.[9] Pausanias has read Plutarch, at least some of the biographies (for instance, the life of Philopoemen, the Achaean general and politician), though he never mentions Plutarch by name.[10] Pausanias was well read in history, as he was in literature (see below, 142ff.).

My own distinct impression is that, except for some long and elaborate digressions (in which he seems to follow closely a single historian), Pausanias does not copy any historian's work, but usually writes history from memory. This method no doubt accounts for most of his errors.[11] In I.6.6, he implies that there was only one winter (instead of six) between the battle of Gaza (312 B.C.), in which Ptolemy defeated Demetrius, and the battle of Salamis (306), in which Demetrius defeated Ptolemy. In I.6.8, he erroneously identifies the Ptolemy honored by the creation of the tribe Ptolemais in Athens as Ptolemy II instead of Ptolemy III.[12] In IV.29.1 and 32.2, he confuses Demetrius the son of Philip V and Demetrius the Illyrian, the associate of Philip V. In IV.27.9 (leaving aside the possibility of a copyist's error), he calls the Athenian archon, Dys*ni*cetus, Dys*ci*netus; in VII.16.10, he calls the Athenian archon, Hagnotheus, Antitheus.

Professional historians nowadays make such mistakes, even the best, and especially in the fields they know best. Just a moment's inattentiveness can change Antiochus to Antigonus, and the mistake may slip past proofreading into the published book.[13] Most of Pausanias' errors are slips of this kind and are pardonable in a man who was not a professional. For instance, in II.8.4 Pausanias inadvertently puts King

---

[9] Hdt. 7.154. Similarly, V.25.11 alludes to Hdt. 7.164.1; see Frazer, p. lxxvi n. 2. Other such allusions ("latente Herodot-Anspielungen," as Robert [p. 98 n. 3] has called them) are, for instance, IX.32.10 (Hdt. 1.137) and VI.3.8 (Hdt. 7.152.3). For a bibliography on the relationship between Pausanias and Herodotus see H.-W. Nörenberg, *Hermes* 101 (1973): 240 n. 16. See further below, pp. 115f., on Phayllus.

[10] That Pausanias has read Plutarch has often been assumed, for instance by K. Ziegler, "Plutarchos," in *RE* (1951), 947, and Regenbogen, pp. 1075–76. It has been demonstrated by Errington (above, n. 2), pp. 238–40; the main passage is Pausanias VIII. 49–52. Plutarch's lost *Epaminondas* seems to be used in IX.13–15. Pausanias may also have known and used Plutarch's *Aratus* (so, tentatively, Regenbogen, p. 1072) and his lost *Aristomenes* (Ziegler, pp. 895, 947).

[11] See also Frazer, p. lxxvii; F. W. Walbank, *Philip V of Macedon* (Cambridge 1940), 286 n. 7; Heer, pp. 85–88.

[12] For the creation of the tribe see Ch. Habicht, *Studien zur Geschichte Athens in hellenistischer Zeit* (Göttingen 1982), 105–12.

[13] Here are a few instances, collected from works on Pausanias. Heberdey (p. 106), commenting on X.34.5, has "Mnesilochos" instead of the correct "Mnesibulos." Hitzig and Blümner (vol. 3, pt. 1, p. 234) say "Antigonos I. Soter" instead of the correct "Antiochos

Antigonus Gonatas down as tutor to Philip V; of course, he knew better, and in VII.7.4 he names the tutor correctly—Antigonus Doson. Pausanias does make more serious errors. He observed that the small Boeotian town of Haliartus was half burned, and tells us, in two different passages (IX.32.5, X.35.2), that it was burned by the Persians in 480 B.C., but the army of Xerxes did not pass through Haliartus; the town was burnt by the Romans in 171 B.C. during their war with Perseus. Maurice Holleaux recognized long ago that Pausanias must have read somewhere that Haliartus was burned ἐν τῷ Περσικῷ πολέμῳ, which he took to mean "during the Persian War" instead of "during the war with Perseus." Holleaux made much ado about this error, and this is a major error, but it does not follow, as Holleaux would have it, that Pausanias cannot be trusted when he turns to history.[14]

In the first book on Elis, Pausanias says, "We know of no Roman

---

I. Soter." Wilamowitz (*Antigonos von Karystos* [Berlin 1881], 192 n. 13) accuses Pausanias of having confused, as Plutarch has (*Mor.* 530C), the two younger sons of King Cassander; however, it is Wilamowitz who is in error—Pausanias (IX.7.3) is correct. Robert (pp. 24, 202) speaks twice of the battle at Arginusae, where that of Aegospotami is meant (Pausanias VI.3.15); he also (p. 15) gives the number of common benefactors of Greece in Pausanias VIII.52 as twelve, instead of ten, by adding Aristides and Pausanias of Sparta, both of whom Pausanias, in fact, explicitly excludes (VIII.52.2). Heer (p. 74) holds that it was not Alexander but his father, Philip, who destroyed the rebellious city of Thebes, and goes on to say that Thebes, reborn, was thereafter able to destroy the power of the Lacedaemonians—which puts the battle of Leuctra (371 B.C.) after 335 B.C. Other cases could easily be cited, among them several from the notes to Levi's *Pausanias* (1 : 28 n. 60, 30 n. 66, 242 n. 30).

[14] M. Holleaux, *RevPhil* 19 (1895): 109–15 (reprinted in *Etudes d'épigraphie et d'histoire grecques*, vol. 1 [Paris 1938], 187–93). See also Regenbogen, p. 1089: "greulicher historischer Fehler." Holleaux soon added another attack, under the title "Apollon Spodios," in *Mélanges H. Weil* (Paris 1898), 193–206 (*Etudes*, pp. 195–209), with the following conclusion: "Voilà longtemps qu'en d'autres pays on a pris la sage habitude de juger le périégète à son vrai mérite, de lui accorder le moindre crédit possible et de ne rien admettre de lui qu'après vérification redoublée." As can be seen from the list of scholars disagreeing with Holleaux's major argument against Pausanias (*Etudes*, p. 209 n. 1, additional note by L. Robert), Holleaux remained far from having established his point; his conclusion, therefore, does not seem justified. See also Holleaux, *REA* 22 (1920): 84 ("Pausanias, dont l'autorité historique est nulle"), where, in particular, the role of the Athenian Cephisodorus as described by Pausanias is doubted—the decree in honor of Cephisodorus found in the Athenian agora has effectively put these doubts to rest (above, p. 92). As Ed. Will says, concerning Holleaux's verdict, "C'est pourtant celui [Pausanias] qui a reçu une confirmation épigraphique" (*Histoire politique du monde hellénistique*, vol. 2, 2d ed. [Nancy 1982], 129–30). Pausanias is also defended against a similar charge by P. Roesch, *Etudes béotiennes* (Paris 1982), 214 n. 37.

before Mummius, whether private person or senator, who dedicated an offering in a Greek sanctuary, but Mummius dedicated a bronze Zeus in Olympia from the spoils of Achaia" (V.24.4). Mummius defeated Achaea in 146 B.C.[15] We, today, happen to know of several Romans who made offerings before 146: in the 190s T. Flamininus and Scipio Africanus each made dedications in Delos and Delphi; Manius Acilius also made one; and L. Aemilius Paullus, the victor over Perseus, made a dedication in Delphi in 167.[16] Only two of these dedications are attested by an author;[17] the others are known only from inscriptions. This is Pausanias' error, but a harmless error, and not so important as his willingness to make such observations.

Pausanias' not being a historian has its disadvantages and its advantages. He is more disposed to use documents than many ancient historians; when he cites historical facts directly from the inscriptions on monuments, as far as the text goes he must be regarded as an eyewitness, just as with any other monument, and he is as trustworthy as the epigraphic evidence. His accounts of the Athenian statesmen Olympiodorus and Cephisodorus derived from decrees have already been discussed in detail in the preceding chapter. I should like to add that one of these passages has given rise to much controversy. Pausanias seems to say that Olympiodorus had once rescued the Piraeus from the Macedonians.[18] For a very long time, the eminent Italian scholar Gaetano de Sanctis stood virtually alone in his conviction that Pausanias was wrong in saying that Olympiodorus recovered for the Athenians the Piraeus sometime between 295 and 270. As more and more inscriptions became known from different years, all of them showing the Macedonians in control of the harbor, the span of time during which Olympiodorus could have rescued the Piraeus became narrower and narrower. Still, de Sanctis was unable to explain the clear statement of Pausanias (Πειραιᾶ . . . ἀνασωσάμενος); he attempted to emend the

---

[15] Full discussion of all relevant questions by H. Philipp and W. Koenigs, "Zu den Basen des L. Mummius in Olympia," *AthMitt* 94 (1979): 193–216.

[16] Flamininus at Delos: *ILS* 8765; at Delphi: Plut. *Flam.* 12.11–12. Scipio at Delos: *IDélos* 442 B, line 102; at Delphi: G. Daux, *Delphes au IIe et au Ier siècle depuis l'abaissement de l'Etolie jusqu'à la paix romaine, 191–31 av. J.-C.* (Paris 1936), 599ff. Acilius: Plut. *Sull.* 12. Aemilius Paullus: *FD* III.4.36.

[17] Plut. *Flam.* 12; *Sull.* 12. See M. Guarducci, "Le offerte dei conquistadori romani ai santuari della Grecia," *RendPontAcc* 13 (1937): 41–58; E. S. Gruen, *The Hellenistic World and the Coming of Rome* (Berkeley 1984), 167–70.

[18] I.26.3: Ὀλυμπιοδώρῳ δὲ τόδε μέν ἐστιν ἔργον μέγιστον χωρὶς τούτων ὧν ἔπραξε Πειραιᾶ καὶ Μουνυχίαν ἀνασωσάμενος. ποιουμένων δὲ Μακεδόνων καταδρομὴν ἐς Ἐλευσῖνα Ἐλευσινίους συντάξας ἐνίκα τοὺς Μακεδόνας.

text, unconvincingly, and in the end rejected Pausanias altogether—"a late and confused writer."[19]

De Sanctis was quite right, as it turns out, that the Macedonians' possession of the Piraeus was not interrupted, but he was certainly wrong to reject Pausanias, because Pausanias was using the evidence in inscriptions about Olympiodorus. Pausanias' sentence has to be interpreted differently: Olympiodorus did not recover the Piraeus from the Macedonians when they held it; he rescued it when they attempted to capture it, sometime before 295 B.C.[20]

The person who judges Pausanias must always be careful to distinguish between what Pausanias has seen (a monument, an inscription), what he may have read in a historical account, and what he may have been told. He frequently adds information of his own to what he draws from inscriptions. The inscriptions prompt him to expand on the persons or events in question and thus to reveal what he has read (and may have misinterpreted). He saw a trophy at Mantinea (in Arcadia) of a battle that, he says, the Spartan king Agis, son of Eudamidas, fought at Mantinea (around the middle of the third century B.C.) against a coalition of Arcadians, Achaeans, and Sicyonians, led by Aratus of Sicyon, Podares of Mantinea, and Lydiadas and Leocydes of Megalopolis. Agis lost the battle and his life.[21] The story cannot stand; either the Spartan was not a king or his name was not Agis or he did not die there. Pausanias may have misrepresented a source, or confused several events.

Certainly Pausanias saw a trophy, and the trophy prompted him to tell the story. The question is, was there ever such a battle,[22] or was the story the result of Pausanias' confusion or his Mantinean informants' invention?[23] Perhaps he saw a trophy from the battle of 418 B.C. at

---

[19] *RivFC* 55 (1927): 495–96: "scrittore tardo e confusionario."

[20] The case has recently been argued at some length: Ch. Habicht, *Untersuchungen zur politischen Geschichte Athens im 3. Jahrhundert v. Chr.* (Munich 1979), 95–112. See also Bultrighini (above, p. 91 n. 102).

[21] The main report is VIII.10.5–10; other mentions occur in VI.2.4; VIII.8.11, 27.14. Operations of the same Agis against Megalopolis and Pellene: VIII.27.13–14, 36.6; II.8.5; VII.7.3.

[22] That the battle occurred has been argued by, for instance, K. J. Beloch, *Griechische Geschichte*[2], vol. 4, pt. 2 (Berlin 1927), 523–27, 609–11; P. Schoch, "Lydiadas," in *RE* (1927), 2202; F. Bölte, "Mantinea," in *RE* (1930), 1326; F. W. Walbank, *Aratos of Sikyon* (Cambridge 1933), 36 n. 1; E. Meyer, "Orchomenos," in *RE* (1939), 899; J. A. O. Larsen, *Greek Federal States* (Oxford 1968), 309; Errington (above, n. 2), p. 3.

[23] So G. Fougères, *Mantinée et l'Arcadie orientale* (Paris 1898), 487; B. Niese, *Geschichte der griechischen und makedonischen Staaten seit der Schlacht bei Chäronea,*

Mantinea, where a Spartan king Agis did fight (but was victorious).[24] This suggestion, too, has its difficulties, and the problem seems insoluble. Pausanias is interested only in Greek history. He includes events scattered through the whole of the seven centuries from the later archaic period, when history supplants mythology, down to his own time, but he has his preferences.[25] He relates little about his own time, the second century A.D., and, in general, little about the history of the Roman Empire, that is to say, the two hundred years from the battle of Actium to the invasion of Greece by the Costoboci and the Danubian wars in the 170s. What little he does have to say usually concerns the reigning emperors[26] or Augustus' changes in the administration of Greece, such as the reformed structure of the amphictyony (the famous old assembly of Greek states around Delphi) and the development of Patras as a Roman colony.[27] Pausanias' interest in the history of Greece seems to stop with the Achaean War of 146 B.C. and the destruction of Corinth by the Romans, with the exception of the catastrophe that befell Athens in 86 B.C., when the army of Sulla sacked the city.

He is almost exclusively interested in the history of *independent* Greece, but even there he does not treat all periods alike. Of the fifth century he writes mostly about the Persian Wars, very little about the fifty years between Xerxes' invasion of Greece and the outbreak of the Peloponnesian War in 431 (which Thucydides called the *pentekontaetia*), and almost nothing about the Peloponnesian War. He has much more to say about the fourth century—the hegemony of Thebes, 371–362; Philip II of Macedonia and Alexander the Great;[28] even

---

vol. 2 (Gotha 1899), 303 n. 1; Hitzig and Blümner, vol. 3, pt. 1 (1907), 146; F. Hiller von Gaertringen, *Klio* 21 (1927): 9–11; Pritchett (above, n. 6), pp. 61–62; E. Gruen, *Historia* 21 (1972): 612 n. 9; R. Urban, *Wachstum und Krise des Achäischen Bundes* (Wiesbaden 1979), 39–43. Undecided is Ed. Will, *Histoire politique du monde hellénistique*, vol. 1, 2d ed. (Nancy 1979), 320: "si la tradition sur ce point est exacte."

[24] Fougères (above, n. 23) and Pritchett (above, n. 23).

[25] For more detail and some statistics, see Regenbogen, pp. 1063–69, who made use of an unpublished manuscript of Heinrich Bischoff (now in the Universitätsbibliothek Heidelberg).

[26] Trajan is mentioned in IV.35.3 and V.12.6. Hadrian occurs in numerous passages (see Rocha-Pereira 3:190, in the "Index historicus"). Antoninus Pius is praised in VIII.43. 1–5, and Marcus Aurelius in VIII.43.6; these eulogies are, according to Robert, pp. 266–69, later additions to the book.

[27] Augustus and the amphictyony: X.8.3–5; Augustus and Patras: VII.17.5, 18.7, 18.9, 22.1, 22.6; X.38.9. Augustus and Laconia: III.21.6, IV.31.1. Augustus and Nicopolis: X.8.3–5.

[28] Regenbogen, pp. 1067–68.

more about the history of Alexander's successors—but by far the most to say about the third and first half of the second century (down to 146 B.C.).[29]

Various factors cause this imbalance. First, the monuments that would prompt Pausanias to give a historical narrative were much more numerous for the Hellenistic than for the classical period. Second, as Pausanias tells us more than once, he did not feel the need to retell what had already been told so well by others—Herodotus and Thucydides (who, together, cover the history of Greece in the fifth century), and Xenophon (who covers the first forty years of the fourth).[30] Third, as he himself says of the time after Alexander:

> The age of Attalus and Ptolemy is so remote that the tradition of it has passed away, and the writings of the historians whom the kings engaged to record their deeds fell into neglect even sooner. For these reasons, I propose to narrate their exploits, and the manner in which the sovereignty of Egypt, of Mysia and of the border lands, devolved on their ancestors. (I.6.1)

Pausanias states this at the beginning of the first book, and he manages with various digressions here and there to incorporate in the first book a complete and sensible, even if much abbreviated, account of the history of the major successors of Alexander down to the death of Pyrrhus (272 B.C., where the work of Hieronymus ended). He includes the Ptolemies (chaps. 6–7), the Attalids (8), Lysimachus (9–10), Pyrrhus (11–13), and Seleucus (16). He has interwoven these accounts, and also inserted Antigonus and Demetrius Poliorcetes, Antipater and Cassander. Athens is the natural setting for the history of these rulers because they all have monuments of various kinds there, and these monuments can serve as transitions to the historical digressions. Pausanias has painstakingly planned and executed this system.[31]

Often he inserts passages in later books to resume the narrative of book I, resuming it at a place more appropriate to its continuation. For instance, the story of Cassander is begun in book I and resumed in

---

[29] Regenbogen, pp. 1068–69.
[30] For Herodotus see I.5.1, 8.5; II.30.4; III.17.7; X.28.6; for Thucydides, I.23.10, VI. 19.5; for Xenophon, I.3.4. The most instructive passage is III.17.7, where the mention of Pausanias, victor in the battle of Plataea, is followed by the statement "His history is well known, and I will not repeat it: the accurate narratives of previous writers are sufficient"; see also I.23.10: "The histories of Hermolycus, the pancratiast [Hdt. 9.105], and of Phormio, the son of Asopichus [Thuc., books 1 and 2, passim], have been told by other writers, so I pass them by." See Gurlitt, p. 50; Frazer, p. lxxiii; Pasquali, p. 194; Meyer, pp. 38–39; Regenbogen, p. 1070.
[31] Regenbogen, pp. 1064–69.

book IX (Boeotia) at Thebes (the Boeotian capital), which had been destroyed by Alexander twenty years earlier and refounded by Cassander in 316.[32] The story of Seleucus and Macedonia in book I (16) ends in 281 B.C., with his murder by one of the sons of Ptolemy, who took Seleucus' place and became king of Macedonia, and resumes in book X (19.7): within a year the assassin had to face the invading Celts—and lost his life in battle against them. Pausanias relegated this part of the story to book X (Phocis) because the sanctuary at Delphi (in Phocis) was the Celts' target and the place where the decisive battle was fought in 279. Without question Pausanias already had the continuation in mind as he wrote book I.

A number of other books contain major narratives: II.8–9, the life of Aratus of Sicyon (the leading Achaean statesman of the third century); IV.4–27, the history of the Messenian wars (covering more than fifty pages of the Teubner text); VII.7–16, a summary of the history of Achaea, 280–146 B.C. (some twenty-four pages); VIII.49–52, the life of the general and politician Philopoemen (a native of Megalopolis in Arcadia); X.2–3, the history of the Third Sacred War, in the fourth century; X.19–23, a long account of the Celtic invasion of Greece (which requires no less than fourteen pages, and is by far the fullest extant account of this event).[33] There are numerous smaller digressions throughout the work.

Pausanias says enough about Greek history to reveal his personal opinions. First and foremost he was a patriot, whose true love was Mother Greece, which he loved even more than the Greek colonial environment that was his home. He cared less about the welfare of Greece than about her freedom, but Greeks had not been free for three centuries—not since the Romans defeated the Achaean League in 146 B.C.—nor could an intelligent man like Pausanias believe that Greece could any longer be free. Pausanias could not deny the situation, and therefore chose to ignore it as best he could. For this reason he includes little Greek history after 146.[34] For instance, the latest of the twenty-two dates indicated by the name of an Athenian archon, which

[32] Various passages in book I, then IX.7.1–3.
[33] For recent bibliography on this see above, p. 84 n. 70.
[34] That Pausanias records relatively few later monuments is well known, and it is principally for this reason that Wilamowitz and others have suspected that he mostly followed a source written in the first half of the second century B.C., viz. the work of Polemo of Ilium, whose date was established by the proxeny awarded to him at Delphi in 175/174 (*SIG*³ 585, no. 114); see app. 1, pp. 165–75. For Olympia, Gurlitt (p. 349) lists monuments mentioned by Pausanias that are later than 150 B.C.; for Delphi, see G. Daux, *Pausanias à Delphes* (Paris 1936), 173ff.

are scattered throughout the work, is the year 146, the year of the loss of Greek freedom.[35] Pausanias is the enemy of all those who ever threatened or diminished the freedom of the Greeks: the Persians, the Macedonians and their kings, the Greek tyrants, the Celts. (The Romans as seen by Pausanias will be discussed in the following chapter.)

The greatest triumph in the struggle of Greek freedom was the Persian Wars. As Pausanias walked through the Altis in Olympia, he could see the image of Zeus dedicated by the Greeks who fought the Persians in 480 and 479. The dedicatory inscription lists all the participating Greek states, including the smallest ones. Pausanias thinks these states should be remembered, and lists the Greek participants (V.23.1–3). His list can be compared with the list on the serpent's column that was sent by the victorious Greeks to Delphi[36] but then transferred by Constantine to his new residence, Constantinople (modern Istanbul), where it can still be seen. The names on the two lists are identical (and so is their sequence for the most part), except that the column at Delphi lists thirty-one states, whereas Pausanias lists only twenty-seven (missing are Thespiae in Boeotia, Eretria, and the islands of Leucas and Siphnos).

Adolf Bauer assumed that the four states are omitted in Olympia because they did not contribute to the costs of the monument. Bauer's explanation has not won general acceptance, and the omission remains to be explained in some other fashion,[37] but Pausanias, as Bauer has shown, did check his list against Herodotus, as is implied by his citing "the Plataeans alone of the Boeotians" (V.23.2): he did realize that the

---

[35] VII.16.10. In addition, in all instances Pausanias also gives the year of the corresponding Olympiad, with two exceptions: IX.1.8, where the omission is probably due to an oversight, and VI.19.13, for the Athenian archon Phorbas, who was elected for life and for whom, consequently, no single Olympiad corresponded. The two archons mentioned in X.23.14, Anaxicrates and Democles, of 279/278 and 278/277, respectively, as shown by such a synchronism, have always been cornerstones for the Athenian chronology of the third century B.C.

[36] M. N. Tod, *A Selection of Greek Historical Inscriptions*, vol. 1, 2d ed. (Oxford 1946), no. 19.

[37] Ad. Bauer, *WS* 9 (1887): 223–28. His view was refuted by Frazer (5:306), who observed that according to Herodotus (9.81) these offerings were financed from the booty taken collectively by the Greeks, and not from contributions of individual states. It remains a puzzle why the four states are omitted in Pausanias' enumeration, but scholars tend to agree that Pausanias was not at fault. See, for instance, W. Gauer, *Weihgeschenke aus den Perserkriegen* (Tübingen 1968), 96–97; F. Eckstein, ANAΘHMATA: *Studien zu den Weihgeschenken des strengen Stils im Heiligtum von Olympia* (Berlin 1969), 23–26, 108–10. The base at Olympia has been identified by W. Dörpfeld (in *Olympia*, ed. E. Curtius and F. Adler, vol. 1 [Berlin 1897], 86; vol. 2 [Berlin 1892], 78).

Thespians were missing. In any case, Pausanias does believe, though 650 years have since elapsed, that all the states that fought for Greece against barbarians deserve to be remembered by name.

In fact, his judgment of the different Greek states always depends first on where they stood when the freedom of Greece was at stake. He cares enormously whether a city (or a region) fought for Greece, remained neutral, or sided with the enemy. Some occasions he uses time and time again as touchstones: the battle of Chaeronea in 338 with Philip of Macedonia, the Lamian War after the death of Alexander, and the invasion of the Celts in 279. The main passages are:

> At last the Messenians formed an alliance with Philip, son of Amyntas, and the Macedonians; and they say it was this which prevented them from taking part in the battle of Chaeronea. But, on the other hand, they would not draw sword against Greece. When, after the death of Alexander, the Greeks took up arms against Macedonia for the second time, the Messenians shared in the war. . . . They did not, however, join with the Greeks in fighting the Gauls, because Cleonymus and the Lacedaemonians declined to conclude a truce with them. (IV.28.2–3)

> When Philip, son of Amyntas, would not keep his hands off Greece, the Eleans, crippled by domestic broils, joined the Macedonian alliance, but they would not fight against the Greeks at Chaeronea. . . . But after the death of Alexander, they sided with the Greeks in the war with the Macedonians under Antipater. (V.4.9)

> The Achaeans took part in the battle of Chaeronea against Philip and the Macedonians, but they say they did not march into Thessaly in the war known as the Lamian War, alleging that they had not yet recovered from the disaster in Boeotia. . . . The march to Thermopylae to meet the army of the Gauls was taken as little notice of by the Achaeans as by the rest of the Peloponnesians; for as the barbarians had no ships, the Peloponnesians thought that they would have nothing to fear from the Gauls. (VII.6.5–7)

If the Arcadians

> did not fight on the Greek side against Philip and his Macedonians at Chaeronea, nor afterwards against Antipater in Thessaly, at least they did not take the field against their countrymen. They say that they were hindered by the Lacedaemonians from hazarding themselves against the Gauls at Thermopylae; for they feared that in the absence of their fighting men the Lacedaemonians might ravage their land. (VIII.6.2–3)

> The Phocians took part in the battle of Chaeronea, and afterwards they fought at Lamia and Crannon against the Macedonians under Antipater. In repelling

the Gauls and the Celtic host, none of the Greeks were more strenuous than the Phocians. (X.3.4)

I have already said that the defeat of Chaeronea was a disaster for the whole of Greece. On the Thebans the blow fell with especial weight, for a garrison was introduced into their city. . . .

The Thebans, of course, were unable to participate in the Lamian War, but they did fight against the Gauls.[38]

The Arcadians avoided the fight against the enemies of Greece on all three occasions; the whole Peloponnese shirked the fight against the Gauls (with the notable exception of the city of Patras).[39] The Achaeans fought only against Philip, the Messenians and Eleans only against Antipater. Of the six tribes only the Phocians fought in all three wars, but they, according to Pausanias, had to atone for former sins: they had seized the sanctuary at Delphi in the fourth century, melted down the gold and silver belonging to Apollo, and kept a mercenary army on the proceeds.[40] Ultimately they were defeated (and heavily punished) by Philip and a coalition of Greeks in the so-called Sacred War. The Phocians fought brilliantly against the Gauls, Pausanias says, "for they felt that they drew sword for the god of Delphi, and they wished, too, I suppose, to wipe out the old stains on their honour" (X.3.4).

Pausanias does not just say that a Greek city or people were absent in these crises; he details their selfish considerations or their justifications—in one case gratitude to Macedonia, in another fear of Spartan aggression—but he does not forgive them: insofar as they were absent, so far they failed in their duty, and eventually they paid—justly—for their failure. The Arcadians, he says, though they did not fight against Philip and Antipater, at least did not take the field against their countrymen, but when they were defeated by the Romans at Chaeronea in 146, "there and then the gods of Greece took vengeance upon them, who were now slaughtered by the Romans on the very ground where they had left the Greeks to fight against Philip and the Macedonians" (VII.15.6; see above, p. 69).

Nor did the Spartans, in Pausanias' view, fulfill their patriotic duty. They did not participate in any of these crises, and even prevented their neighbors from participating by declining to grant a truce.[41] All

---

[38] IX.6.5, with the additional information in I.25.4 and X.20.1.
[39] VII.18.6, X.22.6.
[40] For Alyattes' bowl see Ch. Habicht, *Classical Antiquity* 3 (1984): 47.
[41] The Spartans, of course, lived up to their duty in the Persian Wars. Since it also matters to Pausanias what stand the various Greek tribes took on that occasion, which was even

that Pausanias could find to say in their favor was that they had fought the Macedonians on their own in 331 and had been badly beaten (III.10.5).

Only the Athenians met all their obligations. They stood against the Persians, twice against the Macedonians, and against the Gauls, and, he says, they were also the leaders in the last three crises—which is correct for the battles against Philip and Antipater (I.25.3), but not for the repulsion of the Gauls.[42] The Athenians did fight against them, and they fought bravely, but the Aetolians were the leaders. Nevertheless, as Pausanias sees it, the Athenians were the only Greeks who never failed Greece.

No wonder, therefore, that Pausanias heaps praise upon Athens: the cause of Greece was lost only when Athens no longer had the strength to defend it. After the retreat of the Gauls in 279, he says,

> the condition of Greece was this. There was no longer any state strong enough to take the lead. For the defeat at Leuctra, the consolidation of Arcadia at Megalopolis, and the settlement of the Messenians on her flank, still forbade Sparta to retrieve her shattered fortunes. As for Thebes, so low had the city been laid by Alexander that a few years afterwards, when the people were brought back by Cassander, they were unable even to hold their own. Athens, it is true, had earned the good will of Greece, especially by her later exploits, but she was never able to recover from the effects of the war with Macedonia. (VII.6.8–9)

And then: "Then, like a fresh shoot on a blasted and withered trunk, the Achaean League arose on the ruins of Greece. But the roguery and cowardice of its generals blighted the growing plant."[43] The

---

more distant than the expansion of Macedonia and the invasion of the Celts, here are the main passages: the Messenians, being helots of the Spartans at the time, did not exist (IV.24.5); the Eleans fought on the Greek side (V.4.7); the Achaeans stood aside (VII. 6.3–4); the Arcadians participated (VIII.6.1); the Boeotians were forced to side with the Persians (IX.6.1–2); the Phocians were originally compelled to march with the Persians, but deserted them and ranged themselves on the Greek side at the battle of Plataea (X.2.1).

[42] X.20.5. See recently G. Nachtergael, *Les Galates en Grèce et les Sôtéria de Delphes* (Brussels 1977), 144–45; Habicht (above, n. 20), p. 89ff., esp. p. 91 n. 22.

[43] VII.17.2. He means the last two generals of the league, Critolaus and Diaeus, as is clear from two other passages: VII.14.6 ("But rashness combined with weakness is madness rather than misfortune. It was this that ruined Critolaus and the Achaeans") and VII.16.6, on the occasion of Diaeus' suicide, after the war was lost ("the cowardice of his death"). Since Polybius speaks rather emphatically of the "misfortune" of the Achaeans (38.1.1–7), C. Wachsmuth saw in the first passage of Pausanias quoted here a direct criticism of Polybius (*Leipziger Studien* 10 [1887]: 294–95). See also Heer, p. 67.

crushing defeat the league suffered at the hands of the Romans in 146
B.C. extinguished all hope. The independence of Greece was lost forever. Pausanias saw no reason to comment on later developments.

Pausanias the Greek patriot has no love for those who tormented or
weakened Greece. With harsh words and repeatedly he condemns both
the politics and the personality of Philip II.[44] He calls Cassander the
wickedest of kings,[45] and Philip V, he says, poisoned some of his Greek
rivals and put out a contract on others.[46] All three were oppressors of
Athens. Seleucus I, on the other hand, gets high praise as a just and
pious king (I.16.3)—he restored to Athens statues once taken by the
Persians—and Pausanias praises the Ptolemies, the "real benefactors"
of Athens (I.9.4). He also praises the Attalid kings of Pergamum: they
supported Athens against Philip V, and they defended the Greeks of
Asia Minor against the Galatians (as the Gauls were called after their
arrival in Anatolia) and finally succeeded in repelling the Galatians
from the fertile west coast (inhabited by Greeks) and forcing them to
settle in the interior, which henceforth was called Galatia.[47]

Pausanias was no enemy of monarchy per se: he judged monarchs by
their conduct toward the Greeks, be they in Greece or Asia Minor.
Monarchy, Pausanias believes, is as good as the monarch, but democracy, in general, is suspect. As soon as the Epirots ceased to have kings,
for instance, "the common people grew saucy and set all authority at
naught. Hence, the Illyrians . . . overran and subdued them. . . . No
people ever yet, so far as we know, throve under a democracy, except
the Athenians; and they certainly flourished under it. For in mother-
wit they had not their equals in Greece, and they were the most law-
abiding of peoples" (IV.35.5). But he cannot resist paying even Athenian democracy a left-handed compliment (when speaking of the common burial and commemoration of the free men and slaves who fell at
Marathon): "It seems that even a democracy is capable of a just decision" (I.29.7). And Pausanias scorns the tradition that Theseus was the
founder of Athenian democracy:

There is, indeed, a popular tradition that Theseus handed over the conduct of
affairs to the people, and that the government continued to be a democracy
from his time down to the insurrection and tyranny of Pisistratus. But falsehood, in general, passes current among the multitude because they are igno-

[44] For instance, IV.28.4; V.4.9, 23.3; VIII.7.5–6.
[45] I.6.7. Other passages are, for instance, I.25.6–7, IX.7.2–3.
[46] II.9.4–5, VII.7.5–6, VIII.50.4, X.34.3.
[47] I.4.5–6, 8.1, 25.2; X.15.2.

rant of history and believe all they had heard from childhood in choirs and tragedies. And Theseus, in particular, is the subject of such falsehood. For, in point of fact, not only was he king himself, but his descendants, after the death of Menestheus, continued to bear rule down to the third generation.[48]

In this passage Pausanias almost sounds like Thucydides, and if he had continued in this vein, he might have claimed recognition as a true historian, but he composed this at the very beginning of his career as a writer; he never repeated this sort of passage.[49] If he did, in fact, ever speak as a historian, he soon repented.

Pausanias can take monarchy or leave it, he does not trust democracy, and he does not care for oligarchy either. More than once he accuses the rich and powerful class in the Greek cities of selfishness and corruption. It is they who in Elis accepted bribes from Philip II and caused the civil war (IV.28.4). It is they who in Elatea (in Phocis) accepted bribes from Philip V and acted against the better interests of their city (X.34.3). It is they who in Messene in 183 killed the Greek patriot Philopoemen (whereas the rest of the populace desperately wanted to spare his life).[50]

Tyranny, however, is the form of government that Pausanias abhors more than any other. He paints the tyrants in the darkest possible colors: Lachares in Athens (I.25.7–8, 29.16), the tyrants of Sicyon (II.8.2–3), Machanidas and Nabis in Sparta (IV.29.10), Apollodorus in Cassandrea (IV.5.4–5), Aristotimus in Elis,[51] Hieron in Priene (VII.2.10; see above, p. 84), and others. The Olympic victor Chaeron (from Pellene in Achaea), he says, debased the glory of four Olympic victories by accepting the tyranny of his hometown, "the most invidious of all favours," from Alexander (VII.27.7). He exempts Aristodemus, tyrant of Megalopolis in the third century, who earned the epithet "the Just"[52] (which, however, did not prevent his murder by two doctrinaire assassins who believed that in slaying a tyrant they

---

[48] I.3.3, where C. Robert corrected ὡς of the manuscripts to ὅς: οὐκ ἀληθῆ – λέγεται δὲ καὶ εἰς τὸν Θησέα, ὅς αὐτός τε ἐβασίλευσε (*Hermes* 14 [1879]: 313–14). The cause of Pausanias' remarks is a painting by Euphranor in the Stoa of Zeus Eleutherius showing Theseus, Democracy, and the Demos. For the tradition attacked by Pausanias, see H. Herter, "Theseus," in *RE*, suppl. 13 (1973), 1215–18.

[49] That he was at that time still very much experimenting has often been observed; see above, p. 20 n. 80.

[50] VIII.51.7: "Dinocrates and all the wealthy Messenians advised to put Philopoemen to death; but the popular party were most anxious to save him."

[51] V.5.1 (cf. VI.14.11).

[52] VIII.27.11 (cf. VIII.32.4, 35.5, 36.5).

were obeying the ethical commands of Plato).[53] Two other tyrants receive praise, Aristomachus of Argos (II.8.6) and Lydiadas of Megalopolis (VIII.27.12, 15), but they voluntarily resigned from power, led their cities into the Achaean League, and aided the league in its campaign to free the Greeks from Macedonian rule. In other words, they stopped being tyrants. In short, according to Pausanias, there was— except for Aristodemus—no such thing as a good tyrant.

Pausanias believes that the people are not responsible for the actions of a bad government. For instance, the people of Sparta are absolved from any responsibility for the crimes of their king, Cleomenes III, because "Cleomenes had converted the constitution from a monarchy to a tyranny" (VIII.27.16). Similarly, the people of Thebes are excused for siding with the Persians against the Greeks, "because at the time Thebes was governed by an oligarchy, and not by its hereditary constitution" (IX.6.2).

Pausanias' views on monarchy, tyranny, oligarchy, and democracy reflect little more than the conventions of his time. A monarchical rule was the least unacceptable form of government, provided the monarch meant well, as the Roman emperors of his own time ostensibly meant well. On the course of Greek history Pausanias' views are less conventional.

Perhaps because he was not from Greece proper, Pausanias seldom, if ever, shows partiality toward one Greek state over another. Here he differs markedly from Plutarch (an older contemporary), who wrote a lengthy treatise "On the Malignity of Herodotus" to prove that Herodotus did falsely and willfully malign the Boeotians in that he depicted them as the willing allies of the Persians. Plutarch was a Boeotian. Pausanias, unlike Herodotus, excuses the Boeotians for their medizing, and he does give the excuses of the Greeks who did not do their duty in the national crises, but he is always clear that they did have a duty to Greece and that they failed in that duty. If Pausanias can be said to be partial at all, he is partial to Athens,[54] but Athens, he would point out, in her long history never failed Greece.

---

[53] Polyb. 10.22.2–3; Plut. *Phil.* 1.

[54] A case in point may be IV.27.9–11. Pausanias narrates that in 370 B.C. the Messenians received back their land, after an exile of 287 years. He mentions other cases of prolonged exile: the Plataeans (371–338), the Orchomenians (364–338), and the Thebans (335–316). Conspicuously absent are the Samians, in exile from 365 to 321 (Ch. Habicht, *AthMitt* 72 [1957]: 154ff.), as victims of the Athenians. True enough, Pausanias says that the Athenians expelled the Delians—but their exile lasted only one year, from 421 to 420.

Pausanias does not judge a state or a person by success or failure, or good or bad luck. He praises brave men who failed, such as the Spartan prince Dorieus, who by happenstance lost his right to succeed to the kingship and then perished in Sicily,[55] or the Athenians who tried to recover the Piraeus from the Macedonians, but were betrayed and slaughtered, or those Athenians who attempted and failed to overthrow the tyrant Lachares (I.29.10): "brave men worthy of a happier fate," Pausanias says, commenting on their graves in the public burial ground at Athens. Commenting on the common tomb of the Thebans fallen at Chaeronea, he says, "Their fortune did not match their valour" (IX.40.10). And of the Spartan king at Thermopylae in 480 he says, "To my mind, the exploit of Leonidas outdid all the exploits that have been performed before or since" (III.4.7). He does not, however, fall for the Spartan attempt to turn defeat into victory: "Leonidas was victorious, but had not men enough to annihilate the Medes" (I.13.5). His Leonidas is great in defeat.

Whenever Pausanias has cause to mention a foreign victory over Greeks, such as Chaeronea (338) or Crannon (322), he avoids the word *defeat* ($\mathring{\eta}\tau\tau\alpha$)[56] and uses instead such words as *misfortune* ($\mathring{\alpha}\tau\acute{\upsilon}$-$\chi\eta\mu\alpha$)[57] or *fall* ($\pi\tau\alpha\hat{\iota}\sigma\mu\alpha$),[58] and adds that a demon brought about the calamity (not the virtue of the victorious). Time and again he says that Chaeronea was a "misfortune" for all of Greece, including those Greeks who favored King Philip.[59]

But the calamity at Chaeronea, he would say, grew out of the Peloponnesian War, in which almost all of Greece engaged, Greek against Greek, for three decades, the most painful period of Greek history, and the effects of which made it relatively easy for Philip to conquer Greece

[55] III.16.5. The full story of Dorieus is told by Herodotus, 5.41–48. See A. Graf Schenk von Stauffenberg, *Trinakria* (Munich 1963), 137–54: "Dorieus."

[56] The word for defeat, $\mathring{\eta}\tau\tau\alpha$, occurs only once, in III.5.4, referring to Lysander's last battle in 395 B.C. at Haliartus. This is not surprising: Pausanias disliked the Lacedaemonians in general, and Lysander in particular (below, p. 113).

[57] The word $\mathring{\alpha}\tau\acute{\upsilon}\chi\eta\mu\alpha$ (misfortune) is used twice in connection with the battle of Chaeronea in 338 B.C. (I.25.3, VII.10.5), four times for the catastrophe of the Spartan army in the battle of Leuctra in 371 B.C. (IV.26.4, 32.4; VI.3.3; VIII.6.2). The remaining three instances are IV.35.3, 36.6; X.33.3.

[58] $\pi\tau\alpha\hat{\iota}\sigma\mu\alpha$ (stumble) is used three times for the failure of the Greeks against Philip at Chaeronea (VII.6.5, IX.29.8, X.3.3), four times for that of the Spartans at Leuctra (I.3.4, 13.5; VII.6.8; VIII.27.8). For Chaeronea, Pausanias once uses the synonym $\sigma\varphi\acute{\alpha}\lambda\mu\alpha$ (IX.6.5), whose only other occurrence is in III.5.5, where the plural $\sigma\varphi\acute{\alpha}\lambda\mu\alpha\tau\alpha$ denotes various defeats of the Lacedaemonians.

[59] I.25.3; V.20.10; IX.6.5, 29.8; X.3.3. At age ninety-eight, Isocrates added fame to his name when, having heard about the battle, he committed suicide (I.18.8).

(III.7.11). In a remarkable digression on the men whom he regards as the principal patriots of Greece (VIII.52), Pausanias excludes, first, all those who benefited only their own native land, not Greece as a whole,[60] and, second, all the leading men of the Peloponnesian War, whom he calls "the assassins and almost the wreckers of Greece."[61] And did these men even benefit the fatherland? "For my part, I am of opinion that Lysander did more harm than good to Lacedaemon" (IX.32.10).

His list of national benefactors[62] begins with Miltiades, the victor of Marathon. Next are Leonidas, the hero of Thermopylae, and Themistocles, the victor of Salamis. Pausanias excludes the Athenian Aristides and the Spartan Pausanias (victors at Plataea in 479), Aristides because he imposed tribute on the Greeks in the Athenian League, Pausanias because he became a despot (VIII.52.2). He includes the two Athenians Xanthippus (victor at Cape Mycale in 478 and, incidentally, the father of Pericles) and Cimon, the son of Miltiades. He skips the two generations of the Athenian Empire and the Peloponnesian War, and begins again with Conon of Athens and Epaminondas of Thebes (because they broke the tyranny of Sparta), and the Athenian Leosthenes (VIII.52.5). (Leosthenes rescued the thousands of Greek mercenaries who had taken service with the Persians against Alexander and were then persecuted by Alexander. After Alexander died, Leosthenes was one of the leaders of the revolt against Macedonia.) The last two on the list lived at a time when (according to Pausanias) the hopes of Greece rested no longer with Athens but with the Achaean League: Aratus of Sicyon and Philopoemen of Megalopolis (both of whom tried to salvage what they could of Greek freedom, Philopoemen at a time when the shadow of Rome was growing longer and longer). After Philopoemen's death (in 183 B.C., the year, incidentally, in which two greater men also died—Hannibal and his conqueror, Scipio Africanus), Pausanias says, "from that day, Greece ceased to be the mother of the brave."[63]

His list contains ten names—six Athenians, one Spartan, one Theban, and two Achaeans. None of the names included is surprising, but the omissions are remarkable. The omission of all the kings after

---

[60]VIII.52.1: Οἱ . . . πατρίδας ἕκαστοι τὰς ἑαυτῶν καὶ οὐκ ἀθρόαν φανοῦνται τὴν Ἑλλάδα ὠφελήσαντες.
[61]VIII.52.3: αὐτόχειρας καὶ ὅτι ἐγγύτατα καταποντιστὰς τῆς Ἑλλάδος.
[62]See the remarks of J. Touloumakos, *Zum Geschichtsbewusstsein der Griechen in der Zeit der römischen Herrschaft* (Bonn 1971), 61–62.
[63]VIII.52.1. For Robert's blunder concerning Aristides and Pausanias in this chapter see above, n. 13.

Alexander (as well as Alexander himself) is not surprising (none was Greek, or a benefactor of Greece), but Pericles and Thrasybulus are missing, the Spartan king Agesilaus (whom Xenophon would have included) is missing, and so are Timoleon of Corinth, who liberated Sicily, and Demosthenes, whom Pausanias himself praises.[64]

In contrast to Pausanias, Plutarch and Cornelius Nepos (ca. 99–24 B.C.), when they wrote biographies, chose as subjects men they considered important, whether they were benefactors of Greece or not. Of those individuals expressly excluded by Pausanias, both Plutarch and Cornelius Nepos include in their biographies Alcibiades and Lysander, Plutarch wrote biographies of Pericles and Nicias, and Nepos wrote one of Pausanias. Plutarch and Pausanias agree on Themistocles, Cimon, Aratus, Philopoemen, Leonidas, and Epaminondas (the last two biographies are lost); Nepos and Pausanias agree on Miltiades, Themistocles, Cimon, Conon, and Epaminondas.

Pausanias also gives a list of traitors (VII.10.1–12). At the head of the list are the Samian captains whose defection in the battle of Lade meant the defeat of the Ionian revolt from Darius. He names both individuals, who, mostly, betrayed their own hometown, and groups, such as the Aleuads in Thessaly, who cooperated with Xerxes, and the "friends" of Lysander, or of Philip II, who were spread throughout Greece. Two names stand out: the Athenian Demades and the Achaean Callicrates. The former was the rival of Demosthenes and, after the Lamian War, the mouthpiece of the Macedonian rulers;[65] the latter was the politician who betrayed Greece to the Romans (or such was the accusation made by the historian Polybius, who was a victim of Callicrates' policy).[66]

Pausanias consistently deplores the warfare of Greek against Greek— he calls the leaders of both sides in the Peloponnesian War the assassins of Greece—but he does glorify one particular victory of Greeks over Greeks: Epaminondas' defeat of the Spartans in 371 B.C. "At Leuctra [the Thebans] gained the most splendid victory that ever, to our knowledge, Greek gained over Greek," because "they then put down the decemvirates which the Lacedaemonians had set up in the cities

---

[64] I.8.2–3 and especially II.33.3–4, where Pausanias insists that Demosthenes was innocent in the affair of Harpalus.
[65] VII.10.4. See J. K. Davies, *Athenian Propertied Families* (Oxford 1971), 99ff., no. 3263.
[66] VII.10.5ff. See P. Schoch, "Kallikrates," in *RE*, suppl. 4 (1924), 859–62; J. Deininger, *Der politische Widerstand gegen Rom in Griechenland 217–86 v. Chr.* (Berlin 1971), 135–45.

and they expelled the Spartan governors" (IX.6.4). This was a victory, as Pausanias sees it, for the cause of Greek freedom, which the Spartans, and their supporter, the Persian king, had subverted. The victory resulted in the liberation of the Messenians and to a lesser degree the Arcadians, and in the foundation of Messene and Megalopolis (in Arcadia).

Pausanias praises, or denigrates, other famous individuals insofar as they were devoted to the cause of Greece. Pausanias is aware that Aeschylus has a claim to immortality for other reasons,[67] but he insists that Aeschylus was right in his funeral epigram to stress not his plays but his role in the Persian Wars (I.14.5). And of that group of Panhellenic celebrities, the athletes, Chaeron of Pellene, four times victorious at Olympia, debased his glory by becoming tyrant of his city—and the people of Pellene would not even mention his name (VII.27.7). Chilon, the wrestler from Patras, was twice an Olympic victor and also victorious in the other three Panhellenic contests, but his main claim to glory, Pausanias says, is that he was the only Achaean to participate in the Lamian War (in 322 B.C., just after Alexander's death, between a coalition of Greek states and Macedonia). Chilon was killed. Pausanias quotes in full a posthumous epigram in his honor.[68]

Similarly, about another individual he says (and he mentions Chilon here, too), "I myself know of a Lydian, Adrastus by name, who fought on the Greek side as a volunteer without the sanction of the Lydian community. But the Lydians set up a bronze statue of him in front of the sanctuary of Persian Artemis, and they carved an inscription on it, setting forth how he fell fighting for Greece against Leonnatus" (VII.6.6). Pausanias has seen this inscription, too, although in this case he is content to summarize the text. Pausanias (the preserver of information) had visited the spot. This passage is the *locus classicus* for the existence of the cult of the Persian goddess long after the Persian Empire had been destroyed.[69]

Chilon the Olympic victor and Adrastus the Lydian were obviously inspired to fight as individuals for the Greek cause by the example of another celebrated athlete, Phayllus of Croton, who came from Italy in 480 with a single ship, which he had equipped and manned himself, to fight at Salamis against Xerxes, as every reader of Herodotus knows. The Athenians placed a statue of him on the Acropolis as a token of

---

[67] Pausanias mentions him in eleven passages.

[68] VI.4.6–7. Kalkmann (p. 47) nevertheless undauntedly states that the story is nothing but fiction.

[69] V.27.5–6; cf. L. Robert, *RN*, ser. 6, 18 (1976): 28.

their gratitude (the inscription is extant).[70] Phayllus had won not at Olympia but at the Pythia in Delphi, and it was there that Pausanias saw his statue. Pausanias says explicitly that he will not describe the statues of any athletes at Delphi, since he has already described the two hundred most notable statues of Olympic victors; he makes a single exception for Phayllus, not for Phayllus the famous athlete, but for the man who had done such an exemplary and patriotic deed (X.9.2).

One hundred fifty years later, Alexander the Great, when he had defeated the last of Xerxes' line, sent part of the booty to Croton in remembrance of Phayllus' virtue.[71] And in less than ten years, ironically enough, the two men inspired by Phayllus' example, Chilon and Adrastus, came to fight against Alexander's heirs for the liberty of Greece. But they suffered a different fate from Phayllus': they died fighting for a lost cause. The epigrams in their honor show that they were posthumously honored for their noble deeds, and, I might add, they were memorialized again five centuries later by a writer who still cared about the freedom of Greece.

[70] Hdt. 8.47. The Athenian inscription is *IG* I².655 (*SIG*³ 30). For a dedication of Phayllus at Croton see *NSc*, 1952:167ff.; M. Guarducci, *Epigrafia Greca*, vol. 1 (Rome 1967), 113–15, no. 6.

[71] Plut. *Alex.* 34.

V

THE ROMAN WORLD

OF PAUSANIAS

Pausanias lived and wrote during the second century A.D., specifically between the years A.D. 120 and 180, when the whole of the world in which he lived and traveled was part of the Roman Empire.[1] That world, extending from Britain to the Euphrates, from the mouth of the Rhine to Ethiopia, was a world at peace. Augustus, the first emperor, had put an end to civil war long ago; Hadrian, in Pausanias' own day, foreswore the policy of annexation pushed by his predecessor, Trajan, to the limits of the empire's resources. Instead of expansion, there was to be preservation; the system of static fortification, the so-called *limites*, across Britain, through Germany, along the Danube, and in Syria and North Africa was the most visible expression of this new defensive policy. For half a century Romans fought only minor wars and, with the notable exception of the revolt of Bar Cochba, only wars beyond the Roman frontiers.

The capital itself was mostly undisturbed: Nerva and Trajan had at last composed the long-standing feud between emperor and senatorial nobility; bloodshed and assassination had given way to reasonable cooperation. Pausanias lived in the age of the five good emperors: Nerva, Trajan, Hadrian, Antoninus Pius, and Marcus Aurelius. They treated the Roman aristocracy with respect, and they cared for their non-Roman subjects. They were philhellenes—they adopted the humanitarian ideas widely disseminated by Greeks such as Dio Chrysostom,

---

[1] For a full and representative modern account see A. Garzetti, *From Tiberius to the Antonines: A History of the Roman Empire A.D. 14–192* (London 1974). See also F. Millar, *The Roman Empire and Its Neighbours* (London 1967).

Epictetus, and Plutarch, and modestly acknowledged themselves the pupils of these teachers.[2] The old antagonism between East and West, rooted in the republic's conquest of the Greek world and then rekindled in the wars of the late republic (those between Caesar and Pompey, between Caesar's heirs and his assassins, and between Octavian and Antony), finally was a thing of the past.

As the empire was at peace, so was it prosperous, even if not equally in all its provinces; economic growth was rapid in Asia Minor and North Africa, but relatively slow in Italy and Greece. Nevertheless, the prosperity and peace allowed a man to travel easily from province to province and border to border, not only in an official capacity or on business but also for pleasure or (like Pausanias) for personal reasons. The traveler would not need a passport, visa, or identification papers. He would not need to change his money into different currencies. He would not need to know many different languages: wherever he went, if he spoke either Latin or Greek, he would be understood, not by everybody, but by a sufficient number of people for his needs (and most of those who traveled long distances spoke both languages anyway).

Later generations of Romans would consider the second century the Golden Age of antiquity, and their judgment has stood the test of time. In the late nineteenth century, Theodor Mommsen wrote in the introduction to the Nobel-prize-winning fifth volume of his Roman history, "Even today there is many a region in the East as well as in the West for which the imperial period was the peak of good government, which, limited as it was, still was unrivalled before or thereafter." [3]

This age was idealized, but nonetheless it was by far the best age, considering the overall conditions of life for mankind, in the ancient world. In the final third of the century, however, conditions worsened. First, the Romans had to fight a serious war against the Parthians (A.D. 162–66). The Romans won a victory, but the war brought on a major catastrophe: Roman soldiers carried home the great plague that would devastate the empire's population.[4]

Immediately after the Parthian War the Romans had to fight a much

---

[2] See C. P. Jones, *Plutarch and Rome* (Oxford 1971), 28–38; *The Roman World of Dio Chrysostom* (Cambridge, Mass., 1978), 115–23; P. A. Brunt, "Stoicism and the Principate," *PBSR* 43 (1975): 7–35.

[3] The original (*Römische Geschichte*, vol. 5 [Berlin 1885], 4–5) has, "Noch heute giebt es manche Landschaft des Orients wie des Occidents, für welche die Kaiserzeit den an sich sehr bescheidenen, aber doch vorher wie nachher nie erreichten Höhepunkt des guten Regiments bezeichnet."

[4] J. F. Gilliam, "The Plague under Marcus Aurelius," *AJP* 82 (1961): 225–51.

more serious war, and closer to home, against German and Scythian tribes along the Danube; during this war the enemy invaded northern Italy and Greece, where they set the sanctuary at Eleusis on fire. The emperor, Marcus Aurelius, eventually expelled and overpowered these enemies, but he had personally to lead campaigns for more than a decade (A.D. 167–80).

These barbarian attacks foreshadowed the grim struggle for survival the empire would face during most of the third century, but Pausanias, who lived through these campaigns, although he does allude to the wars (in a single sentence: VIII.43.6), and to the short-lived invasion of Greece (in another sentence: X.34.5), nevertheless gives no indication whatsoever that he is aware of a new, more dangerous threat or a growing crisis in the empire.[5] Pausanias is a witness to the brighter side of his age; he is a man convinced of the unimpaired power and the unmenaced security of the Roman world.

Pausanias' world was Roman. At the time of his birth, Asia, his homeland, had been ruled by the Romans for some two and a half centuries, and Greece, when Pausanias began to write his work, had been under the direct control of the Romans for almost three centuries. But Pausanias was a Greek, he thought of himself as a Greek, not a Roman, and he had definite opinions about Rome and the Romans.

Most scholars have assumed that his view was adverse or hostile,[6] but Jonas Palm, in an interesting chapter in his book on Rome, the Roman Empire, and Greek literature under the empire,[7] has challenged this opinion, and concludes, first, that Pausanias does not blame the decline of Greece on the Romans, but on Philip and the Macedonians, second, that Pausanias is a neutral and detached reporter on Roman interventions in Greek affairs, and, third, that since Pausanias castigates only individual Romans (for instance, his condemnation of Caligula and Nero is well in line with the consensus of both Romans and Greeks, as is his praise of the emperors of his own time), he has no original views about Rome. J. H. Oliver and others agree with him.[8]

Furthermore, Palm has eliminated what had long been regarded as a key passage: "Megalopolis is the newest city not only in Arcadia, but in Greece, if we except the case of cities whose inhabitants were ex-

---

[5] He does not mention the plague, or the revolt of Avidius Cassius in A.D. 175, or, for that matter, that Marcus Aurelius had Lucius Verus as co-ruler from A.D. 161 to 169.

[6] For instance, Gurlitt, p. 87 n. 43; Regenbogen, pp. 1069–70.

[7] J. Palm, *Rom, Römertum und Imperium in der griechischen Literatur der Kaiserzeit* (Lund 1959), 63–74.

[8] J. H. Oliver, *Gnomon* 32 (1960): 503; Ch. Pietri, *REG* 74 (1961): 525.

pelled by the calamity of the Roman domination [κατὰ συμφορὰν ἀρχῆς τῆς 'Ρωμαίων]" (VIII.27.1).[9] Palm proves that E. Clavier, in the early nineteenth century, was right in inserting ἐπὶ after συμφορὰν, which changes the meaning to ". . . if we except the case of cities whose inhabitants were forced to move because of a catastrophe occurring in the time of Roman domination."[10] Pausanias means natural catastrophes, such as earthquake or flood; he does not blame Rome for earthquakes or floods, but only says that they occurred *at the time* when Rome was master of Greece. This is a sound and valuable observation, and the passage, therefore, can no longer serve as evidence of an anti-Roman bias in Pausanias.

In general, however, Palm seems to have gone too far. Pausanias may not display open hostility toward the Romans, but he does show plenty of resentment and animosity,[11] though not because they are Romans but because they dominate Greece. He resents the imperialistic policy of republican Rome, and he laments the fact that it is the fate of Greece to be ruled by foreigners, even if under the foreigners Greece is peaceful and prosperous. Roman rule is just as deplorable as Macedonian rule.

At an assembly of the Achaeans in 198 B.C., the Achaeans had to choose between honoring their alliance with Philip and defecting to Rome. They were deeply divided, and Flamininus' offer to switch alliances provoked a heated debate. Opportunism pointed to the Roman side. Pausanias says:

But the Achaeans deeply resented the conduct of Flamininus and Otilius before him, both of whom had behaved with merciless severity to ancient Greek cities that had never done the Romans any harm, and had been loath to yield to the Macedonian rule. They foresaw also that, like the rest of Greece, they were only about to exchange the dominion of Macedonia for that of Rome. (VII.8.2)

Pausanias emphasizes the brutality of the Roman commanders Sulpicius Galba, the enigmatic Otilius, Flamininus, and, later, Sulla.[12] Otilius was, to be sure, reprimanded by the senate, and Sulla's ruthless

---

[9] Accepted as such as late as 1956 by Regenbogen, p. 1070. The translation in the text is my own, since Frazer seems to have accepted Clavier's emendation.
[10] Palm (above, n. 7), pp. 72–74. This has now been accepted by Rocha-Pereira in vol. 2, p. 277, of her edition (1977).
[11] This has been well observed by Heer (pp. 66–69), who speaks of "cette amertume secrète" (p. 68), which sensitive readers will notice in the pages of Pausanias.
[12] Galba: VII.17.5; "Otilius": VII.7.8–9, X.36.6; Flamininus: VII.8.1–2; Sulla: I.20. 4ff.; IX.7.5, 30.1, 33.6. See also App. *Mac.* 7; A. M. Eckstein, *Phoenix* 30 (1976): 126, 138.

cruelty was "worse than what could be expected from a Roman" (I. 20.7), but they were Romans representing Rome abroad, and Galba and Flamininus were never censured.

Pausanias expresses his opinion quite clearly: the Achaeans had to choose between two evils, Macedonian or Roman rule, and chose Rome.[13] And with equal clarity Pausanias describes, in a long account of Achaeo-Roman relations, what an evil that choice was in the next fifty years:[14] once they had chosen the Roman side, the Achaeans stood loyally by Rome, they helped her in her wars against Philip, Antiochus the Great, and other enemies, and for their pains they received increasingly arrogant and unjust treatment, which culminated with the senate's order in 146 B.C. that Sparta, Corinth, Argos, and other states be dismissed from the Achaean League. Roman policy drove the Achaeans into the unwinnable war against Rome and sealed their fate and the fate of Greece.

Pausanias does not, as Palm maintains, occasionally depict the Romans as liberators;[15] all he says is that the Romans prevented Athens from being captured by the Macedonian king in 200 B.C. (VII.7.8, X.36.6) and that they rewarded the Phocian town of Elatea for their brave resistance against the forces of Mithridates in 87 B.C. (X.34.4). Though both the Macedonians and the Pontic king, who were attacking these cities, were, as far as Pausanias is concerned, barbarians, he is not thereby partial to the Romans, who crushed the aggressors. The Romans are no better than other barbarians.

In no less than six different passages he describes Sulla's cruelty—he destroyed Athens, he massacred the population, he violated the divine rules of asylum, and so on. Sulla, Pausanias says, acted "with a cruelty you would not expect from a Roman."[16] Even if Pausanias meant, as Palm suggests, that Sulla was atypical, the implication still is not that all other Romans are good. Pausanias does not mean to say that Romans are so noble that Sulla's cruelty is unexpected, but that you would not expect even a Roman to act so viciously. And he adds that Athens' recovery from the wounds inflicted by Sulla took two hundred years: Athens flourished again only in the reign of Hadrian.[17] It is hard

---

[13] VII.8.2.

[14] VII.7.7–16.10.

[15] Palm (above, n. 7), p. 65.

[16] I.20.7: ἀγριώτερα ἢ ὡς ἄνδρα εἰκὸς ἦν ἐργάσασθαι Ῥωμαῖον. Here, for once, is Frazer's translation misleading: "with a cruelty unworthy of a Roman."

[17] I.20.7: Ἀθῆναι μὲν οὕτως ὑπὸ τοῦ πολέμου κακωθεῖσαι τοῦ Ῥωμαίων αὖθις Ἀδριανοῦ βασιλεύοντος ἤνθησαν.

not to see in such a statement, detached though it may appear, a judgment on Roman rule in Greece.

The Romans plundered Greece of thousands of famous works of art. Palm finds significance in Pausanias' emotionless accounts of these robberies,[18] but as Pausanias includes at least a dozen passages on the subject,[19] he must have considered it a serious matter. He does not name all the guilty Romans, but he does name Mummius, in connection with the sack of Corinth in 146, and Sulla, too, of course, and Augustus, Caligula, and the thief of thieves, Nero. (Nero alone carried off no less than five hundred works from Delphi.)[20] The robberies affected the major centers of Greek civilization—Olympia, Delphi, Athens, and Corinth—and also a good many smaller places, like Tegea, Thespiae, Argos, Tritaea, Pharae, Alalcomenae.

Pausanias did not need to be emotional. The facts were well known, mostly of the distant past, and they spoke for themselves, though in the case of Augustus Pausanias considered it necessary to give some explanation (VIII.46.2–4): Augustus was not the first to do such things, nor were the Romans. Greeks had plundered Troy, the Persians had plundered Greece, and Greeks had plundered each other. But just because others had committed robbery does not mean that Pausanias found robbery excusable. On the contrary, what he thought is quite clear: both Caligula and Nero were sinners against the god (Caligula had removed Lysippus' image of Eros from Thespiae to Rome, Claudius had returned it, and then Nero had taken it back), and both came to a dreadful end.[21] His otherwise rather detached manner of speaking about these thefts is, it seems, more Thucydidean—he exposes human vices as they are, with no expressed judgment, but still creates the impression that these acts are wrong and so are the men who commit them. Pausanias gets his point across—the Romans were thieves who robbed Greece of thousands of masterpieces.

Pausanias thinks the Romans, like the Persians, the Macedonians, the Gauls, and the Pontic king Mithridates, are foreigners who do not belong in Greece and ought not to rule there. They had not contributed to Greek culture, as expressed in religion, literature, art, and phi-

---

[18] Palm (above, n. 7), p. 67. Similarly, B. Forte, *Rome and the Romans As the Greeks Saw Them* (Rome 1972), 427.

[19] V.25.8, 26.3; VI.9.3; VII.16.8, 22.5, 22.9; VIII.46.1–4; IX.27.3–4, 33.6; X.7.1, 19.2. See in general M. Pape, "Griechische Kunstwerke aus Kriegsbeute und ihre öffentliche Aufstellung in Rom" (diss., Hamburg 1975).

[20] X.7.1; cf. X.19.2.

[21] IX.27.3. See Ch. Habicht, *Classical Antiquity* 3 (1984): 48–49.

lo̞sophy. In 198 B.C. the Achaeans had one last option open: a choice between Macedonian and Roman rule. In 146 B.C. Roman domination became permanent, irreversible, and final. As far as Pausanias is concerned, Greek history ends in 146 B.C. with the catastrophic defeat of the Achaeans and the destruction of Corinth. Therefore, "Philopoemen, who shut the Romans out of Sparta, and warned the Achaeans that pro-Roman elements were 'hastening . . . the doom of Greece,' is praised as a hero, and the last benefactor in common of all Greece." [22]

Two hundred years later, the emperor Nero summoned the Greeks to the shrine at Isthmia, where Flamininus, in 196 B.C., had made the famous declaration that Greece was free (free from Macedonian rule, that is). [23] In a boastful and pathetic speech, which is preserved in an inscription, Nero declared that Greece was free once more; the Roman province of Achaea ceased to exist. [24] For a moment Greeks must have thought they could be free, but they started quarreling with each other again and their freedom was withdrawn by Nero's successor, Vespasian (VII.17.4). Pausanias does not quarrel with Vespasian's measure, [25] although he does praise Nero's gesture (which proved, as far as he is concerned, that Nero had been born with a noble nature, but it was debased by a vicious upbringing), and he does not disagree with Vespasian's remark "that Greece had forgotten what it was to be free" (VII.17.3–4). By then Greece had been under Roman rule for more than two hundred years, and all that Greeks (and Pausanias) could do about it was resign themselves to it.

The picture becomes a little brighter in Pausanias' own time, owing to the fact that the good emperors succeeded not only in reconciling the monarchy with the ideology of the republic [26] but also in reconciling the Greek world to its fate. As Nero had done before, though by rather erratic and irrational moves, they showed respect, love, and care for the Greeks and their heritage. Their philhellenism achieved a great deal, and this was acknowledged by the Greeks. Pausanias is no exception. He was born in the reign of Trajan, around A.D. 112; at that time his homeland in the province of Asia was governed by the proconsul

---

[22] VIII.51.4, 52.1, 52.6. The quotation is from Forte (above, n. 18), p. 420.

[23] Polyb. 18.46; Livy 33.32; Plut. *Flam.* 10; *Phil.* 15.

[24] Published with full commentary by M. Holleaux, *Discours prononcé par Néron à Corinthe en rendant aux Grecs la liberté* (Lyon 1889) (reprinted in *Etudes d'épigraphie et d'histoire grecques*, vol. 1 [Paris 1938], 165–85); *SIG*³ 814.

[25] Palm (above, n. 7), p. 67.

[26] Tac. *Agr.* 3. See Ch. Wirszubski, *Libertas as a Political Idea at Rome during the Late Republic and Early Principate* (Cambridge 1950), 124ff.

Cornelius Tacitus[27] and the neighboring province, Bithynia, by Pliny the Younger,[28] luminous stars of Roman *humanitas*. That an emperor would select men like these to govern Greeks indicated a change in climate, and Pausanias, like all the rest, could feel it. He often speaks of the three emperors of his adult life in glowing terms—Hadrian was the benefactor of Athens, the Greeks, and all his subjects.[29]

Of Antoninus Pius he says:

> The Emperor bequeathed another memorial to himself, and it was this: In virtue of a certain law, all provincials who were Roman citizens, but whose children were Greeks, had only the alternative of distributing their property among strangers, or of giving it to swell the Emperor's wealth; but Antoninus allowed them to transmit their property to their children, for he would rather enjoy a character for humanity than uphold a law which brought money into the treasury.[30]

The measure must have benefited many thousands of Greeks. Such acts and such emperors made Roman domination a much lighter burden than it had ever been before.

Even so, Pausanias nowhere gives the slightest hint that Roman rule in Greece was anything better than tolerable. He never says, or implies, that Roman rule was natural or logical for Greece, as other Greeks of his time did. His contemporary, the sophist Aelius Aristides, born and raised in northwestern Asia Minor not far from Pausanias' own birthplace, delivered his famous (and extant) speech in praise of Rome in A.D. 143 before the emperor Antoninus Pius.[31] In the speech, he com-

---

[27] The year of his governance of Asia was, in all probability, 112/13: D. Magie, *Roman Rule in Asia Minor* (Princeton 1950), 1442; R. Syme, *Tacitus*, vol. 2 (Oxford 1958), 664–65; W. Eck, *Chiron* 12 (1982): 353.

[28] Pliny's term in Bithynia was either 111–13, as Magie (above, n. 27), p. 1454, and B. Thomasson, *Laterculi praesidum*, vol. 2, pt. 2 (Göteborg 1978), 27, have it, or 110–12, as Eck (above, n. 27), p. 349 and n. 275, points out; hardly 109–11.

[29] I.3.2, 5.5, 20.7, 36.3, and other passages.

[30] VIII.43.5. See W. Hüttl, *Antoninus Pius*, vol. 1 (Prague 1936), 110–11. B. Frier informs me that the same law is meant in S.H.A. *Ant. Pius* 8.5, where, however, the traditional text makes no sense ("hereditates eorum, qui filios habebant, repudiavit") and can be understood only with the help of Pausanias' sentence. It is worth mentioning that Gaius says nothing about this where one would expect him to (*Inst.* 2.218, 285).

[31] Ael. Aristides *or.* 26 (Keil), interpreted by J. H. Oliver, "The Ruling Power: A Study of the Roman Empire in the Second Century after Christ through the Roman Oration of Aelius Aristides," *Transactions of the American Philosophical Society*, n.s., 43 (1953): 871–1003 (translation pp. 895–907), and by J. Bleicken, "Der Preis des Aelius Aristides auf das römische Weltreich," *NAkG*, 1966: 225–77. For the date, see R. Klein, *Historia* 30 (1981): 337–50.

pares Rome's rule on earth with that of Zeus above it: both have established peace and law and order in their realms. The gods, he says, will give divine sanction to the Roman Empire and guarantee Rome's rule forever. And no longer is there any distinction between Romans and non-Romans: the best elements in the whole of the empire are now Roman citizens, and the term *Roman* no longer denotes a place of origin but a certain personal quality or value.[32] Aristides, of course, is speaking of, and concerned only with, the upper class, the Greek elite, the small minority that by his time had acquired Roman citizenship, but even so his picture is idealized.

A comparison between Pausanias and Aristides may seem inappropriate, because Aristides was hired to deliver just such a panegyric, Pausanias was not. Aristides was paid to praise Rome; Pausanias had no such obligation. Nevertheless, Aristides did agree to deliver this panegyric, as he delivered others in praise of Athens,[33] or of this god, or that one. Aristides, like other sophists, was quite prepared to employ his rhetorical faculties wherever the price was right, and whatever the topic might be, whereas Pausanias was pursuing a lifetime work, one single topic that he himself had chosen, that was dear to his heart, but that paid no dividends.

But Pausanias, I dare say, could never have been able under any conditions to bring himself to such flattery of Rome as Aristides did, and yet it is Aristides, the versatile rhetorician, whose views are typical of the age, not the sober Pausanias. Pausanias was prepared to give credit to the emperors of his day, but his attitude toward Rome remained reserved, and, no matter how liberal the policy had become of granting Roman citizenship to the Greek elite, to him Greeks were Greeks and Romans Romans: he was writing a "Description of Greece"—the land of the Greeks.[34]

Pausanias could regret the past even as he lived comfortably in the present, the Roman world of his own day, at peace, secure, prosperous, free of major tensions, a time labeled by posterity the Golden Age of

[32] §103, 109, 63, for which see A. N. Sherwin-White, *The Roman Citizenship* (Oxford 1939), 259; Bleicken (above, n. 31), 226, 242ff.

[33] J. H. Oliver, "The Civilising Power: A Study of the Panathenaic Discourse of Aelius Aristides against the Background of Literature and Cultural Conflict, with Text, Translation, and Commentary," *Transactions of the American Philosophical Society*, n.s., 58 (1968): 1–223.

[34] It is unfortunate that American archaeologists these days speak of Pausanias as "the *Roman* traveler" (St. G. Miller, flier of the American School of Classical Studies, Athens, dated October 2, 1982; T. L. Shear, Jr., *Hesperia* 53 [1984]: 18).

antiquity. It was also an age, however, that, as far as any contribution to the literary and artistic heritage of mankind goes, was perhaps the poorest in all of antiquity between the early archaic period and the fall of the Roman Empire. It was the heyday of superficial intellectual activity.

Intellectuals and artists had never been esteemed so highly by society, and never did they perform so poorly. New and original ideas were not appreciated, nor the penetrating search for truth, nor a poetry of passion or pity. The age applauded form, not content; it praised the technical brilliance of oral expression,[35] not the ideas expressed; it valued entertaining literature, not demanding literature. It was a complacent age, pleased with itself, an age of rhetoric, of unimportant topics delivered to an audience who wanted extemporaneous speeches of impeccable Attic and who graded the speeches by the number of mistakes.

The orators were virtuosi in a rhetorical opera performed for the benefit of ticket holders in auditoriums, not in the people's assembly or the forum. Under the monarchy, there were no longer assemblies of a sovereign people, no political trials hotly debated in public, and no decrees of the senate deciding the fate of kings, pretenders, or entire nations. Nothing real was at stake when the sophists pleaded: not how the Athenians should deal with the deserters in Mytilene, not whether Socrates should live or die. It was not for the sophists to persuade a jury to find Verres guilty, to make the Roman people vote that Pompey be given the command against the pirates, or to convince a reluctant senate that Mark Antony be declared an enemy of the republic.

True enough, they all did speak on such and similar topics, but the issues were no longer real. They were borrowed from the past, preferably the distant past of the fifth century B.C. In discussing them, these sophists were just displaying art for art's sake, and yet the fault lies not with them alone; they were meeting popular demand. This age looked to the past, was more interested in times long gone than in its own.[36] The present was without tensions and conflicts, void of strong emo-

[35] U. von Wilamowitz, "Die griechische Literatur des Altertums," in *Die Kultur der Gegenwart*, ed. P. Hinneberg, vol. 1, pt. 8 (Berlin and Leipzig 1905), 164: "Niemals ist die formale Technik der Prosarede . . . mit grösserer Vollkommenheit geübt worden."
[36] Ed. Norden, *Die antike Kunstprosa vom 6. Jahrhundert bis in die Zeit der Renaissance*, vol. 1, 3d ed. (Leipzig and Berlin 1915), 345: "Denn die Menschen dieses und der folgenden Jahrhunderte haben ihre Augen nach rückwärts gewendet. Wie Greise erinnern sie sich einer glücklicheren Kindheit."

tions. So people turned to more agitated phases of history. And a predilection for the old was exactly to the taste of the time. The emperor
Hadrian preferred Cato as an orator to Cicero; he preferred the historian Coelius Antipater to Sallust, the poet Ennius to Vergil.[37] The future emperor Marcus Aurelius was expressly warned by his teacher,
the Latin sophist Cornelius Fronto, not to read such writers as Seneca
or Lucan (who, in fact, had a lot more to say than poor Fronto
himself).[38]

This predilection for the archaic past produced some strange results.[39] Cities claimed they were founded by the autochthonous people
of their region and invented mythical founders; ludicrous as their
claims often were, the Roman authorities were obliged to take them
seriously. Even in the time of Augustus, Marcus Agrippa (his junior
partner in the administration of the empire) addressed a letter to the
Council of the Elders at Argos, "the offspring of Danaus and Hyper-
mestra."[40] Noble families traced their pedigrees back to such famous
men as Themistocles and Alcibiades,[41] to heroes such as Heracles, or
to gods. Sparta reinstituted what it thought was the Lycurgan constitution and the traditional way of educating boys.[42] In Athens, the
Areopagus played a greater role in the government than it had since
the early fifth century, when it lost its power.

The cities in the Greek part of the empire fought against each other
like demons for the right to bear such pompous titles (bestowed by the
emperors) as "the first and largest and most beautiful city of Asia, warden of two imperial temples, sole warden of the goddess Artemis, the
metropolis of Ionia," and on and on.[43] Their most celebrated sophists
would plead their cases before the emperors, who were as annoyed by

---

[37] S.H.A. *Hadr.* 16.6.

[38] Fronto ad M. Antoninum *De orationibus* 2ff. (p. 149ff. van den Hout).

[39] For the following see, above all, U. von Wilamowitz, *Der Glaube der Hellenen*, vol. 2
(Berlin 1932), 462–66: "Spielen von Althellas," where much of the evidence is collected.

[40] *Mnemosyne* 47 (1919): 264, no. 28: Ἀγρίππας Ἀργείων γέρουσι τοῖς ἀπὸ Δαναοῦ
καὶ Ὑπερμήστρας χαίρειν. See Pausanias II.19.6.

[41] Herodes Atticus claimed to be a descendant of Miltiades, and therefore named a
daughter Elpinice. An Athenian Diogenes, son of Hermolaus, claimed to be a descendant
of Pericles (*SEG* 11, p. 216, no. 77). For a Samian claiming to be a descendant of Alcibiades see *AthMitt* 44 (1919): 43, no. 34, line 8.

[42] V. Ehrenberg, "Sparta," in *RE* (1929), 1450–53.

[43] See, for instance, Ch. Habicht, *Die Inschriften des Asklepieions*, Altertümer von Pergamon, vol. 8, pt. 3 (Berlin 1969), 72–74, 158–61; C. P. Jones, *The Roman World of
Dio Chrysostom* (Cambridge, Mass., 1978), 77–78.

these quarrels as they were patient in listening to the "Greek aberrations" (as Dio Chrysostom characterizes the Roman view of these Greek orgies of vanity).[44]

The true representatives of the culture, taste, and intellectual life of the age were the sophists, mostly Greek, like Antonius Polemo and Aelius Aristides from Asia Minor, and Herodes Atticus from Athens, or, on the Latin side, the African-born Cornelius Fronto.[45] Valuable information about them is contained in Philostratus' "Lives of the Sophists,"[46] and their impact on the age has been admirably assessed in G. W. Bowersock's *Greek Sophists in the Roman Empire.*[47] Wherever they spoke (or, rather, performed), they attracted large crowds and collected enormous fees. They were unoriginal, mediocre figures, shallow, arrogant, and full of vanity, but they exerted influence on the emperor and barely acknowledged him as their equal; the most celebrated were granted audiences or asked to deliver lectures in his presence; some were high-ranking officials in the imperial administration.

When, for instance, Aelius Aristides delivered his panegyric of Rome before the emperor in A.D. 143, another sophist, Herodes Atticus, was *consul ordinarius*, a third, Cornelius Fronto, *consul suffectus.*[48] They enjoyed such privileges as freedom from taxation, customs, and billeting; in their hometowns they could not be forced to undertake liturgies or to serve as elected officials, jurors, or tutors of minors.[49] Chairs of rhetoric were endowed by the emperor in Athens and Rome for the most famous sophists. Their statues were placed in the most prestigious shrines.

---

[44] Dio Chrys. *Or.* 38.38: Ἑλληνικὰ ἁμαρτήματα.

[45] For Polemo see below, n. 50; for Aristides, A. Boulanger, *Aelius Aristide et la Sophistique dans la province d'Asie au deuxième siècle de nôtre ère* (Paris 1923); C. A. Behr, *Aelius Aristides and the Sacred Tales* (Amsterdam 1968); for Herodes Atticus, P. Graindor, *Un Milliardaire antique: Hérode Atticus et sa famille* (Cairo 1930); H. Halfmann, *Die Senatoren aus dem östlichen Teil des Imperium Romanum bis zum Ende des 2. Jh. n. Chr.* (Göttingen 1979), 155ff., no. 68; W. Ameling, *Herodes Atticus*, 2 vols. (Hildesheim 1983); for Fronto, E. Champlin, *Fronto and Antonine Rome* (Cambridge, Mass., 1980).

[46] 2 : 1–127 Kayser.

[47] G. W. Bowersock, *Greek Sophists in the Roman Empire* (Oxford 1969). See also L. E. Bowie, "The Importance of Sophists," *YCS* 27 (1982): 29–59.

[48] R. Syme, "The Greeks under Roman Rule," *Proceedings of the Massachusetts Historical Society* 72 (1957–60): 11.

[49] Bowersock (above, n. 47), pp. 30–42. "Special Privileges." In addition, see the new inscription from Ephesus, dating from the triumviral period, *ZPE* 44 (1981): 1–10; *IEphesos* 4101, with the important discussion of K. Bringmann, *Epigraphica Anatolica* 2 (1983): 47–75, esp. 69ff.

Antonius Polemo provides a good example of how these sophists used to conduct themselves.[50] When the ruler of the Bosporan kingdom, an ally of the emperor, came to Smyrna to visit Polemo and pay his respects, Polemo demanded ten talents in advance for an audience. Once this shining star returned to his home to find that the governor of Asia, none other than the future emperor Antoninus Pius, had, in the course of a journey, taken lodging in Polemo's house; he kicked him out.

Polemo was indeed a star. When Hadrian dedicated the temple of Olympian Zeus in Athens, a project begun by the Pisistratids in the sixth century, advanced by Antiochus IV in the second century, and completed by Hadrian, Polemo delivered the inaugural address.[51]

He was invited by Herodes Atticus to deliver three public lectures in Athens. The three topics he chose for his performance were a defense of Demosthenes, who had been accused of accepting bribes from Alexander's treasurer, Harpalus; an analysis of the peace of Nicias in 421 B.C.; and a declamation on the situation of Athens in 404 B.C. after her decisive defeat in the Peloponnesian War. The most recent of his subjects was 450 years in the past—not exactly hot news.

For these three speeches he was offered an honorarium of fifteen talents; he demanded and received twenty-five.[52] Twenty-five talents is equivalent to the annual pay of five hundred Roman legionnaires, and six times the annual salary granted by the emperor Vespasian to the excellent Quintilian.[53]

This age has been called the age of quietude, the beginning of senility in the empire.[54] There was no Latin writer of the depth and temper of Tacitus, the brilliance of Juvenal, no Greek writer of stature with the compassion for mankind and human values of Epictetus or Plutarch. There are, of course, the *Meditations* of Marcus Aurelius, written during his campaigns on the Danube, certainly a decent attempt by a decent man who was working to improve his character, but his self-absorption is not to everybody's taste.[55] In the field of literature, only

[50] Philostr. *VS*, pp. 42–54; *PIR*[2] A.862; W. Stegemann, "Polemon," in *RE* (1952), 1320–57; Habicht (above, n. 43), p. 75, no. 33.
[51] The information is from Philostr. *VS*, pp. 46, 44–45, 44.
[52] The information is from Philostr. *VS*, pp. 48, 49.
[53] Suet. *Vesp.* 18; cf. Hieron. *Chron.*, p. 190, line 20 Helm (p. 272, line 19 Fotheringham). See also A. Kappelmacher, "Fabius (Quintilianus)," in *RE* (1909), 1849.
[54] Norden (above, n. 36), p. 344ff.; Wilamowitz (above, n. 35), p. 164ff.
[55] See, however, P. A. Brunt, "Marcus Aurelius in His Meditations," *JRS* 64 (1974): 1–20. Wilamowitz, too, spoke in defense of the *Meditations*: "Der Wert des Buches

two names stand out: the Greek satirist Lucian from Samosata on the Euphrates and the Latin novelist Apuleius from North Africa, author of the delightful work *The Golden Ass*. Neither man was a sophist (though Lucian once had been) or involved in the sophists' professional circles and personal feuds.[56] They were outsiders with enough talent to go their own way, and they were the only two who produced works that have appealed to generation after generation of readers down to the present day.

First-rate people were, to be sure, at work in some fields of knowledge—in medicine especially, with Galen of Pergamum, who became the physician of the imperial family under Marcus Aurelius, and in Roman law, with such men as Juventius Celsus, consul for the second time in A.D. 129, and Salvius Julianus, consul in A.D. 148, men who continued to produce creative work in law and even brought the discipline to its peak.[57] Nevertheless, works of lasting value were produced only in the area of useful knowledge and in professions serving a certain purpose, not in the field of pure literature. After Tacitus, history in the second century was abandoned to obscure writers (at least to judge from what Lucian has to say about contemporary historians in his "How to Write History"),[58] poetry was dead, philosophy mediocre.

How does Pausanias fit into this general picture? What is his place within his age? Was he really, as is often believed, just a typical product of his time, reflecting no more than the general trend?[59] Or was there, perhaps, something original in him that was not in harmony, but rather at odds, with the prevailing trend? No doubt Pausanias, like the vast majority of his contemporaries, held the past, as compared with

---

kann nicht ärger verkannt werden als durch Harnacks unbegreifliche Bezeichnung als 'oberflächliches Räsonnement und moralisierende Selbstbespiegelung.' Von dieser steckt in Augustins Confessionen wahrhaftig mehr" ("Kaiser Marcus" [1931], in *KlSchr*, vol. 3 [Berlin 1969], 502). The last remark is beside the point; in my opinion, Harnack's judgment is valid (*Augustins Konfessionen* [Giessen 1895], 9).

[56] For Lucian as the prototype of sophists see G. Anderson, "Lucian: A Sophist's Sophist," *YCS* 27 (1982): 61–92. See, on the other hand, W. Schmid, *Geschichte der griechischen Literatur*, vol. 2, pt. 2, 6th ed. (Munich 1924), 710: "Die übliche äusserlich glänzende Karriere der Sophisten hat er sich gründlich verdorben."

[57] See W. Kunkel, *Herkunft und soziale Stellung der römischen Juristen*, 2d ed. (Graz 1967), 146–47 (Celsus), 157–66 (Julianus).

[58] G. Avenarius, *Lukians Schrift zur Geschichtsschreibung* (Meisenheim 1956); H. Homeyer, *Wie man Geschichte schreiben soll* (text, translation, and commentary) (Munich 1965).

[59] Kalkmann, p. 11: "Er ist überhaupt ein Kind seiner Zeit, ein Dutzendmensch ohne Originalität."

the present, in high esteem, in particular the archaic and classical periods for their art, architecture, and literature. He mentions no fewer than 179 different sculptors, some only once, others several times, a good many repeatedly.[60] Most often, he just mentions the sculptor's name to attribute the statue, but in quite a few instances he gives his judgment of the work; for instance, of a wooden image of Heracles in Corinth ascribed to Daedalus (a sculpture of the archaic period), he says, "The works of Daedalus are somewhat uncouth to the eye, but there is a touch of the divine[61] in them for all that." Pausanias has the discernment, despite the sculpture's lack of elegance and refinement, to recognize a kind of sublime inspiration and to value that.

Pausanias, in general, recognizes the quality of some sculpture of the sixth century. He praises unequivocally the sculptors of the fifth century, notably Alcamenes, Calamis, Myron, Naucydes, Onatas, Phidias, and Pythagoras.[62] He is little less enthusiastic about two artists of the fourth century, Cephisodotus and Praxiteles.[63] Of later sculptors he compliments only Damophon of Messene (IV.31.10)—if calling Damophon "the only Messenian sculptor of note that I know of" is a compliment.

He has nary a word of praise for such famous artists as Polyclitus, Paeonius, and Agoracritus in the fifth century, Scopas, Lysippus, and Leochares in the fourth, and, of course, all the postclassical sculptors, including those of the so-called Pergamene baroque. Pausanias, it seems, rates Phidias the highest, and Phidias' pupil Alcamenes second (V.10.8).[64] By comparison, Lucian, his contemporary, gives, as the unrivaled models of Greek sculpture, Phidias, Alcamenes, and Praxite-

---

[60] They can easily be found in Rocha-Pereira 3:261–65 ("Index artificum").

[61] II.4.5: ἔνθεόν τι.

[62] I.19.2, V.10.8 (Alcamenes); IX.20.4 (Calamis); IX.30.1 (Myron); VI.9.3 (Naucydes); V.10.8, VI.4.5 (Phidias); VI.4.4, 6.6 (Pythagoras). Pausanias calls Onatas' Apollo, which he had seen at Pergamum, "one of the greatest marvels both for size and workmanship" (VIII.42.7). The statue had been taken from Onatas' hometown of Aegina after Aegina had become part of the Pergamene kingdom ca. 208 B.C. It was probably on this occasion that the statue received a new base, with Onatas' signature reengraved, since the base found at Pergamum with his name dates from ca. 200 B.C. (*IPergamon* 48). Antipater of Thessalonica, in the time of Augustus, dedicated an epigram to this famous statue (*Anth. Pal.* 9.238).

[63] IX.16.2 (Cephisodotus); I.20.1–2, IX.39.4 (Praxiteles).

[64] On the gables of the temple of Zeus at Olympia: "The figures in the front gable are by Paeonius, a native of Mende in Thrace: the figures in the back gable are by Alcamenes, a contemporary of Phidias, and only second to him as a sculptor." Cf. I.28.2, on the *Athena Lemnia*: "This image of Athena is the best worth seeing of the works of Phidias."

les.[65] Pausanias' taste, as far as sculpture is concerned, seems well in line with the taste of his time.

Pausanias has much less to say about painters; he mentions only sixteen,[66] and seems to have been impressed by no more than two, the Athenian Nicias of the fourth century, who is mentioned four times ("the greatest animal painter of his time": I.29.15), and, above all, Polygnotus of Thasos (a contemporary of Cimon and Pericles), who did the painted Stoa in Athens and the hall that the Cnidians dedicated at Delphi. The subjects were the destruction of Troy and Odysseus' voyage to the underworld. Pausanias consumes nineteen pages of text in describing these works (X.25–31). His painstaking description is in itself a tribute to the art of the classical period.

His views on architecture follow the same pattern. Of the four buildings he likes the best, two belong to the fifth century and two to the fourth. The first pair are the Propylaea in Athens—"for the beauty and size of the blocks [the work] has never yet been matched" (I.22.4)— and the temple of Apollo at Bassae in Arcadia—"of all the temples in Peloponnese, next to the one in Tegea, this may be placed first for the beauty of the stone and the symmetry of its proportions" (VIII.41.8). The architect, Ictinus, also designed the Parthenon.[67]

The two fourth-century buildings are the temple of Alea in Tegea, a work of the sculptor Scopas—"the present temple far surpasses all other temples in Peloponnese, both in size [this is wrong] and style" (VIII.45.5)—and the theater in Epidaurus, by Polyclitus of Argos— "most especially worth seeing. It is true that in size the theatre of Megalopolis in Arcadia surpasses it, and that in splendour the Roman theatres far transcend all the theatres in the world; but for symmetry and beauty what architect could vie with Polyclitus?" (II.27.5). Today's experts would hardly quarrel with Pausanias about the artists and works he admires most.

His views on literature accord with his views on art and architecture. Of the some 125 authors he names—and he quotes from a good many of them[68]—he all but ignores philosophy; he alludes once or

---

[65] Lucian *Hist. conscr.* 51.

[66] They, too, can be found in Rocha-Pereira's "Index artificum" (3 : 261–65).

[67] While F. E. Winter (*AJA* 84 [1980]: 399–416) argues that the attribution of the temple at Bassae to Ictinus is unlikely to be correct, according to B. Wesenberg ("Wer erbaute den Parthenon?" *AthMitt* 97 [1982]: 99–125) Ictinus built the temple at Bassae and the Telesterion at Eleusis, but in Athens only the so-called Vorparthenon, the Parthenon itself being the work of Callicrates.

[68] Rocha-Pereira 3 : 252–59 ("Index auctorum"). Cf. Meyer, p. 36.

twice each to Plato (with just two quotations), Aristotle, Zeno, Chrysippus, Diogenes the Cynic, and Arcesilaus. He is just as meager in Greek drama; he quotes from Aeschylus and Euripides more than once, and mentions Sophocles, and, in comedy, Aristophanes, Phrynichus, Eupolis, and Menander. Among historians there are only two he quotes from often—Herodotus (his model) and Thucydides—though he does insert brief quotations here and there from a good many others, mostly historians of the fifth or fourth century, with the exception of Polybius (of the second century). However, when Pausanias refers to Polybius by name, he seems to refer to Polybius the political figure rather than Polybius the author, although most of the long account of the history of Achaea in book VII, where Polybius' name does not appear, is, in fact, based on his history.[69]

Pausanias gives more space to lyric and epic poets. He cites and quotes from a long list of lyric poets, ranging from the seventh century to the fourth; his favorite is Pindar (with twenty-three quotations from his poems and five additional citations), followed by Stesichorus (whose verses are quoted thirteen times). He can pass judgment on a city for its attitude toward this form of literature: "It seems to me that in all the world there is no people so dead to poetry and poetic fame as the Spartans" (III.8.2), though even the Spartans had one great poet, "Alcman, the sweetness of whose songs was not impaired by the Laconian dialect, the least musical of languages" (III.15.2). He praises the Orphic hymns: "For poetical beauty they may rank next to the hymns of Homer, and they have received still higher marks of divine favour" (IX. 30.12). And he is full of contempt for the poor quality of some epigrams that the Eleans set up in Olympia on athletic fraud.[70]

In epic, naturally enough, Pausanias puts Homer first (with some 250 citations and twenty-two quotations) and Hesiod second (with some fifty citations and eight quotations). Homer and Hesiod are the classics, but Pausanias says of the *Thebais*, "Next to the Iliad and Odyssey, there is certainly no poem which I esteem so highly."[71] He prefers the archaic period, which, after all, was the heyday of Greek epic, but he also likes two epic poets of the Hellenistic age, Apollonius of Rhodes and Aratus of Soli, both from the third century B.C. (II.12.6, I.2.3).

[69] Polybius is mentioned often, mostly in connection with honors he received: VIII.9.1, 30.8, 37.2, 44.5, 48.8. Cf. *IOlympia* 302, 449, 450, 486, 487.

[70] V.21.2–16, esp. 21.4, 21.6; H.-V. Herrmann, "Zanes" in *RE*, suppl. 14 (1974), 977–81.

[71] IX.9.5. For Pausanias' knowledge of Homer and for the significance of Homer's work for his own, see Robert, p. 25ff., and below, p. 143 nn. 11, 12.

In art and literature Pausanias shares the taste of his time.[72] He scarcely mentions Hellenistic artists, architects, poets, or other writers, and certainly values them less than their predecessors (nor would many, today, disagree with that judgment). In his day Pausanias could still see Hellenistic buildings and statues in large number; Hellenistic literature was less accessible. Nevertheless, despite the difficulties, he has included a large amount of Hellenistic history in his work, and he states the reason unequivocally: the Hellenistic period was almost forgotten in his time, whereas everybody knew the history of the fifth century (I.6.1).

He has read Hellenistic historians and has used their work, even though he does not often quote them directly. In his time, the general public no longer read these historians, and so they were no longer copied, and now are lost. In appreciating what they had to offer and including them in his work, Pausanias does, at least in the field of history, represent something more than was to be expected of a man of his time; though he did share the general taste, he was less one-sided than the larger public.

He, too, may have despised the style of these Hellenistic historians, but he was concerned not so much with the aesthetic value of these historians as with the information they could furnish him, so he could bring his descriptions of places and works to life. Nevertheless, among the 120 to 130 authors he names, there is not a single contemporary Greek, and not a single Latin writer at all!—neither Cicero nor any historian nor any Latin poet. In this, at least, he shares the attitude common among Greek intellectuals of his age.[73]

His preference for the distant past is also revealed in his selection of monuments to describe. Few are later than the first half of the third century B.C. In Athens, for instance, although he admits that the stadium of Herodes Atticus is "wonderful to see" (I.19.6), he does not mention the Stoa of Eumenes or the Stoa of Attalus (which dominated the Agora) or the monument of Agrippa; in Olympia he ignores the splendid Exedra of Herodes Atticus;[74] in Delphi he discusses no monu-

---

[72] Meyer, p. 26.

[73] For the absence of Greek contemporaries see A. Diller, *TAPA* 86 (1955): 273; for that of Latin authors, J. Crook, *CR*, n.s., 11 (1961): 69: "One of the most obvious peculiarities about the Greek writers of the Empire is the way in which they ignore Roman literature."

[74] This, of course, has often been observed, and there have been numerous attempts to explain the fact, the most elaborate by S. Settis, "Il ninfeo di Erode Attico a Olimpia e il problema della composizione della Periegesi di Pausania," *AnnPisa*, ser. 2, 37 (1968):

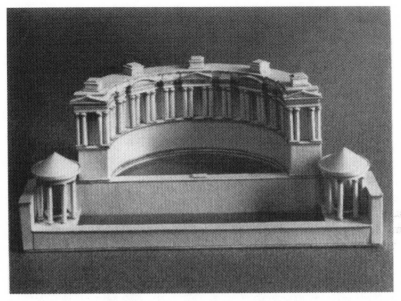

Fig. 31. Olympia, Exedra of Herodes Atticus (courtesy Deutsches
Archäologisches Institut, Abteilung Athen).

ment, no statue, no base, no object that is later than 260 B.C., except
the "third temple" in the sanctuary of Athena and "several statues of
emperors."[75] Except for the "third temple," these were not sacred
buildings, and sacred buildings did mean more to him than civic monuments.[76] Moreover, as Wilamowitz put it, "as was the spirit of his
time, his interest was completely attracted by the distant past of Greece;
the age of the heroes was closer to him than the recent past."[77]

1–63. The omission can hardly be anything but deliberate. E. N. Gardiner (Olympia:
Its History and Remains [Oxford 1925], 192) holds that Pausanias' taste was offended
by the display of such luxurious architecture at this sacred spot (see fig. 31; see also the
bust of Herodes shown in fig. 32); H.-V. Herrmann agrees with him (Olympia: Heiligtum und Wettkampfstätte [Munich 1972], 192, 262 n. 779). This seems to me to be the
right explanation. See below, on the monument of Philopappus.

[75] G. Daux, Pausanias à Delphes (Paris 1936), 173.

[76] F. H. Sandbach, in CAH, vol. 11 (1936), 689; Meyer, pp. 47–48; R. E. Wycherley,
GRBS 2 (1959): 24; Heer, p. 112. H. Brunn correctly observed, a century ago, that the
taste of Pausanias and his time determined the selection of objects to be discussed or
excluded ("Pausanias und seine Ankläger," Fleckeisens Jahrbücher, 1884:23–30 (reprinted in KlSchr, vol. 3 [Leipzig and Berlin 1906], 210–16, on pp. 213–16).

[77] Wilamowitz (above, n. 39), p. 501.

Fig. 32. Louvre, bust of Herodes Atticus.

When he does mention a monument of his own time, such as the mausoleum of Philopappus on the Museion Hill in Athens (even today an Athenian landmark), he may give the description a peculiar twist. The man buried there was the son of the royal family of Commagene (on the Euphrates), a great benefactor of Athens, and a Roman consul in 109, as well as the recipient of a treatise by Plutarch;[78] Pausanias,

---

[78] *PIR*² J.151; Halfmann (above, n. 45), p. 131, no. 36; D. E. E. Kleiner, *The Monument of Philopappos in Athens* (Rome 1983). See fig. 33.

however, shows his disdain by saying, "Afterwards a monument was built here to a Syrian man."[79]

A writer of Pausanias' day must write in Attic, and Pausanias is, this far, a product of his own time. He writes in the fashionable Attic style, but he faces a particular problem. The nature of his work demands repetition, while high style demands variety, and so he constantly goes out of his way to vary his expression, sometimes at the cost of clarity. This variation is particularly obvious in, for example, the list of the two-hundred-odd bases for victorious athletes at Olympia (VI.1–18). In his style, unfortunately, he fails. It does not relieve the monotony, and often does confuse the meaning, especially his trick of using a highly unusual word order.[80]

Pausanias, incontestably, is a man of his time, and not a deep thinker, certainly, but some scholars have refused to credit Pausanias with any originality.[81] They have put a label on him: "Pausanias the sophist" or "a scissors-and-paste author"—like Aulus Gellius, Aelian, and Athenaeus, authors who compiled what seemed to them to be memorable features of a motley range of subjects: religion, myth, law, history, institutions, science, language, customs, food, drink, prostitutes, and so on.[82]

Nothing could be farther from the truth than to apply either label to

---

[79] I.25.7. See above, n. 74, on his failure to mention the Exedra of Herodes Atticus in Olympia. It is likewise with disgust that Pausanias, in his description of the Athenian agora, remarks, "The names on the statues of Miltiades and Themistocles have been altered into those of a Roman and a Thracian" (I.18.3). The practice was common and often criticized, for instance by Dio Chrysostom in his Rhodian speech (*Or.* 31). See H. Blanck, *Wiederverwendung alter Statuen als Ehrendenkmäler bei Griechen und Römern* (Rome 1969). Dio also criticizes the extravagance of the Athenians in bestowing high honors (*Or.* 31.116–18); see C. P. Jones, *The Roman World of Dio Chrysostom* (Cambridge, Mass., 1978), 31–32.

[80] Robert, pp. 201–16: "Einiges vom Stil des Autors"; see also Strid, passim, where earlier contributions on Pausanias' style and language are cited. As so often, Wilamowitz is extremely rude: "der Stil so zerhackt und verzwackt, so altbacken und muffig. . . . [Das Buch] ist eines der bezeichnendsten, also auch unerquicklichsten Erzeugnisse einer kernfaulen Zeit" (Wilamowitz [above, n. 35], p. 163).

[81] See above, n. 59.

[82] Pausanias as a "sophist": Kalkmann, p. 280; Gurlitt, p. 20 (who nonetheless assigns him a special place among the sophists with respect to his aim and style); Pasquali, pp. 165, 194; H.-W. Nörenberg, *Hermes* 101 (1973): 236 n. 6; Heer, p. 16, and passim. Pausanias as a "Buntschriftsteller": U. von Wilamowitz, *Homerische Untersuchungen* (Berlin 1884), 339; Robert, p. 8; Pasquali, p. 192 ("im Rahmen der Periegese eine παντοδαπὴς ἱστορία").

Fig. 33. Athens, monument of Philopappus.

Pausanias.[83] Pausanias differs from the compilers of *Variae historiae*, "Attic Nights," and "Learned Banqueteers." He has one theme, the "Description of Greece"; it is an important theme and one he pursues no matter how often he digresses (as Herodotus digressed even as he pursued his main theme). And, as for the sophists, Pausanias is worlds apart from them. They were famous, wealthy, influential, and often vicious. A sophist would talk on any subject; he was as willing to deliver an extemporaneous speech as to recite on a topic of his choice, after laborious preparation. A sophist wanted to show off, to display his brilliant rhetoric, to get a big hand—and an even bigger payoff. A sophist was a prima donna whose ego required the stage.[84] Even on the road from engagement to engagement, a sophist played the great man, accompanied "by luggage-carts, horses, slaves and several packs of hounds, while he himself [this is Polemo once more] rode a silver-bridled horse."[85] A sophist could deliver a portrayal of Demosthenes struggling for the freedom of Greece on one day and a panegyric of Rome on the next.

How could Pausanias be stuck among these? Pausanias kept the lowest possible profile, spent twenty years or more in the pursuit of one single goal close to his heart, a goal he could not know he would attain: "The facts which I ascertained about the latter incident [Heracles and Apollo wrestling] I will narrate in that part of my description of Phocis which relates to Delphi, if I ever get so far" (VIII.37.1). Pausanias was not touring Greece to receive the plaudits of the crowd, nor did he limit his travels to the amenities of the cities. Once he made his laborious way to Phigalia in the mountainous heart of Arcadia in order to see the famous statue of Demeter, carved by Onatas some six hundred years before, and found, when he arrived, that it no longer existed: "The oldest man we met said that three generations before his time some stones from the roof had fallen on the image . . . ; and sure enough in the roof we could still clearly see the places from which the stones had broken off."[86]

[83] A. Lesky, *Geschichte der griechischen Literatur*, 2d ed. (Bern and Munich 1963), 912: "Dieser Perieget ist ein Vielgereister, der über zahlreiche Dinge aus eigener Anschauung spricht; er ist daneben auch ein Vielbelesener, aber in besserem Sinne als die Buntschriftsteller."

[84] They have been called "Konzertredner" by Ludwig Radermacher (quoted by Lesky [above, n. 83], p. 891).

[85] The quotation is from F. H. Sandbach (above, n. 76), p. 682, who in turn resumes Philostr. *VS* 2 : 43 Kayser.

[86] VIII.42.1–13. This chapter has been a favorite playground of Pausanias' critics. Although he expressly says that his main incentive for going to Phigalia was this Demeter

At least once, it seems, Pausanias draws a line between himself and these sophists: "Though I have investigated very carefully the dates of Hesiod and Homer, I do not like to state my results, knowing as I do the carping disposition of some people, especially the professors of poetry at the present day" (IX.30.3). Partly in harmony, partly at odds with his own day, Pausanias retains an individuality of his own.

Thank God his work has lasted rather than the mass of the sophists' speeches!

(VIII.42.11), Wilamowitz and others categorically denied that he ever went there (for instance, U. von Wilamowitz, *Der Glaube der Hellenen*, vol. 1 [Berlin 1931], 402–3), and declared his description of the statue a mere fiction. Others disagreed, and Regenbogen eventually struck the balance: "Man kann die ganze Auseinandersetzung nur als abschreckendes Beispiel törichter Hyperkritik benutzen" (p. 1042). The most recent discussion does not even mention Wilamowitz' name (J. Dörig, *Onatas of Aegina* [Leiden 1977], 8–9).

VI

A PROFILE OF PAUSANIAS

Pausanias does not often speak about himself, and when he does he usually does not reveal much. Although he makes it clear that he has traveled widely, not only around Greece but also to the Near East, Egypt, Italy, and elsewhere,[1] he does not give the slightest clue to the dates, sequence, or number of his major journeys. Pausanias does not complain about the hardships of ordinary travel or the difficulties in reaching remote places, except for a few offhand remarks like "The voyage from Peloponnese to Creusis is tortuous and stormy" (IX.32.1). He does not even suggest that traveling was not always or everywhere entirely safe. (His contemporary Apuleius has a lot to say about brigands in Greece.)[2] He never mentions accommodations, be they an inn or a private home where he was a guest. He does not name a single personal acquaintance, not even a companion on one of his journeys, although he must have met, known, and befriended a good many important and famous people.

Dedicated as he is to his work, his own person never comes into the foreground—beginning to end, Pausanias keeps a low profile—but no one can write a book of almost nine hundred pages without injecting, here and there, some signs of his own personality. The signs are not

---

[1] See above, p. 17 n. 71.
[2] See F. Millar, "The World of the *Golden Ass*," *JRS* 61 (1981): 64. Other contemporary witnesses are Lucian, *Dial. Mort.* 27.2 (see Frazer, p. xiv), and Artemidorus of Daldis, who in numerous passages reveals that encounters with robbers were almost to be expected on journeys (see R. Hercher's index to Artemidorus, s.v. λῃσταί); B. D. Shaw, "Bandits in the Roman Empire," *Past and Present* 105 (1984) 3–52.

easy to find, and often not easy to assess, since he rarely makes open statements and his incidental remarks, while numerous, are less revealing. The signs need to be followed and Pausanias cornered before his personality can be caught. It is no doubt for this reason that the first book on the subject was not published until 1979.[3]

Pausanias came from a wealthy family; he grew up in western Asia Minor in the vicinity of Mount Sipylus, not far from Pergamum, at that time one of the liveliest centers of cultural activity in the whole empire.[4] He received a solid education, was an extremely well-read man, and continued to read all his life. The list of writers he quotes is long, and it speaks to his honesty that he tells the reader when, in fact, he has not read what he quotes. Twice he cites verses from a pair of obscure poets, whose works, he explains, were lost, but the verses had been quoted by Callippus of Corinth in his history of Orchomenus (in Boeotia), and Pausanias has copied them from this work.[5] With the same honesty he tells the reader when he has not visited a certain site himself, or seen a certain object (I.38.2, VIII.10.2). As Frazer puts it, "if we take the word of Pausanias for what he tells us he did not see and did not read, we must take it also for what he tells us he did see and did read."[6]

Pausanias is at home with the major classical writers (as was every educated man of his time); his memory is excellent, and his ability to synthesize good. For instance, on the dedication at Olympia by the Myanians he says, "I recollected that Thucydides, in his history, mentions various cities of the Locrians . . . and amongst others the city of the Myonians." He concludes that the Myanians and the Myonians are the same, and this is correct.[7] He saw two trophies from the Persian Wars on the Athenian acropolis: "the corselet of Masistius, who commanded the cavalry at Plataea, and a sword said to be that of Mar-

---

[3] J. Heer, *La Personnalité de Pausanias* (Paris 1979); see Ch. Habicht, *Gnomon* 56 (1984): 177–79.

[4] For Pergamum, especially the sanctuary of Asclepius, as a center of intellectual and cultural life in the second century A.D. see Ch. Habicht, *Die Inschriften des Asklepieions*, Altertümer von Pergamon, vol. 8, pt. 3 (Berlin 1969), 15–18.

[5] IX.29.1–2 from the *Atthis* of Hegesinus (*FGrHist* 331); IX.38.9–10 from Chersias of Orchomenus.

[6] Frazer, p. lxviii.

[7] VI.19.4–5 (cf. X.38.8), referring to Thuc. 3.101.2. Myania has been located at Haghia Efthymia by L. Robert, *Etudes épigraphiques et philologiques* (Paris 1938), 237–42. Since then, a treaty between Myania and Hypnia has been published (*BCH* 89 [1965]: 665–81; *FD* III.4.352), and also a decree of Delphi in honor of a citizen of Myania (*SEG* 27.124), both documents dating from the second century B.C.

donius." From his knowledge of Herodotus he can deduce which trophy could be genuine: "Masistius, I know, was killed by the Athenian
cavalry; but as Mardonius fought against the Lacedaemonians, and
fell by the hand of a Spartan, the Athenians could not have got the
sword originally, nor is it likely that the Lacedaemonians would have
allowed them to carry it off."[8] In these two passages knowledge and
logic are combined, as they often are in Pausanias.

Verses from the third-century epic poet Apollonius of Rhodes help
him evaluate a story some locals had told him, according to which
Phlias, the eponym of Phlius, was a son of Cisus: "But I cannot agree
with them, for I know that he is called a son of Dionysus, and is said to
have been one of those who sailed in the Argo. And the verses of the
Rhodian poet bear me out: 'After them came Phlias from Araethyrea, /
Where he dwelt in wealth through Dionysus / His sire: his home was
by the Asopus.'"[9]

A Nemean ode by Pindar comes to mind when he speaks of Lynceus,
"of whom Pindar said (believe it who likes) that his sight was so sharp
that he saw through the trunk of an oak."[10] When Pausanias reports a
local tradition in a part of Laconia that Achilles had been a suitor of
Helen, he has at his fingertips three passages from the *Iliad* and the
Odyssey that prove "that this is a sheer impossibility" (III.24.10–11).[11]
In IV.1.3–4 he uses no less than four Homeric passages (one from the
catalog of ships in the *Iliad*, the other three from the *Odyssey*) for a
conclusive demonstration that at the time of these poems there was no
city, only a region, called Messene.[12] Pausanias is certainly entitled to
say, "Like every attentive reader of Homer, I am persuaded that . . ."
(II.4.2).

Apart from the works he already knew as a well-rounded man, he
read others solely for the purposes of his work, to verify or clarify
what he had been told by local guides. The mythology of Messenia, in
which King Polycaon and his wife, Messene of Argos, play a dominant
role, piqued his curiosity: "Wishing very much to learn who were the
sons of Polycaon by Messene, I read the poem called the 'Eoeae' and
the epic called the 'Naupactia,' and, moreover, all the genealogies
composed by Cinaethon and Asius. But they had nothing to say on the
subject" (IV.2.1).

---

[8] I.27.1; the references are to Hdt. 9.22 (Masistius) and 9.64 (Mardonius).
[9] II.12.6; Ap. Rhod. *Argon.* 1.115–17.
[10] IV.2.7, referring to Pind. *Nem.* 10.61–63.
[11] He refers to 1.158–60 and 23.790 of the *Iliad* and to 11.630–31 of the *Odyssey*.
[12] *Il.* 2.591ff.; *Od.* 21.18, 21.15–16, 3.488–89.

In collecting material for his book, Pausanias examined hundreds of statues carved by hundreds of sculptors, whose names were usually written on the bases, and so, naturally enough, he read literary works on sculptors in order to be able to tell the reader, "The statue is by Pythagoras of Rhegium. . . . They say that Pythagoras was taught by Clearchus, who was himself a native of Rhegium and a pupil of Euchirus; and Euchirus, it is said, was a Corinthian, and studied under two Spartan masters, Syadras and Chartas." [13] He could not have learned these details from a local guide; he had to search for them in a library where he could find biographical works on famous artists.

Apart from the general knowledge Pausanias had acquired in school and what he had researched in libraries for the sake of his book, he was eager to learn as much as he could at a site, and was the recipient of a stream of oral information. He did not always succeed in learning something, nor did he always believe what he was told. The construction of the Pelasgian wall on the Athenian acropolis was ascribed to two characters named Agrolas and Hyperbius: "Inquiring who they were, all I could learn was that they were originally Sicilians who migrated to Acarnania" (I.28.3). He wondered why Artemis was called wolfish in Troezen ("I could learn nothing from the guides": II.31.4) and Coccoca in Olympia ("Why they give the surname of Coccoca to Artemis I was not able to learn": V.15.7). In other instances, he did better: "Such is the genealogy of the kings of Arcadia as I ascertained it by careful inquiry from the Arcadians." [14]

Pausanias often refers (though rarely by name) to the educated people whom he met or with whom he stayed and from whom he obtained a good deal of information: "a man of Mysia said"; "I have heard a Cyprian say"; "I heard from a man of Byzantium"; "an Egyptian assured me"; "if the old man whom I questioned spoke the truth"; "thus I have been told by a Phoenician man"; "I heard this from a man of Ephesus, and I give his statement for what it is worth"; "I have been

---

[13] VI.4.4. See A. Rumpf, "Pythagoras (14)," in *RE* (1963), 305–7. Other passages with obvious allusions to biographical works on sculptors include VI.3.5, 3.11, 9.1; VIII. 42.7–10. See Kalkmann, pp. 184–99; S. Settis, *AnnPisa*, ser. 2, 37 (1968): 38ff., who argues (p. 41) that Pausanias did not yet know such works when he wrote book I.

[14] VIII.6.1. See J. Roy, "The Sons of Lycaon in Pausanias' Arcadian King-List," *BSA* 63 (1968): 287–92, who concludes that the statement is true: "It is possible and even likely that other parts of his king-list equally owe their form to him, the more so since he says explicitly that he took great trouble to learn the history of the Arcadian kings from the Arcadians" (p. 291).

told by a man who made a trading voyage to Temesa [in Italy] that the town is inhabited to this day"; "so my Larisaean friend told me"; "I have heard a like story from a Phoenician man."[15] Very occasionally he gives a name: "Euphemus, a Carian, said that when he was sailing to Italy he was driven by gales out of his course and into the outer ocean, into which mariners do not sail."[16] On a few occasions such a reference, anonymous or not, is to a written source: the "man from Ephesus" is none other than the well-known geographer Artemidorus.[17]

His other group of informants comprised, of course, the guides who dwelt around the well-visited sites.[18] He sometimes refers to them as antiquarians,[19] but most often as guides.[20] They could be quite useful; they could provide valuable information, measurements of buildings, and local traditions. But not always were they helpful. Frazer gives a vivid sketch of the way they used to operate:

We know from other ancient writers that in antiquity, as at the present day, towns of any note were infested by persons of this class who lay in wait for and pounced on the stranger as their natural prey, wrangled over his body, and having secured their victim led him about from place to place, pointing out the chief sights to him and pouring into his ear a stream of anecdotes and explanations, indifferent to his anguish and deaf to his entreaties to stop, until having exhausted their learning and his patience they pocketed their fee and took their leave. An educated traveller would often have dispensed with their explanations. . . . That Pausanias should have fallen into their clutches was unavoidable. He seems to have submitted to his fate with a good grace, was led by them to see the usual sites, heard the usual stories, argued with them about some, and posed them with questions which they could not answer about others.[21]

Pausanias himself says, "The Argive guides themselves are aware that not all the stories they tell are true; yet they stick to them, for it is not easy to persuade the vulgar to change their opinions" (II.23.6). He

---

[15] The quotations are from I.35.5, 42.5; III.17.7; VI.20.18, 24.9; IX.28.2; V.5.9; VI.6.10; IX.30.9; X.32.18.

[16] I.23.5; other instances are II.37.6, X.4.6.

[17] V.5.9; A. Enmann, *Fleckeisens Jahrbücher*, 1884:512, as quoted by Gurlitt, p. 137. The Cleon from Magnesia (X.4.6; see preceding note) may also have been an author; see F. Jacoby, "Kleon (7)," in *RE* (1921), 718.

[18] A collection of testimonies on guides in antiquity can be found in L. Casson, *Travel in the Ancient World* (London 1974), 264–67.

[19] οἱ τὰ ἀρχαῖα μνημονεύοντες, or similar: VII.18.2; VIII.14.12; IX.18.2; I.27.4, 1.4.

[20] ἐξηγηταί occurs very often.

[21] Frazer, p. lxxvi.

seems to mean that the guides themselves were quite prepared to discard their fictions, but that the public was not: visitors preferred the known fictional story to the unfamiliar truth.

The quality of the guides must have varied greatly, and quite respectable men could be found among them (and quite the opposite). In the only instance in which Pausanias gives a guide's name—"Aristarchus, the guide at Olympia"—the name reveals that the man belonged to the illustrious family of the Iamids, who are attested for almost one thousand years as the priests and seers of the Eleans.[22] The story told by this distinguished man may well be the most fantastic in the entire work.

Although Pausanias is often described as naive, he is not prepared to accept everything he has read or been told—not, for instance, the story about the king of the Ligurians named Cycnus (Swan), skilled in the Muses' art, who at his death was transformed by the will of Apollo into a swan (*cycnus*): "That a votary of the Muses was king of the Ligurians I believe, but that a man should be turned into a bird is to me incredible" (I.30.3). Nor is he prepared to believe the story, sworn to by the most respectable men in Elis, that during the annual festival of Dionysus the god filled empty kettles in a sealed building with wine; this story has, as Pausanias himself remarks, analogies in other parts of the Greek world.[23] Unfortunately, he could not test the truth of the story, because he did not happen to be in Elis during the festival.

Several times he expresses his skepticism with the phrase "believe it who likes"[24]—about a statue of Hermes ("They say that Hercules leaned his club against this image, and the club, which was of wild olive wood, struck root in the ground and sprouted afresh and the tree is still growing"); on Pindar's statement that Lynceus' sight was so sharp that he saw through the trunk of an oak; and about a place in Thebes "where they say that Cadmus sowed the teeth of the dragon which he slew at the fountain and that from the teeth the earth brought forth men."[25]

In one instance, Pausanias attributes and explains the motive behind

---

[22] V.20.4. See *IOlympia* 62.6; H. Hepding, "Iamos," in *RE* (1914), 687–88; *FGrHist* 412.1. For the story see also Pausanias V.27.11.

[23] VI.26.1–2. See Kalkmann, pp. 41–42; M. P. Nilsson, *Griechische Feste von religiöser Bedeutung* (Leipzig 1906), 291–93 ("irgendein Priesterbetrug"); K. Preisendanz, "Thyia," in *RE* (1936), 680–81.

[24] ὅτῳ πιστά: II.5.1, 31.10; IV.2.7; V.1.8; IX.10.1.

[25] The same story is called a ridiculous legend by Artemidorus of Daldis, *Oneirocrit.* 4.47.

an incredible story about the Hydra in Lerna: "I believe that this beast was larger than other water-snakes, and that its venom was so deadly that Hercules poisoned the barbs of his arrow with its gall; but I do not think it had more than one head. The poet Pisander, of Camirus, multiplied the Hydra's heads to make the monster more terrific, and to add to the dignity of his own verses" (II.37.4).

In many other passages, Pausanias shows his skepticism—as he puts it once (concerning an event of the Persian Wars), "I am bound to record the Greek traditions, but I am not bound to believe them all."[26] This is an echo of his model, Herodotus (on communications between the Persians and the Argives: 7.152.3): "I am bound to report all that is said, but I am not bound to believe it all alike."

Since he is not writing fiction, but a report on present survivals and the past (and for him, as for most ancients, the time of myth was a real part of the past), he has to be judged not by his brilliance of thought or expression, or even his imagination,[27] but by his accuracy and honesty. Pausanias nearly always takes pains to separate the factual report from any comments he might have on the subject.[28] His reader, therefore, can almost always distinguish the passages in which Pausanias reports what he has seen, heard, or read from the passages in which he reflects upon the facts. Very often in his personal comments Pausanias applies his depth of knowledge and intelligence to reach a valid critical conclusion. Sometimes, however, the result is not successful.

A lack of knowledge can lead him astray. Pausanias quotes the inscription on the chariot of Gelo in Olympia, where he had won a victory in the chariot race. Pausanias reports that earlier writers had identified Gelo as the tyrant of Sicily, but this cannot be, since the inscription (which is extant) reads, "Gelo son of Deinomenes, of Gela."[29] The victory was dated by the official lists to 488 B.C., but Gelo had captured Syracuse in 491, and would thereafter have called himself "Gelo son of Deinomenes, of Syracuse." Therefore, the inescapable conclusion is that this was a homonymous man, originating from Gela like the tyrant, whose father bore the same name as the tyrant's father.

---

[26] VI.3.8. Cf. II.17.4: "This and similar stories of the gods I record, though I do not accept them."

[27] As Casson (above, n. 18) observed: "Wit and originality have no place in such an assignment; in fact, they might very well get in the way. What he requires above all are the matter-of-fact virtues of thoroughness, diligence, and accuracy. And these were the virtues *par excellence* of a certain Pausanias . . ." (p. 292).

[28] Slight reservations on this in G. Daux, *Pausanias à Delphes* (Paris 1936), 187.

[29] VI.9.4–5. The inscription is *IOlympia* 143 (*SIG*³ 33).

Pausanias' reasoning is flawless: inscriptions confirm that Gelo, once he had taken Syracuse, did not style himself "of Gela" any longer, but "of Syracuse." Unfortunately, however, Pausanias' facts are confused: Gelo became master of Syracuse not in 491 but in 485, that is, after his Olympic victory; 491 is the year he rose to power in his native Gela.[30]

Sometimes his reasoning leaves something to be desired. One of the gods worshipped in the Laconian town of Amyclae was Dionysus, the god of wine, who there bore the epithet Psilax. Pausanias thinks that the epithet is appropriate, "for the Dorians call wings *psila*, and wine uplifts men and raises their spirits, as wings do birds" (III.19.6). Pausanias is absolutely right that *psilax* is a Dorian word, but his explanation is patently false (though modern scholarship has not done any better in its attempts to explain the epithet).[31]

An occasional error of fact or wild speculation does not detract substantially from a large work filled with accurate information and sober comment. Georges Daux judges that the total number of errors in Pausanias remains far below the number found in many modern works of scholarship despite the many tools of reference now at a scholar's disposal.[32] Another French scholar, Georges Roux, says that in the whole of Pausanias' work modern scholarship has not found a single topographical error.[33]

Hundreds of excavations testify to the solidness of Pausanias' work, be it the Agora in Athens, the sanctuary of Apollo at Delphi, the sanctuary of Asclepius at Epidaurus, the shrine of Zeus in Olympia, or the shrines of the goddesses in Arcadia, the cities of Corinth, Messene, and many other cities. When Wilamowitz launched his first vicious attack on the integrity, honesty, and veracity of Pausanias, the excavations had hardly begun: Wilamowitz' paper was published in 1877, the first campaign in Olympia was begun in 1875, and the traumatic expe-

---

[30] B. Niese, "Gelon," in *RE* (1910), 1012–13. Gelo as Syracusan: *SIG* ³ 34, from Delphi. By contrast, the same pattern of argument (the use of the form of an ethnic for chronological purposes) is put to good effect in V.25.11: the artist Aristocles must have made the statue of Hercules and the Amazon before the city of Zankle changed its name to Messene (494 B.C.), since the dedicant of this group to Olympia calls himself a citizen of Zankle.

[31] G. Radke, "Psilax," in *RE* (1959), 1398–1400 and bibliography cited there.

[32] Daux (above, n. 28), p. 187. See also F. Chamoux, in *Mélanges Dion*, ed. R. Chevallier (Paris 1974), 87: "D'autres inexactitudes sont indiscutables: reconnaissons qu'elles sont rares et généralement mineures."

[33] G. Roux, in J. Pouilloux and G. Roux, *Enigmes à Delphes* (Paris 1963), 16.

rience that triggered Wilamowitz' attack happened in 1873 at Olympia (see below, pp. 169f.).

In the first eighteen chapters of book VI, Pausanias describes, one by one, some two hundred statues of Olympic victors.[34] (He also mentions many more in other parts of his work.) Each description usually includes the name of the athlete, his patronymic, his ethnic, the contest of which he was victor, and the sculptor who carved the statue, and often the date of the victory and other bits of interesting information. One hundred fifteen inscribed bases of statues of victors have been found so far, the last one (known to this writer) in 1982;[35] in no less than thirty-four instances the original inscription and Pausanias' summary can be compared, and there are numerous other sources with which his account can be compared, such as partial copies of the official lists of victors,[36] or the many inscriptions of other kinds found at Olympia and either copied word for word or summarized by Pausanias.

It is hard to understand how an Italian scholar could write in 1978 that Pausanias perhaps, in the case of Olympia, made use of an epigraphic collection put together by others and that his quotations of lines of metrical inscriptions are secondhand.[37] (Wilamowitz looms large here.) On the contrary, the comparison proves that Pausanias copied the essentials of the hundreds of inscriptions himself, and that he did it with the greatest care, in that he had to read various old alphabets and dialects and often had to overcome the difficulties weathered stones presented.

Naturally enough, he occasionally makes mistakes, though not all the mistakes in his work are his. For instance, in VI.8.5 he correctly calls the boy who was victorious in boxing in 376 Critodamus, but a few lines later he slips and calls him Damocritus.[38] In VI.12.4 the name of the artist who made the statue of Hiero II of Syracuse is written

---

[34] See above, p. 65 n. 4.

[35] Most of them were published in *IOlympia*, 142–243; for those found later see *Olympiaberichte*. See also *Archaeological Reports*, 1982:30 (*JHS* [1983]). In general, see W. W. Hyde, *Olympic Victor Monuments* (Washington, D.C., 1921); G. Lippold, "Siegerstatuen," in *RE* (1923), 2265–74; J. Wiesner, "Olympia," in *RE* (1939), 156, no. 48, and 161ff., nos. 61–94; H.-V. Herrmann, *Olympia: Heiligtum und Wettkampfstätte* (Munich 1972), 114ff.; H. Buchmann, *Der Sieg in Olympia und in den anderen panhellenischen Spielen* (Munich 1972); J. Ebert, *Griechische Epigramme auf Sieger an gymnischen und hippischen Agonen*, *AbhAkLeipzig* 63, no. 2 (1972).

[36] For instance, *POxy* 222 (*FGrHist* 415), 2082 (*FGrHist* 257a); Phlegon, *FGrHist* 257; *FGrHist* 416.

[37] See above, p. 64 n. 3.

[38] The original base is preserved: *IOlympia* 167.

"Mico, son of Niceratus, of Syracuse," whereas the original inscription has "Mic*io*, son of Niceratus, of Syracuse"; certainly this is the fault of the copyist.[39] More interesting is VI.10.5, a description of statues of two victors, father and son, made by two Argive sculptors, Eutelidas and Chrysothemis. From the base Pausanias quotes the two verses that give their names and background—they learned their art "from those who went before" (τέχναν εἰδότες ἐκ προτέρων). Scholars have long suspected that the words ἐκ προτέρων must be corrupt, since they are all but meaningless: artists must of necessity learn their craft "from those who went before." The editor J. H. C. Schubart in 1853 therefore proposed instead ἐκ πατέρων, "from their fathers." This emendation made good sense, since family tradition among Greek sculptors was strong, even if it was not the rule for a young artist to be taught by his own father. Scholars were divided on the merits of the conjecture; some accepted it, others rejected it (among the latter, the most recent editor).[40] In March 1980, a bronze tablet dating from ca. 500 B.C. was found with the greater part of these two lines preserved; it contains the name Chrysothemis and at the end the incontestable phrase ἐκ πα-τέρων, "from their fathers," exactly as Schubart had conjectured.[41] Here it is Pausanias, not a copyist, who is to blame, since the remark "The epigram does not say by whom they were taught" makes it quite clear that Pausanias read and copied ἐκ προτέρων. It could be, however, that a few letters of the text were damaged and hard to read.

However that may be, on the whole Pausanias has done an excellent job of transmitting the essence of more than two hundred athletic inscriptions, the oldest of which were almost 750 years old in Pausanias' time. By chance we know the names and ethnics of all thirteen victors from the year 472.[42] Pausanias has summarized the inscriptions of five of them,[43] and for four of these five the excavations have yielded the originals.[44] Nine victors are known from the year 464, among them

[39] *Olympiabericht* 6 (1958): 204.

[40] J. H. C. Schubart, edition of 1853, p. 24: "ἐκ πατέρων malim." This was accepted by Th. Bergk and Th. Preger, *Inscriptiones Graecae Metricae* (Leipzig 1891), 174. Against, Hitzig and Blümner, vol. 2, pt. 2, p. 583.

[41] Olympia Inventory B.10471. I am grateful to A. Mallwitz and P. Siewert, who kindly granted permission to quote from this text before its publication.

[42] They are recorded in *POxy* 222 (*FGrHist* 415).

[43] Ergoteles (VI.4.11), Euthymus (VI.6.4), Hiero (VI.12.1), Callias (VI.6.1), and Tellon (VI.10.9).

[44] *Olympiabericht* 5 (1956): 153ff. (Ergoteles); *IOlympia* 144 (Euthymus), 146 (Callias; cf. his dedication in Athens, *IG* I².606), 147, 148 (Tellon).

three attested both by other sources and by Pausanias.[45] In all cases where we can check on him, his care and accuracy have been vindicated. Incidentally, he must have spent many weeks on the Olympic victors, first copying the inscriptions from the statue bases at Olympia and then formulating each entry for his book.

So much may be said for Pausanias the intellectual. As for Pausanias the human being, he is a modest man. Just as he does not mention any acquaintance or boast of any important connection (see above, p. 18), so does he refrain, with the same modesty, from mentioning himself; as Joyce Heer has put it, he is "remarkably discreet."[46] For instance, only through offhand and incidental remarks can even the location of his native home—close to Mount Sipylus—be deduced. And he is an honest man. He readily admits what he does not know or could not learn or has to guess or what he cannot even guess. He may, from time to time, lecture like a schoolmaster, but he never boasts, nor is he ever rude. His whole approach is businesslike and direct.

Pausanias is constantly aware that he has set himself a long and arduous task that will require total commitment if he is to finish it.[47] He does incorporate numerous digressions, short and long, and he does admit sometimes that "this has been a digression,"[48] but, in fact, only a few of those passages can be dismissed as superfluous or inept deviations from his purpose. The most notorious of these is the thirteen paragraphs on the island of Sardinia. Pausanias' starting point is a dedication that the Sardinians sent to Delphi; he then summarizes what he had read about the island, and he concludes the chapter, "My reason for introducing this account of Sardinia into my description of Phocis is that the island is but little known to the Greeks" (X.17.13).

Pausanias seldom loses sight of his goal, but he is, as has often been observed (see above, p. 23), attracted by sacred buildings, and his interest in religion is documented on every page of his work; it is here that he most reveals his personality.[49] Although he was a learned and skeptical man, he still had faith in the gods, or rather, perhaps, in the

---

[45] Diagoras (VI.7.1; *IOlympia* 151), Ergoteles (VI.4.11; *Olympiabericht 5* [1956]: 153ff.), and Pherias (VI.14.1; *Olympiabericht 2* [1938]: 129).

[46] Heer, p. 13.

[47] Casson (above, n. 18), p. 295: "It turned out to be, as he probably knew it would, a lifetime's work."

[48] VIII.7.8: Τόδε μὲν ἡμῖν ἐπεισόδιον ἐγένετο τῷ λόγῳ. (This is the only occurrence of ἐπεισόδιον in Pausanias.) Cf. IV.24.3, I.26.4: "But I must proceed. . . ."

[49] Heer has devoted two-thirds of her book on Pausanias' personality to his views on Greek religion (pp. 127–314).

divine. He praises the Athenians because "they are more pious than other people" (I.17.1) and their zeal "in matters of religion exceeds that of all other peoples" (I.24.3), and the Boeotians of Tanagra because "no Greek people . . . have regulated the worship of the gods so well as the people of Tanagra; for at Tanagra the dwelling-houses are in one place, and the sanctuaries are in another place . . . , in a clear space away from the haunts of men" (IX.22.2).

Gods and men belong to two distinct spheres, and Pausanias adheres to the traditional belief that the boundary between the two is the mortality of men; when he relates the story that Semele was rescued from Hades by Dionysus, he says, "I do not believe that Semele ever died, seeing that she was the wife of Zeus" (II.31.2). Nor does he question the popular belief that gods are superior to and stronger than men; when mortal men challenge the gods, they are bound to fail. Thus the Cnidians, and later Alexander the Great, failed to dig through the promontory of Mimas, and Nero failed to turn the Peloponnese into an island by cutting through the Isthmus of Corinth: "So hard is it for man to do violence to the works of God" (II.1.5).

Pausanias believes an insuperable barrier exists between men and gods; he says so explicitly in an acid criticism of the practice of the deification of mortals, Roman emperors as well as Hellenistic rulers. "Men are not changed into gods, save in the hollow rhetoric which flattery addresses to power." [50] However, in the past, when men were so righteous and pious that the gods visited them, sat with them at the table, and openly honored the good and punished the bad, Heracles, Amphiaraus, the Dioscuri, and other mortals had been elevated to the ranks of the gods. "But in the present age, when wickedness is growing to such a height, and spreading over every land and every city," the gods no longer visit mortals, and even "the wrath of the gods at the wicked is reserved for a distant future when they shall have gone hence" (VIII.2.5).

In the past, Pausanias implies, gods and heroes actively intervened in human affairs: Artemis overtook the Persians in the land of Megara and rendered them helpless (I.40.2–3), Heracles, Apollo, and Hermes came as allies to the city of Themisonium in Asia Minor when the country was ravaged by the Galatians (X.32.4), and Athena helped the people of Elatea against Mithridates (X.34.6). Four local heroes con-

---

[50] VIII.2.5. Cf. I.9.4, on Hellenistic kings, and see Gurlitt, p. 33 ("qualificierte Majestätsbeleidigung"); Frazer, p. l; Regenbogen, pp. 1089–90; J. Palm, *Rom, Römertum und Imperium in der griechischen Literatur der Kaiserzeit* (Lund 1959), 70–71; Heer, p. 98.

tributed to the disaster that befell the Gauls when they attacked Delphi (X.23.2), and Marsyas helped the citizens of Celaenae (in Phrygia) to repel the Galatians (X.30.9). The Greek gods and heroes rose to defend Greeks against barbarians.

The gods are even more active when they have been offended. Then their divine wrath—Pausanias always uses the Homeric word for divine wrath, μῆνιμα—destroys the guilty. Alexander's father, Philip, "always trampled on oaths, violated treaties on every opportunity, and broke faith more shamefully than any other human being. However, the wrath of God did not tarry, but overtook him with unparalleled speed"; the assassination at a fairly young age was vengeance from the gods, by whose names he had sworn (VIII.7.5–6).

"When the heralds whom king Darius had sent to Greece to demand earth and water had been murdered, the wrath of Talthybius at the crime was manifested against Lacedaemon as a state; but at Athens it fell on the house of . . . Miltiades. . . . For it was Miltiades who caused the Athenians to kill the heralds" (III.12.7).

The city of Megara, where Hadrian was regarded not only as a benefactor but also as a second founder, and had a tribe, Hadrianis, named after him,[51] still suffers, says Pausanias, from a wrongful act committed six hundred years before. The Athenian Anthemocritus "was the victim of a most foul crime perpetrated by the Megarians; for when he came as a herald to forbid them to encroach on the sacred land, they slew him. And the wrath of the two goddesses [Demeter and Kore] abides upon them for that deed to this day; for they were the only Greek people whom even the Emperor Hadrian could not make to thrive" (I.36.3).

The usurpation of sacred property, as in this story, is the cause of divine punishment in other instances, too. The Phocians seized Apollo's sanctuary at Delphi and used the proceeds to bribe King Archidamus of Sparta; he was killed by barbarians in Italy, "and the wrath of Apollo prevented his corpse from receiving burial" (III.10.5). Punishment also fell on Mithridates and his general for their attack on Delos, the sacred island of Apollo (III.23.5), and on the Spartan king Cleomenes I, who "incurred his death in a mad fit: seizing a sword he wounded himself and then proceeded to hack and mangle his whole body. . . . The Athenians declare it was a punishment for ravaging the Orgas"[52] (III.4.5). In the case of Cleomenes I, "who was generally out

[51] *IG* VII.70–74; cf. Pausanias III.4.6.
[52] That is, the sacred land belonging to the goddesses Demeter and Kore.

of his mind" (III.4.1), Greeks agreed that he had been punished by the gods, but they differed on the cause—the Delphians said the punishment was inflicted because he bribed the Pythia; the Argives, because he burned a sacred grove and with it the Argives who had sought sanctuary there.[53]

The worst crime of all, according to Pausanias, was a crime against those who came to a shrine as suppliants (ἱκέται); it called for the vengeance of both the offended god and Zeus Hikesios (protector of suppliants). It was the cause of the complete destruction of the Achaean city of Helice in a flood (VII.24.5–6), of the dreadful ends of the Spartan leader Pausanias (III.17.9) and the Roman dictator Sulla, who had the Athenian leader Aristion dragged out of the shrine of Athena and murdered (I.20.7), and of divine punishment for others.[54]

There are some twenty instances where the word μήνιμα occurs. All but one concern mythical times, and in all but one a superhuman being shows his wrath. The single exception is Alexander the Great, who, in his wrath, destroyed the city of Thebes (VII.17.2).

Instead of μήνιμα, Pausanias may use δίκη ἐκ θεῶν, divine "justice" or "vengeance," as for the slaughter of the Arcadians (by the Romans) at Chaeronea, where they had once failed the Greek cause.[55] Sometimes divine punishment is given on the same spot; in other cases the culprit is punished as he had punished others, and this is called "the retribution of Neoptolemus," because, as Pausanias explains, Neoptolemus, son of Achilles, slew Priam at the altar and was himself slain at Delphi beside the altar of Apollo (IV.17.4–5).

Pausanias' beliefs are conventional;[56] they do not differ from, for instance, those of Herodotus, writing six hundred years earlier. And Pausanias, too, like Herodotus, is fond of oracles—the oracle of Amphilochus at Mallus in Cilicia, he says, is the most trustworthy of all the oracles of the present day (I.34.3). He underwent considerable difficulty so he could consult another famous oracle, Trophonius in Boeotia, and he gives a detailed and vivid description of the procedure.[57]

---

[53] The three conflicting causes in III.4.5–6, and already in Hdt. 6.75.3.

[54] VII.25.1. See, in general, J. Gould, "Hiketeia," *JHS* 93 (1973): 74–103, esp. 77–78.

[55] VII.15.6.

[56] The culprit who, through divine punishment, suffers the same that he has done to others occurs, for instance, in 2 Macc. 4.26, 5.9–10, 9.6, 9.28, 13.8; the culprit who is punished on the same spot where he has made others suffer occurs in 2 Macc. 4.38, 4.42, 15.32–33.

[57] IX.39.5–14. This is the oracle that contributed to the boom of the city of Lebadeia in the second and third centuries A.D., as mentioned by Pausanias, IX.39.2. Kalkmann (pp.

As all the oracles were not of equal quality, so all the traditional gods were not of equal stature. It had always been true that some cities, or individuals, would prefer certain gods, but by the second century A.D. some of the Olympians had become shadowy figures. Oriental gods were on the upswing—Sarapis and Isis, Mithras, and Cybele—though Pausanias does not care for them,[58] nor does he mention either Jews or Christians. He was deeply attracted to Asclepius (the healer), who was the most venerated of the traditional gods though he was a rather late addition to the Greek pantheon.[59] Of the places where the cult of Asclepius flourished, Pausanias puts Epidaurus first. From Epidaurus, he says, the cult of the god spread throughout the Greek world—to Athens, Pergamum, Smyrna, Cyrenaica, and Crete (II.26.8–9)—and at Epidaurus "tablets stood within the enclosure. There used to be more of them: in my time six were left. On these tablets are engraved the names of men and women who have been healed by Aesculapius together with the disease from which each suffered, and the manner of the cure. The inscriptions are in the Doric dialect" (II.27.3). Four of them, each containing some 140 lines, are still preserved, and all date from the fourth century B.C.

Again, at Epidaurus, Pausanias' assiduousness can be seen (and proven). Did he read but a few lines of the inscriptions? No. He sees the name of the small town of Halieis: "Mention is made of natives of Halieis on the Epidaurian tablets, which record the cures wrought by Aesculapius, but I know of no other authentic document in which mention is made of the town or its inhabitants" (II.36.1). In fact, the town had gone out of existence around 300 B.C.,[60] but the ethnic of a man from Halieis appears in line 19 of one of the extant tablets, and again in line 69ff., and on another tablet the same ethnic is mentioned in line 120.[61]

273–74) doubts that he ever went there—the description, according to him, "is covered with the dust of Pausanias' library." His doubts are unfounded; see A. Schachter, *AJP* 105 (1984): 268.

[58] Gurlitt, p. 31.

[59] The famous description of the god's sanctuary at Epidaurus (II.26.3ff.) is well known. On his way from Corinth to Sicyon, Pausanias made a detour in order to visit the sanctuary of Asclepius at Titane (II.11.3, 27.1; Heberdey, p. 41), and he went out of his way in order to see the Asclepieium at Pellene (Heberdey, p. 58f.). In general, see Heer, pp. 254–61, for the significance Asclepius had for Pausanias.

[60] M. H. Jameson, *Hesperia* 38 (1969): 313–15; *BSA* 76 (1981): 245.

[61] *IG* IV.1².122.19, 69ff.; IV. 1².121.120. See O. Weinreich, *Antike Heilungswunder* (Giessen 1909), 103–6; F. Hiller von Gaertringen, comments on *IG* IV.1².121.69.

Pausanias' admiration is even higher for Zeus,[62] and still higher for the two goddesses to whom his heart belongs, Demeter and Kore. He himself had been initiated into their Eleusinian mysteries and thereby become the peer of the emperors Augustus, Hadrian, and Marcus Aurelius.[63] However, these mysteries were open also to common people and even to slaves. This initiation meant more to him than any worldly approbation (I.37.4, 38.7). "Many a wondrous sight might be seen," Pausanias says, "and not a few tales of wonder may be heard in Greece; but there is nothing on which the blessing of God rests in so full a measure as the rites of Eleusis and the Olympian games" (V.10.1). What exactly these rites were only the initiates knew, and they were obliged to keep them strictly secret. Time and again, Pausanias feels the urge to tell about the miracles, of which his heart is so full, but he always, reluctantly, refrains: "I was prevented from describing this by a vision in a dream," and "but it would be sinful for me to divulge them" (I.14.3, 38.7; cf. I.37.4). And he has the same scruples about other mysteries, be they the mysteries of the Great Goddesses in Messenia (which, in point of sanctity, he regards as second only to the Eleusinian mysteries: IV.33.5), or the nighttime rites performed in honor of Dionysus (II.37.6), or other cult secrets.[64]

In only two or three passages does Pausanias openly state beliefs of his own that go beyond the conventional. He explains how he changed in his convictions (VIII.8.3). He tells the story of Cronus and his wife, Rhea, and how Cronus would devour his children as they were born. According to Arcadian legend, however, Rhea tricked him and rescued Poseidon and then Zeus—in place of Zeus she gave Cronus a stone wrapped in swaddling clothes.

When I began this work I used to look on these Greek stories as little better than foolishness; but now that I have got as far as Arcadia my opinion about them is this: I believe that the Greeks who were accounted wise spoke of old in riddles and not straight out; and, accordingly, I conjecture that this story about Cronus is a bit of Greek philosophy. In matters of religion I will follow tradition.[65]

---

[62] See Heer, pp. 211–21.

[63] F. Millar, *The Emperor in the Roman World* (London 1977), 449–50. See also D. Kienast, "Hadrian, Augustus und die eleusinischen Mysterien," *JfNG* 10 (1959–60): 61–69; for Hadrian also *IG* II².3575.

[64] V.15.11, VIII.37.9, IX.25.5–6.

[65] It seems obvious that the Greek of the last sentence, τῶν μὲν δὴ ἐς τὸ θεῖον ἡκόντων τοῖς εἰρημένοις χρησόμεθα, ought to be emended to τῶν . . . ἐς τὸ θεῖον ⟨ἀν⟩ηκόντων.

His earlier position seems to be expressed, for instance, in II.17.4. The image of Hera in the Argive Heraeum has a cuckoo on the scepter—the story goes that when Zeus was in love with the maiden Hera, he changed himself into a bird and Hera caught the bird to play with it. Pausanias says, "This and similar stories of the gods I record, though I do not accept them."

Frazer is certainly right in concluding that such a total change of attitude was more probably an affair of years than of weeks or months;[66] one could probably even say an affair of many years. But what kind of a change was it? Frazer says that Pausanias has lost his youthful skepticism, that paralysis of age has led him to accept what he had spurned in youth, that "the scoffer had become devout."[67] Joyce Heer is correct: Pausanias has not lost his skepticism, he does not now believe the literal truth of such legends, but he has acquired insight—they may be more than foolish tales, they may be symbols of a mystery he does not pretend to understand.[68] His initiation into the Eleusinian mysteries may have had a great deal to do with his change of mind.

Pausanias met a man from Sidon in a sanctuary of Asclepius at Aegium in Achaea:

In this sanctuary a man from Sidon entered into a discussion with me. He maintained that the Phoenicians had juster views of the divine nature than the Greeks, and he instanced particularly the Phoenician legend that Aesculapius had Apollo for his father, but no mortal woman for his mother. "For Aesculapius," said he, "is the air and as such is favourable to the health, not only of mankind, but of every living thing; and Apollo is the sun, and most rightly is he called the father of Aesculapius, since by ordering his course with due regard to the seasons he imparts to the air its wholesomeness." "Agreed," cried I, "but that is just what the Greeks say too. For at Titane, in the land of Sicyon, the same image is named both Health and Aesculapius, clearly because the sun's course over the earth is the source of health to mankind." (VII.23.7–8)

Scholars have explained this passage in many ways. W. Gurlitt calls the explanation of the gods in terms of natural forces without parallel in the work and Pausanias' reply nothing but an expression of Greek arrogance responding to the claim that Greeks could learn anything

---

See, for instance, *IMagnesia* 61.23–24 (καὶ τῶν ἄλλων τιμίων τῶν ἀνηκόντων εἰς τὸ θεῖον), or, for Pausanias' use of the composite verb, III.1.2 (ἐς Δία . . . ἀνήκοντα); I.39.3, X.32.1 (τὰ ἐς συγγραφὴν ἀνήκοντα). The simplex ἥκω in Pausanias always means "come," never "refer to," "be connected with," or "belong."

[66] Frazer, p. lviii.   [67] Frazer, p. lviii.   [68] Heer, pp. 252–53.

from foreigners.[69] Frazer, on the other hand, states that Pausanias here, at least once, had a glimpse of a higher truth: that there were no gods and that the Olympians were needed no more—"It was only a flashlight that went out leaving him in darkness."[70] Wilamowitz stressed that if Asclepius can evaporate, that is, the only god who still had a recognizable individuality and who still communicated personally with man, Pausanias must have already discarded his faith in the old Olympian gods.[71] Carl Robert and Joyce Heer detect here (as in the passage discussed before) the influence of Stoicism.[72] Peter Levi judges the statement "not incredibly *avant-garde* for any professional man in the age of Hadrian, and in philosophical circles it would have been very ordinary."[73]

But for Pausanias the statement is surprising—first, because he readily abandons the concept that the gods have a distinct personality, and, second, because his reply does not really correspond to the Phoenician's statement. Greeks agreed that Apollo was Asclepius' father, and most, including Pausanias (II.26.6–7; cf. IV.3.2), believed that Asclepius' mother was a mortal woman, Coronis, which he denies here. Whereas the Sidonian identifies Apollo with the sun, Pausanias says that the sun is the source of health, that is (presumably), the father of Health, and that Health and Asclepius are one and the same. This explanation is neither lucid nor convincing.

In this passage Pausanias seems not to conceive of the gods (though he retains their names) as divine beings with distinct personalities, anthropomorphic traits, and individual histories as narrated in the old myths. They exist, they are powerful, they deserve to be venerated, but their true nature is beyond human comprehension. Therefore, one might as well follow tradition (as the old Pausanias says he will), since tradition is sanctified by its age, though it must not be understood as literally true. This dialogue, then, would fall into line with the passage previously discussed (in which Pausanias says that the myths are nothing more than riddles or allegories), and Pausanias' views, as Levi observed,[74] would fall into line with the perception prevailing in his time

[69] Gurlitt, p. 86 n. 43. For the same attitude of snobbery toward Phoenicians in a Greek contemporary see C. P. Jones, *The Roman World of Dio Chrysostom* (Cambridge, Mass. 1978), 75.
[70] Frazer, pp. lvii–lviii.
[71] *Der Glaube der Hellenen*, vol. 2 (Berlin 1932), 510.
[72] Robert, p. 70; Heer, p. 251.
[73] Levi 1 : 290 n. 122.   [74] Levi 1 : 290 n. 122.

that the gods are divine beings with unspecifiable natures. He would, then, seem to have been influenced by Stoic doctrines.

There is another aspect to this dialogue—Pausanias the treasure house of rare information. The Sidonian's thesis is one of very few substantial testimonies about Phoenician religion. The others are, almost exclusively, excerpts preserved by Eusebius from the work of Philo of Byblus (another contemporary of Pausanias).[75] An edition of Philo's Greek text, with an English translation and a thorough commentary by Albert I. Baumgarten,[76] discusses the passage in question. A Phoenician, and especially a Sidonian, speaking of Asclepius means Eshmun; the two were commonly identified and Eshmun was worshipped primarily at Sidon. Baumgarten concludes that the views expressed by the Sidonian in Pausanias do, in fact, represent Phoenician beliefs, but in a form that was current during the early empire.[77]

Besides religion, art is the other predilection of Pausanias, and crit-ics disagree on his artistic sense. Frazer says, "The artistic taste of Pausanias was sound and good, if somewhat austere" (p. lxvi). Georges Daux says, "His artistic sense is almost nonexistent."[78] But Pausanias had a keen eye (how else could he have distinguished the pieces of classical art from all the later ones?),[79] and several times he says that he could tell just by looking at a statue who the artist was: Calamis in Olympia, Endoius in Erythrae (V.25.5, VII.5.9). The Apollo in Aegira is so similar to the Heracles in Sicyon that it, too, must be the work of Laphaes; the statue of Ismenios in Thebes resembles the Apollo of Didyma so much that whoever sees the one will ascribe the other to the same sculptor, Canachus, although the Apollo is of bronze, the Ismenios of cedar (VII.26.6, IX.10.2). Pausanias poses, just a little, as a connoisseur, but, as Otto Regenbogen neatly put it, he is far less arrogant than some of his critics claim—and are themselves.[80]

---

[75] Collected in *FGrHist* 790.

[76] A. I. Baumgarten, *The Phoenician History of Philo of Byblus* (Leiden 1981).

[77] Baumgarten (above, n. 76), pp. 264–65. Kalkmann (p. 261) had already pointed to Philo in this connection.

[78] Daux (above, n. 28), p. 177.

[79] He speaks more than once of works "in contemporary style" (τέχνη ἡ ἐφ᾽ ἡμῶν): III.16.1, V.21.15, VII.26.4. Of these, the monument mentioned in V.21.15 is dated to Olympiad 226 or A.D. 125.

[80] Regenbogen, p. 1081. A good example of the arrogance of Pausanias' critics in matters of art can be seen in Kalkmann, pp. 194–99. It is well known that the identification of the statue found in the temple of Hera at Olympia as the Hermes of Praxiteles is due to Pausanias (V. 17.3). It is less well known that it was his note (VII.26.4) that allowed O.

Fig. 34. Aegira, Zeus of Euclidas
(courtesy A. F. Stewart).

In general, whatever his subject, he is sober and restrained, never exuberant or passionate. If he had a temper, he does not show it. If he had a sense of humor, he restrained it, perhaps because he thought humor was incompatible with the seriousness of his topic; humorous pas-

Walter (*ÖJh* 27 [1932]: Beiblatt, p. 223ff.) to identify the cult image of Zeus that he found at Aegira in Achaea as the work of the Athenian sculptor Euclidas, of the second century B.C. (fig. 34). In fact, nearly all surviving Greek statues that are mentioned by ancient writers and are securely identified owe their identification to Pausanias (F. Brommer, *Gymnasium* 59 [1952]: 115–25; see Ch. Habicht, *Classical Antiquity* 3 [1984]: 49–50).

sages are next to nonexistent and the humor he does reveal is reserved. Some Greeks numbered the Scythian Anacharsis among the seven sages, but the Pythia greeted Socrates as the wisest of men, "a title which she did not give even to Anacharsis, though he was quite willing to receive it, and had indeed come to Delphi for the purpose" (I.22.8). Sometimes the humor is unintentional. In the Arcadian sanctuary of Aphrodite (the goddess of love) Aphrodite is called Aphrodite Melaina, Black Aphrodite: "The goddess is so surnamed simply because men mostly indulge in sexual intercourse by night, instead of, like the beasts, by day" (VIII.6.5).[81]

In general, Pausanias is dry, sober, and pedantic.[82] He can also be dull, and, if read superficially, might give the impression that he was a rather heavy-handed fellow; a few of his remarks show that he was not.[83] He is always on guard not to give himself away; he would never reveal that he had once suffered a broken heart, but of the river Selemnus in Achaea he writes, "I have also heard say that the water of the Selemnus is a cure for love in man and woman, for they wash in the river and forget their love. If there is any truth in this story, great riches are less precious to mankind than the water of the Selemnus" (VII. 23.3). Would he have made this remark if he had not experienced the sweetness, as well as the bitterness, of love?

In the same book Pausanias relates two tragic love stories (VII.19.1 –

---

[81] In the following passage I am not so sure that Pausanias wanted to be funny: "The Moon, they say, loved Endymion, and he had fifty daughters by the goddess. Others, with more probability, say that Endymion married a wife: some say that she was Asterodia . . ." (V.1.4). It looks, rather, as if some sort of an allusion to Hecataeus (*FGrHist* 1 F 19) was intended, since both passages express the same rational skepticism toward the number of fifty children: "Aegyptus himself did not come to Argos, only his sons did, according to Hesiod they were no less than fifty; according to me, however, less than twenty."

[82] Gurlitt calls him "pedantisch" (p. 126), and Petersen emphatically states, "wohl uns, dass er ein Pedant und kein Phantast war" (p. 490 n. 1). His pedantic endurance has preserved, among other things, the 203 résumés from the inscriptions of Olympic victors (VI.1–18); the names of all thirty-seven figures represented on the victory monument of Lysander at Delphi (X.9.7–10; above, p. 73); the names of all forty communities that were absorbed into the new city of Megalopolis (VIII.27.3–4; Diod. 15.72 gives the same number but no names); the names of the Greek states on the victory monument of 479 B.C. at Olympia (above, p. 105); and all the necessary information about no less than sixty-nine altars standing in the Altis of Olympia (V.13.4–15.12; Herrmann [above, n. 35], p. 187; A. Mallwitz, *Olympia und seine Bauten* [Munich 1972], 10). Furthermore, we have the detailed descriptions of the throne at Amyclae (III.18.9–19.5), of the image of Zeus (V.11.1–11) and chest of Cypselus (V.17.5–19.10) at Olympia, and, above all, of the Lesche of the Cnidians at Delphi (X.25.1–31.12).

[83] Heer (pp. 55–57) has correctly sensed that.

5, 21.1–5), and not only does he display warmth, but he concludes the first story in a remarkable way. The two young lovers had taken their fill of love in the only place available to them, the sanctuary of Artemis, and they were sacrificed to the goddess in expiation of the sacrilege. "But the lovers, I take it, were beyond the reach of sorrow; for to man, and to man alone, better it is than life itself to love and to be loved." Our author, after all, must have been a warm and gentle human being.

He was sensitive to the vicissitudes of human life, and, it seems, more of a pessimist than an optimist. He knew that people may bring disaster upon themselves by their own actions—"many men and more women are shipwrecked on the shoal of foolish desires"—but even if one is not at fault, "it is given to no man to see all his wishes fulfilled" (VIII.24.9, II.8.6).

I heard a story of a man . . . called Aglaus, a contemporary of Croesus the Lydian. The story was that Aglaus had been happy all the days of his life; but I did not believe it. No doubt, one man may have fewer ills to bear than the men of his time, just as one ship may be less buffeted by the tempest than another; but a man who has always been out of the reach of misfortune, or a ship that has always sailed with a fair breeze, is not to be found. (VIII.24.13–14)

Surpassing the will, the power, and the endeavors of man, a much stronger force is at work: "But the affairs and especially the purposes of man are hidden by Fate as a pebble is hidden by the slime of a river" (IV.9.6).

Much can be said in Pausanias' favor—he was well educated, widely read, fairly intelligent, and not uncritical—but it has to be admitted that he did not have a brilliant mind. He lacked originality and the creative spark; there were, in his time, better and more elegant writers—Aristides for one, and Lucian. Where Pausanias is superior to most of his contemporaries (and to many others) is this: he selected a worthwhile topic, he pursued it assiduously for more than twenty years, and he was always serious, always honest, and almost always accurate.

Why did he choose the topic he chose? Albino Garzetti suggests that the book was "probably the result of the stimulus, given by the travelling Emperor's [that is, Hadrian's] memorable visits, to the tourist and antiquarian exploitation of the Greek monuments."[84]

Maybe Hadrian did have some influence on Pausanias, and certainly

---

[84] A. Garzetti, *From Tiberius to the Antonines: A History of the Roman Empire A.D. 14–192* (London 1974), 393.

the wave of philhellenism, so characteristic of the second century A.D., must have played its part, but the main reason for his choice of topic, and for his endurance, must certainly be found in his own state of mind. He was well aware that Greece, especially the Ionians (whom he thought came from Achaea), had shaped his own homeland. Greece and Asia Minor both had been parts of the Roman world for a long, long time, and Pausanias was driven to revive the past by describing what was left of it in the present. In my opinion, the American scholar Herman Louis Ebeling made the point neatly seventy years ago: "While there is a certain antagonism between his historical and his periegetical plans, both were united in his aim to connect the past with the present."[85]

Pausanias knew all too well that many Greek treasures had already disappeared: hundreds of famous statues had been carried off to Italy, others were lost while being transported there, others had been destroyed at their original sites. Many of the famous sites, if they even still existed, had become deplorable ruins; others were threatened by a similar fate. If Pausanias gives any indication of his motives, it may perhaps be found in the following chapter of his book on Arcadia:[86]

Megalopolis, the foundation of which was carried out by the Arcadians with the utmost enthusiasm, and viewed with the highest hopes by the Greeks, now lies mostly in ruins, shorn of all its beauty and ancient prosperity. I do not marvel at this, knowing that ceaseless change is the will of God, and that all things alike, strength as well as weakness, growth as well as decay, are subject to the mutations of fortune, whose resistless force sweeps them along at her will. Mycenae, which led the Greeks in the Trojan war; Nineveh, where was the palace of the Assyrian kings; Boeotian Thebes, once deemed worthy to be the head of Greece; what is left of them? Mycenae and Nineveh lie utterly desolate, and the name of Thebes is shrunk to the limits of the acropolis and a handful of inhabitants. The places that of old surpassed the world in wealth, Egyptian Thebes and Minyan Orchomenus, are now less opulent than a private man of moderate means; while Delos, once the common mart of Greece, has now not a single inhabitant except the guards sent from Athens to watch over the sanctuary. At Babylon the sanctuary of Bel remains, but of that Babylon which was once the greatest city that the sun beheld, nothing is left but the walls. And it is the same with Tiryns in Argolis. All these have been brought to

---

[85] *CW* 7 (1913): 139.

[86] VIII.33. Much of the contents of this chapter is topical, beginning with Hdt. 1.5.4; see the comments of Hitzig and Blümner, vol. 3, pt. 1, pp. 233–35. It is nonetheless significant that Pausanias expresses these thoughts.

nought by the hand of God. But the city of Alexander in Egypt, and the city of Seleucus by the Orontes, founded but yesterday, have attained their present size and opulence because fortune smiles on them. . . . So transient and frail are the affairs of man.[87]

Pausanias, then, was out to preserve as much for posterity as he could of the inheritance of the past.[88] The tools at his (or anybody's) disposal for such an undertaking were limited, but he put them to good use, much better use than could be expected in the general intellectual climate of his day. Is it not time, then, to forego that scholarly attitude that is satisfied in exposing his shortcomings and so quick in its high-handed condemnation of the work and the man?

He has put into our hands a mass of information. Important work still remains to be done on that information; a balanced assessment is called for, not rash and malicious slander. Fortunately, there have always been other scholars ready to appreciate Pausanias' achievement. One of these is Frazer, who says, "Without him the ruins of Greece would for the most part be a labyrinth without a clue, a riddle without an answer. His book furnishes the clue to the labyrinth, the answer to many riddles."[89] Another, in our time, is Ernst Meyer, who says, "One can safely say that no other book from antiquity shows us so much of the reality of ancient Greece as this one."[90]

I wish my voice to be counted among theirs.

---

[87] VIII.33.4: οὕτω μὲν τὰ ἀνθρώπινα πρόσκαιρά τε καὶ οὐδαμῶς ἐστιν ἐχυρά.

[88] B. P. Réardon, *Courants littéraires grecs des IIe et IIIe siècles après J.-C.* (Paris 1971), 221, comparing Pausanias to Arrian: "Plus facile à reconnaître, cependant, est le mobile qui l'a poussé à entreprendre cet énorme travail: ces auteurs veulent, tous les deux, plaire en rappelant, et pour ainsi dire en stabilisant, un héritage."

[89] Frazer, p. xcvi.

[90] Meyer, pp. 11–12.

APPENDIX ONE

PAUSANIAS AND HIS
CRITICS

Little did he foresee the disposition of certain other professors who were to sit in judgment on him some seventeen hundred years
later. Had he done so he might well have
been tempted to suppress the *Description of
Greece* altogether, and we might have had to
lament the loss of one of the most curious
and valuable records bequeathed to us by
antiquity.

Frazer, *xviii–xix,*
on Pausanias IX.30.3

Pausanias' reputation, more than that of any other ancient writer, has
suffered greatly from the animosity and (it must be said) the arrogance
of modern scholars, among whom German authorities on Greek literature clearly had the lead. He became the prime victim of misguided
scholarship. The main accusations against him were that, though he
quotes a large number of earlier writers, he had, in fact, read extremely
little, that most of his quotations were secondhand from anonymous
handbooks, and that even where he claims personal reading he is often
lying. Furthermore, of the descriptive parts of his book, it was stated
that Pausanias had, in fact, seen very little of what he claims to be describing, and had mostly copied earlier writings by Polemo of Ilium,
who lived in the second century B.C. Therefore, it was concluded, the
Greece described in the pages of Pausanias was not the Greece of his
time, but Hellas some 300 to 350 years earlier. The infrequency with
which he mentions monuments later than the third century B.C. seemed
to find a natural explanation with this theory.

It is well known that it was young Wilamowitz who started the attack, and the charges he blasted against Pausanias had such a strong
and lasting effect because of his great authority. At the age of twenty-

seven, in a paper entitled "Die Thukydideslegende," Wilamowitz formulated his accusations for the first time, opening not the debate but, as has been recently said, "the hostilities."[1] The main instruments of his attack were two dedications from the Athenian acropolis mentioned by Pausanias and still preserved.[2] Wilamowitz, after a series of rash statements, concluded that for the whole of book I Pausanias thoughtlessly copied a very full periegetic source, into which he wove a few recollections of what he had seen, and more of what he had read, all of which he then wrapped about with sophistic simplicity and infantile imitation of Herodotus.[3] Wilamowitz also named Polemo as his periegetic source.

Although Wilamowitz conceded that his verdict of Pausanias was of such significance that a full-scale justification was needed,[4] he never cared to undertake this, but was content to renew and widen the attack whenever he sensed an occasion. In 1881, he pointed again to Polemo as Pausanias' source;[5] in 1884, he insisted that Pausanias had not read what he says he had read,[6] that he had not seen what he says he had seen,[7] and that some of the sources he cites were invented by him.[8] He did not care that, after the first attack, R. Schöll had immediately taken away the foundations on which it was built, and that Schöll, at the same time, had demanded better proof for such a devastating verdict.[9]

[1] U. von Wilamowitz, *Hermes* 12 (1877): 326ff.; the pages on Pausanias are 344–47. The quotation about Wilamowitz is from Heer, p. 18.

[2] I.23.9 (*IG* I².135; A. E. Raubitschek, *Dedications from the Athenian Akropolis* [Cambridge, Mass. 1949], 124, no. 120) and I.23.10 (*IG* I².527; Raubitschek, p. 141, no. 132).

[3] Wilamowitz (above, n. 1), p. 346: "Der ganze Rattenkönig von Widersprüchen und Verkehrtheiten, den die Ἀττικά bieten, ist schlechterdings nur durch die Annahme erklärlich, dann aber verliert er jedes Auffällige, dass er eine als Periegese gehaltene sehr ausführliche Vorlage gedankenlos ausschreibt, einzeln mit den Reminiscenzen eigener Anschauung, durchgehends mit denen anderer Lectüre versetzt und schliesslich mit dem Rococomäntelchen sophistischer ἀφέλεια und kindischer Herodotimitation umkleidet."

[4] Wilamowitz (above, n. 1), p. 347 n. 31: "Ich weiss wohl, dass diese Schätzung des Pausanias von so weittragender Bedeutung ist, dass sie umfassende Begründung erfordert."

[5] *Antigonos von Karystos* (Berlin 1881), 12–14.

[6] U. von Wilamowitz, *Homerische Untersuchungen* (Berlin 1884), 338, says that Pausanias has not read the poems he cites, not even where he says ἐγὼ ἐπελεξάμην.

[7] Wilamowitz (above, n. 6), p. 339: "Wenn . . . Pausanias sagt θεασάμενος οἶδα, so hat das nur stilistischen Wert."

[8] Wilamowitz (above, n. 6), p. 24, on Pausanias VI.6.10; p. 339 on IX.29.1–2 and IX.38.9–10. See now F. Jacoby, *FGrHist*, comments on 331.

[9] *Hermes* 13 (1878): 434–38. See Regenbogen, p. 1094: "Die ruhige Entgegnung von R. Schöll . . . scheint keinen Eindruck hervorgebracht zu haben."

For some time, Wilamowitz attracted followers who, like himself, were stronger in language than in arguments in this matter. The most vehement was A. Kalkmann.[10] He barely admitted that Pausanias had visited Greece, and had seen Olympia for himself, but it was clear to him that only very few, and minor, features of the book resulted from personal observation; Pausanias had taken from earlier writers whatever is essential or excellent in his work.[11] Polemo, whom Wilamowitz had already named, was now identified as Pausanias' source for Athens, Olympia, Delphi, and parts of book III. Other principal sources, according to Kalkmann, were a geographer of the time of Augustus, a catalog of artists, and a handbook on mythology.[12] Kalkmann categorically denied that Pausanias could be trusted in what he says he has seen for himself, and on the last page of his book he renders the final verdict that Pausanias possessed neither talent nor diligence.[13]

Among others who argued in a similar manner were several scholars working at Olympia[14] and, somewhat later, Carl Robert[15] and Giorgio Pasquali. Both were students, the former also a lifelong friend, of Wilamowitz'. Robert claimed that Pausanias never meant to write a guidebook, but a collection of manifold and colorful stories, a παν-τοδαπὴ ἱστορία. In his view, the descriptive, periegetic parts (the θεωρήματα) were nothing but an artificial frame for these stories (the λόγοι). In Robert's opinion, only the stories mattered to Pausanias; the topographical thread, if at all recognizable, played only a minor and subordinate role.[16] Pasquali, for his part, correctly acknowledged that the periegetic parts were of much greater importance than Robert was

[10] *Pausanias der Perieget* (Berlin 1886).

[11] Kalkmann, p. 275: "Dass Pausanias überhaupt in Griechenland gereist ist, und vereinzelte Reise-Reminiscenzen in seine Periegese einstreute, kann man nicht bezweifeln"; for Olympia, pp. 102–3, 276: "Indess schienen auch in der Beschreibung der Altis einzelne Bemerkungen des Periegeten Autopsie zu verrathen"; p. 271: "darüber kann kein Zweifel mehr obwalten, dass Pausanias alles Wesentliche, das Beste, was er uns giebt, aus anderen Autoren geschöpft hat."

[12] Kalkmann, pp. 59 (Athens), 102–3 (Olympia), 111–12 and 116 (Delphi), 119ff. (book III), 155ff. (the geographer, perhaps Menippus of Pergamum [p. 182]), 184ff. (artists), 200ff. (mythology).

[13] Kalkmann, passim, for instance pp. 14, 49 (and all of the first chapter), 273, 274. The final judgment, on p. 282: "Pausanias zeichnet weder Begabung noch saubere Arbeit aus."

[14] See Regenbogen, p. 1094, who refers to papers of W. Dittenberger, G. Hirschfeld, and G. Treu published in *AZ* in 1880 (Dittenberger) and 1882 (Hirschfeld and Treu).

[15] *Pausanias als Schriftsteller* (Berlin 1909).

[16] Robert, pp. 6 (on the book: "Es ist nichts als eine grosse Zusammenstellung von λόγοι, für die die Periegese ebenso nur den Rahmen abgiebt, wie bei Athenaios das Gast-

willing to admit, and he pointed to Hecataeus and Herodotus as the ultimate models for all periegetic literature, including Pausanias. He nevertheless agreed with Robert that Pausanias' ultimate goal was a παντοδαπὴ ἱστορία.[17] Pasquali concluded that in blending history and other stories into his descriptions Pausanias was following, but abusing, the old format of periegetic literature.[18]

By the time Robert's and Pasquali's contributions appeared, the tide had already turned toward a vindication of Pausanias. He had always had his defenders, among whom J. H. C. Schubart, H. Brunn, and H. Hitzig may be mentioned,[19] and while he had always been highly regarded by archaeologists, he was more and more valued by them as excavations continued in more and more places.[20] As for scholars of literature, however, the reversal of opinion was mainly the result of the appearance of a well-researched and thorough book by W. Gurlitt,[21] whose position was soon thereafter shared (and transmitted to the English-speaking scholarly world) by Frazer.[22] R. Heberdey's study, too,

---

mahl"), 8 (παντοδαπὴ ἱστορία), 82 (minor role of the topographical principle), 110 (the book not a guide).

[17] "Die schriftstellerische Form des Pausanias," *Hermes* 48 (1913): 161–213. For the statements made in the text see Pasquali's own words: "Die Kunstform der Periegetik ist die Kunstform der altionischen Geographie und Historiographie, die des Hekataios und des Herodot" (p. 187); "Pausanias will . . . im Rahmen der Periegese eine παντοδαπῆς ἱστορία schreiben" (p. 192). He also says (pp. 191–92) that Pausanias still clings to a major characteristic of the Ionians, the habit of personal inquiry and exploration.

[18] Pasquali, p. 194: "Pausanias, der Sophist, will seinem nach allgemeiner Bildung durstigen Publikum allgemeine Bildung, vornehmlich Geschichte, aber auch Anderes, beibringen: dafür missbraucht er die althergebrachte Form der Periegese; denn Missbrauch ist es sicher"; p. 196: "Pausanias hat freilich eine althergebrachte Form missbraucht; er kann nicht Mass halten. Aber die Neigung zu Exkursen, die Neigung zur Polyhistorie wohnte der Form inne, wie sie schon Polemon handhabte; sie lud förmlich den Pausanias zu seinen Abschweifungen ein."

[19] J. H. C. Schubart, "Pausanias und seine Ankläger," *Jahrbücher für Philologie*, 1883 and 1884 (*non vidi*); H. Brunn, "Pausanias und seine Ankläger," *Fleckeisens Jahrbücher*, 1884:23–30 (reprinted in *KlSchr*, vol. 3 [Leipzig and Berlin 1906], 210–16); H. Hitzig, "Zur Pausaniasfrage," in *Festschrift des philologischen Kränzchens in Zürich zu der in Zürich tagenden 39. Versammlung deutscher Philologen und Schulmänner* (Zurich 1887), 57–96.

[20] Instructive is the angry remark with which Wilamowitz, in old age, reacts to this fact: "der auch jetzt noch von den meisten Archäologen kanonisierte Sophist" (*Erinnerungen, 1848–1914* [Leipzig 1928], 155).

[21] *Über Pausanias* (Graz 1890). It is hard to believe that Gurlitt, whose book is nothing but a refutation of Wilamowitz' views, has recently been called Wilamowitz' most bizarre follower (Levi 1:363 n. 156, where Kalkmann must be meant).

[22] Frazer, pp. xiii–xvi and esp. pp. lxvii–lxix, lxxxiii ff.

contributed to this reversal of opinion. And Robert's book provoked the sharp criticism of Eugen Petersen, who wrote in defense of Pausanias (or rather attacking some of his colleagues), "And why can he be expected to know everything as well as a German professor?"[23]

Today, Pausanias has been vindicated of all charges expressed by Wilamowitz and his followers.[24] Moreover, the comparison between Pausanias and Strabo, often made, turns out to be no longer in favor of the latter, as it was when Wilamowitz wrote of Strabo that, "as a sensible man," he "manages to describe regions that he has not visited in much more precise fashion than the always confused Pausanias."[25] On the contrary, the verdict is, today, that Strabo is the better and more elegant writer, but that Pausanias is by far the more reliable authority.[26]

The question, today, is therefore no longer what Wilamowitz said about Pausanias,[27] but what had caused him to be so furious against him. This question seems never to have been asked. And yet it is Wilamowitz himself who provides the answer. In spring of 1873 he had made a fool of himself while acting as a guide for a group of people, and since this happened in Greece he blamed Pausanias, who, he thought, had served him ill. To make things worse, this occurred at about the time when Heinrich Schliemann, whom the young Wilamowitz despised, struck gold at Troy, and not long before Schliemann again, this time with Pausanias as his acknowledged guide, had an-

---

[23] "Pausanias der Perieget," *RhM* 64 (1909): 481–538; the quotation is from p. 491.

[24] Among those expressing the new position: R. Heberdey, *Die Reisen des Pausanias in Griechenland* (Vienna 1894); Petersen; F. H. Sandbach, in *CAH*, vol. 11 (1936), 689–90; A. Diller, *TAPA* 87 (1956): 84; Meyer, pp. 36, 41ff.; Regenbogen, pp. 1093–95; G. Roux, *Pausanias en Corinthie (II 1–15)* (Paris 1958), 12; A. Lesky, *Geschichte der griechischen Literatur*, 2d ed. (Bern and Munich 1963), 912; Heer, pp. 17–21; R. E. Wycherley, *Hesperia*, suppl. 20 (1982): 182.

[25] *GGA*, 1906:638 (reprinted in *KlSchr*, vol. 5, pt. 1 [Berlin 1937], 373): "Strabon, der als ein verständiger Mann die Gegenden, die er nicht besucht zu haben behauptet, sehr viel präziser beschreibt als der Erzkonfusionar Pausanias." This statement is perhaps the source for the passage of G. de Sanctis in which he calls Pausanias "scrittore tardo e confusionario" (above, p. 101 n. 19).

[26] Gurlitt, pp. 201–2, 431; R. Weil, *BPW* 10 (1890): 1107; Heer, pp. 20–21; W. K. Pritchett, *Studies in Ancient Greek Topography*, pt. 4 (Berkeley 1982), 101, who subscribes to W. M. Leake's appraisal of 1841: "The description of Greece, therefore, by Strabo, although luminous and accurate in particular instances, is extremely imperfect, when compared with that which Pausanias has left us" (*The Topography of Athens*, vol. 1, 2d ed. [London 1841], 32).

[27] It seems symptomatic, for instance, that A. E. Raubitschek, in his discussion of the two dedications that provoked Wilamowitz' attack (above, n. 2), still lists Wilamowitz in the bibliography but does not find it worthwhile to quote his views on the matter.

other great success at Mycenae. That was more than Wilamowitz cared to bear. In the year following Schliemann's good fortune at Mycenae, he published his first attack on Pausanias.

Wilamowitz gives the first hint of what had happened in 1873 thirteen years later, in his book on Isyllus. He says that he first suspected Pausanias of not having reported from autopsy, but of having copied from another writer's periegetic work, when he tried to follow Pausanias on his route from Olympia to Heraea in Arcadia, that is to say, Pausanias VI.21.3f. He adds that Pausanias, in fact, describes the way coming from the opposite direction.[28] Matters become much clearer in Wilamowitz' *Erinnerungen, 1848–1914*, published in Leipzig in 1928. Wilamowitz narrates that, coming from Italy, where he lived from August 1872 to April 1874, he visited Greece for the first time from March to May 1873. On a trip to the Peloponnese, he joined the young Erbprinz Bernhard von Meiningen and his entourage. It was only natural that he was considered the expert on geographic and topographical matters, and Wilamowitz, after some preparatory study in Athens, set out, his Pausanias ready at hand.[29] When the group left Olympia on its way to Arcadia, nothing in Pausanias seemed to make sense, and Wilamowitz frankly admits that his low opinion of Pausanias stems from this experience.[30] It is easy to speculate that he must have made a very poor guide of his group that day, and that he perhaps was ridiculed, and certainly humiliated. In time, he discovered that he had only himself to blame, since it had been known for some time (though not to him) that Pausanias had come to Olympia from the South and that he had described the way from that direction.[31] This discovery, however, did not soothe Wilamowitz' feelings toward Pausanias.

[28] *Isyllos von Epidauros* (Berlin 1886), 184 n. 43.

[29] Wilamowitz (above, n. 20), pp. 153 (trip to the Peloponnese, description of the group), 155 (Olympia, traces of some digging by the French, then: "Weiter ging es flussaufwärts. Es hatte sich schon so gefügt, dass die geographischen und topographischen Fragen mir vorgelegt wurden; ich hatte den Pausanias mit, auch in Athen mich etwas vorbereitet").

[30] Wilamowitz (above, n. 20), p. 155: "Aber hier am Alpheios wollte nichts stimmen. . . . Meine geringe Schätzung des . . . Sophisten stammt von dieser Erfahrung." Through the kindness of Professor W. M. Calder, III, I have recently seen the (unpublished) diary that Wilamowitz kept during this visit to Greece. The incident at Olympia that seems to have caused his hatred for Pausanias is there dated April 18, 1873. I am most grateful to Professor Calder for sharing his find with me.

[31] After the words quoted in n. 30 ("Aber hier am Alpheios wollte nichts stimmen"), Wilamowitz continues: "konnte es auch nicht, denn Pausanias beschreibt den Weg in umgekehrter Richtung. Das war zwar schon früher bemerkt, aber davon wusste ich

Wilamowitz could not have stated more clearly where the very personal roots of his vendetta against Pausanias lay. But to make things worse for him, it was only a few weeks later, in May 1873, that Schliemann found at Hissarlik the famous "treasure of Priam." It is well known how strongly Wilamowitz reacted to this, how he mocked Schliemann and Mrs. Schliemann at a Christmas party given at the German Archaeological Institute in Rome in 1873, and what he wrote about the Schliemanns to his parents in September and December 1873.[32] Schliemann's success and Wilamowitz' reaction have been recently thus described: "A Mecklenburg peasant outsmarted the professors. The mandarins never forgave Schliemann."[33]

What most angered Wilamowitz toward Schliemann was the latter's confidence in a tradition that was nothing but pure myth to Wilamowitz. And it was a piece of that tradition—a chapter of Pausanias (II.16)—that helped Schliemann strike gold again at Mycenae, where a few lines of Pausanias correctly interpreted led him to the excavation of the royal tombs in the last three months of 1876.[34] Within a few months, Wilamowitz told the world what he thought of Pausanias.

Wilamowitz is not the only intellectual who once lost his way between Olympia and Heraea. It had happened long before to Dio Chrysostom, who, however, came from the South and was going to Olympia—he could have benefited from Pausanias' description, had it already been written.[35]

---

nichts, und meine geringe Schätzung des auch jetzt noch von den meisten Archäologen kanonisierten Sophisten stammt von dieser Erfahrung." It is disarming to see how Wilamowitz lets Pausanias take the blame for what was his own mistake: he does not try to hide his own ignorance at the time of the event, but still manages to blame Pausanias—and to get in a shot at the archaeologists at the same time.

[32] Wilamowitz (above, n. 20), p. 148 (where he is in doubt whether the Christmas party took place in 1872 or 1873—it took place in 1873, after his own visit to Greece). The letters and more about all this in W. M. Calder, III, "Wilamowitz on Schliemann," *Philologus* 124 (1980): 146–51.

[33] Calder (above, n. 32), p. 150.

[34] See above, pp. 29f.

[35] Dio Chrys. *Or.* 1.52ff., translated by J. G. Frazer, *Pausanias and Other Greek Sketches* (London 1900), 289–90:

Going on foot from Heraea to Pisa by the side of the Alpheus, I was able, up to a certain point, to make out my path. But by and by I found myself in a forest and on broken ground, with many tracks leading to sheepfolds and cattle-pens. And meeting with no one of whom I could ask the way I strayed from the path and wandered up and down. It was high noon; and seeing on a height a clump of oaks, as it might be a grove, I betook myself thither, in the hope that from thence

As for Wilamowitz, it has been said, correctly, that some of his later remarks on Pausanias are more moderate.[36] It may be added that a lecture given by Wilamowitz at the Berlin Academy in November 1930 contains a few sentences that suggest that he might be about to forget about his hypothesis regarding Pausanias and Polemo.[37] And, as early as 1891, he makes a very surprising statement. After making a polemical remark on a passage in Gurlitt's book on Pausanias, which had just been published, he says, "Against Gurlitt, however, I do not want to say anything without acknowledging that his book is gratifying and useful."[38] Taken at face value, this would mean that Wilamowitz, under the influence of Gurlitt's book, has withdrawn whatever he had said about Pausanias. But he certainly has not, as, for instance, his words from *Erinnerungen* quoted in note 31 above clearly show. He still disliked Pausanias, he still had a low opinion of him; but he was no longer (or, perhaps, not always) sure whether all the bad things he had said about him were true.

However that may be, the damage to Pausanias' reputation was certainly done. While it is true that for a long time scholars who take a special interest in Pausanias, for instance those cited in note 24, have come to regard those old views put forward by Wilamowitz, Kalkmann, Robert, and others as an aberration, it also remains true that these views continued to prevail with many others who are not specialists on Pausanias, among them first-rate scholars.[39] It is the more

---

I might spy some path or home. Here then I found stones piled carelessly together, and skins of sacrificed animals hanging up, with clubs and staves, the offerings, as I supposed, of shepherds; and a little way off, seated on the ground, was a tall and stalwart dame, somewhat advanced in years, in rustic attire, with long grey hair. Of her I asked what these things might be. She answered very civilly, in a broad Doric accent, that the spot was sacred to Hercules. . . .

For the significance of this episode, see C. P. Jones, *The Roman World of Dio Chrysostom* (Cambridge, Mass., 1978), 51.

[36] Regenbogen, p. 1094, who refers to *Der Glaube der Hellenen*, vol. 2 (Berlin 1932), 508–10.

[37] A summary, by Wilamowitz himself, was published as "Reiseerlebnisse des Pausanias," *Forschungen und Fortschritte* 7 (1931): 50–51.

[38] *Hermes* 26 (1891): 228 n. 2 (*KlSchr*, vol. 5, pt. 1 [Berlin 1937], 63 n. 1): "Übrigens will ich nicht gegen Gurlitt etwas sagen, ohne sein Buch als ein erfreuliches und nützliches anzuerkennen."

[39] These include, to mention only a few, W. Dittenberger, quoted in this connection by Regenbogen, p. 1094; M. Holleaux, *RevPhil* 19 (1895): 109–15 and *Mélanges H. Weil* (Paris 1898), 193–206 (both articles are reprinted in *Etudes d'épigraphie et d'histoire grecques*, vol. 1 [Paris 1938], 187–93, 195–209); M. P. Nilsson, *Geschichte der*

remarkable that Otto Regenbogen, himself a pupil of Wilamowitz, was able to come to a verdict in this matter that is contrary to his master's.[40]

Even more interesting is the way in which another great scholar and leading authority on Pausanias, Sir James George Frazer, once reacted to Wilamowitz' attacks. When, in 1898, he published his monumental work on Pausanias, he had read, among other things, the books by Gurlitt and Heberdey that had done so much to restore Pausanias' credit.[41] He also cites the recent excavations of Lycosura in Arcadia as further proof of his reliability.[42] Frazer, in his long general introduction, is quite firm in his view of the matter, but he is also very restrained when he comes to mention Wilamowitz' role in it.[43] From what he says no one would guess that Frazer was offended by the manner in which Wilamowitz used to condemn Pausanias. A passage in volume 3 of Frazer's *Pausanias*, to which Robert Ackerman has recently drawn attention,[44] goes a little further: it is written in somewhat stronger language and has an ironic tone. This is not surprising, since Frazer, in fact, is exposing an egregious blunder by Wilamowitz, one, moreover, that seems characteristic of his frivolous method of dealing with Pausanias. The passage that provoked Frazer's remarks is II.17.1, which mentions a spring called the Water of Freedom. Wilamowitz had devoted a paper to it, in which he accused Pausanias of having used, and misrepresented, a written source, while insinuating that he is reporting from personal observation.[45] Frazer examines Wilamowitz' arguments and summarizes:[46]

It would thus appear, on Prof. von Wilamowitz-Möllendorff's own showing, that the book from which Pausanias copied made a mistake, and that Pausanias, in copying it, made another mistake, which fortunately cancelled the original error of his authority, with the net result that he finally blundered into

---

griechischen Religion, vol. 2 (Munich 1950), 51 (3d ed. [1974], 54); F. Jacoby, *FGrHist*, vol. 3 (1955), introduction to "Elis and Olympia," pp. 147–48, nn. 24, 31.

[40] Regenbogen, pp. 1093–95.
[41] Frazer cites both books, for instance p. xvi n. 9, p. xx n. 2, p. xxiii n. 2 (Gurlitt); p. lxxvii n. 8, p. lxxviii n. 3 (Heberdey).
[42] Frazer, p. xcvi. He was quite right in this; see E. Meyer, "Lykosura," in *RE* (1927), 2419.
[43] Frazer, p. lxxxix n. 3.
[44] R. Ackerman, "Sir James G. Frazer and A. E. Housman: A Relationship in Letters," *GRBS* 15 (1974): 339–64. I owe the knowledge of this paper to the kindness of H. A. Thompson.
[45] *Hermes* 19 (1884): 463–65.
[46] Frazer 3:179–81; the actual quotation is from p. 180.

placing the water quite correctly. . . . It requires less credulity to suppose that Pausanias saw the water for himself.[47]

Critical as Frazer is in this passage, nothing indicates animosity against Wilamowitz. A few years thereafter, when he and Mrs. Frazer visited Berlin late in 1902, they were introduced to, and politely received by, Wilamowitz. In 1905 and 1906, the two scholars exchanged books, and a few letters that are full of courtesies.[48] They do not, on either side, contain any indication of warm feelings, but no sign of antipathy either. It was only much later, in a letter of October 1927 to the famous Latin scholar A. E. Housman, his friend for some thirty years, that Frazer let himself go and openly stated how he felt about Wilamowitz. Moreover, he clearly says that Wilamowitz' attacks on Pausanias, more than any other matter, were the cause of his animosity.[49] He writes of Wilamowitz, "He has always seemed to me a sophist with an infallible instinct for getting hold of a stick by the wrong end. I do not forget how, with the stick (wrong end up, as usual), he belaboured my poor old friend Pausanias and no doubt many a better man."

Robert Ackerman, to whom we owe the publication of this letter, of Housman's reply to it, and of Frazer's reaction to the reply, correctly sensed that Frazer's rage must date from a much earlier time, when he was working on Pausanias. Naturally, Ackerman attempted to identify the cause of what he calls a "striking and gratuitous attack."[50] Unfortunately, however, he took the wrong road. Being a historian of Frazer's life and works, he looked for clues in Frazer's *Pausanias*, not in Wilamowitz' writings. He finally persuaded himself that it was Wilamowitz' paper on the Water of Freedom that made Frazer so angry: "Wilamowitz' suggestion that Pausanias had clumsily tried to pass off a literary reference as a personal observation might well have gone further with Frazer than the trivial matter of the location of the Water of Freedom would seem to warrant. It very likely struck Frazer as undercutting Pausanias' reliability."[51]

---

[47] Similar objections against Wilamowitz' view can be found in Hitzig and Blümner, vol. 1, pt. 2 (1899), 563–64. They conclude, "Unter solchen Umständen ist es natürlicher zu glauben, Paus. habe sich an Ort und Stelle über die Sache unterrichtet." F. Zucker did well to exclude Wilamowitz' paper from vol. 3 of the latter's *Kleine Schriften*. See also above, p. 20 n. 82, for Frazer's comments on Pausanias VI.21.3, the very passage that baffled Wilamowitz in 1873 and enraged him toward Pausanias.

[48] R. Ackerman and W. M. Calder, III, "The Correspondence of Ulrich von Wilamowitz Moellendorff with Sir James George Frazer," *PCPS* 204 (1978): 31–40.

[49] Ackerman (above, n. 44), p. 361.

[50] Ackerman (above, n. 44), p. 348ff.; the quotation is from p. 349.

[51] Ackerman (above, n. 44), p. 352ff.; the quotation is from p. 354.

It seems likely that the brief paper referred to by Ackerman in fact added to Frazer's irritation, but this paper was not important, not weighty enough to have been the cause of Frazer's outburst. There had been, in fact, several earlier and much stronger condemnations of Pausanias by Wilamowitz, beginning with the paper in *Hermes* in 1877 (see above, n. 1). Frazer was well aware of all these attacks when he wrote his commentary on Pausanias. But his reactions were, for several decades, strictly controlled and never went beyond some fine irony, as in his assessment of Wilamowitz' blunder on the Water of Freedom. When he finally expressed his real feelings, it was in a letter to an intimate friend; they were hardly meant to become public knowledge.

However that may be, Frazer was not prepared, once he had formulated his opinion, to change his mind. When Housman, replying the following day, rose to Wilamowitz' defense in emphasizing his singular abilities "in verbal scholarship and textual criticism," Frazer, two days later, somewhat stubbornly replied, "From Mommsen I, of course, learn much, but with Wilamowitz, so far as I can remember, I have never found myself in agreement about anything. Hence I am apt to regard him as a brilliant, but misleading, rhetorician rather than historian." [52]

Frazer, indeed, had not forgotten what Wilamowitz, beginning exactly fifty years before this correspondence, had done to Pausanias. Another fifty years (and more) have elapsed since then, and further progress has been made toward a vindication of Pausanias: in the end, the author triumphs over his critics.

[52] Ackerman (above, n. 44), p. 362, nos. 8, 9.

PAUSANIAS' USE
OF THE EXPRESSION
"IN MY TIME"

Pausanias very often speaks about matters as they were in his time (as opposed to the past), or as they were when he saw them. He also very often mentions things as they were "still in my time," or as they remained "down to my time" or "to the present day." An attempt must be made to define more clearly what he means by such expressions and, most important, to determine how far back in time such an expression can refer.[1]

There are no less than 144 instances where Pausanias uses the expression "in my (our) time": ἐπ᾽ ἐμοῦ (27), κατ᾽ ἐμέ (26), ἐφ᾽ ἡμῶν (85), or καθ᾽ ἡμᾶς (6). It goes without saying that there is no meaningful difference between these four expressions, and both ἐφ᾽ ἡμῶν (II.26.9) and κατ᾽ ἐμέ (VII.5.9) are, in fact, used to designate one and the same event. The unique ἐπὶ ἡμῶν in VI.10.8 should be emended to ἐφ᾽ ἡμῶν.

Most often the expression is used to say that a site is either more or less well preserved or that it is now in ruins or deserted. In most of these instances there is no explicit connection with an absolute date or with any datable event. Some passages, however, give certain hints as to the dates Pausanias is referring to when he says "in my (our) time." They confirm what was to be expected: that he means "since I was born." It was "in his time" that

---

[1] This research was greatly facilitated by the tape of Pausanias' vocabulary produced at the Thesaurus Linguae Graecae at Irvine and by the Ibycus computer that made the tape readable.

1. the Athenians created the tribe Hadrianis (A.D. 121/22 or 124/25);[2]

2. Hadrian built the new sanctuary of Poseidon Hippius near Mantinea (A.D. 117–38);[3]

3. Herodes Atticus adorned the temple of Poseidon at Isthmus;[4]

4. the people of Smyrna were building a shrine for Asclepius (building activity is attested for A.D. 150–52);[5]

5. the Roman senator Sextus Iulius Maior Antoninus Pythodorus erected buildings in the sanctuary of Asclepius at Epidaurus;[6]

6. another Roman senator dug to make a foundation for a monument commemorating his Olympic victory (after A.D. 129);[7]

7. the number of votes in the Delphic amphictyony was thirty;[8]

8. the Costoboci invaded Greece (A.D. 170 or 171).[9]

Furthermore, it was "down to his time" that

9. 217 years had gone by since the refoundation of Corinth by Julius Caesar (A.D. 174).[10]

It results from these figures that the expression "in my time" can refer back to at least A.D. 124/25, if not beyond. And when Pausanias says that the tribe Hadrianis in Athens was created "already in my time," he obviously implies that he was already born by then, that is, by A.D. 121/22 or 124/25. Instead of "before my time," there occurs "before I was born" in IX.29.2, and occasionally Pausanias says "one generation (two, three generations) before me," as in VII.21.10, VIII.32.3, VIII.9.9, and X.32.10.

In addition to the 144 occurrences of "in my time" there are almost as many instances—a total of 136—where Pausanias says something like "down to my (our) time," "until now," or "still at present."[11] And there are still other expressions with which Pausanias refers to the time

[2] I.5.5. See above, p. 12 n. 58. [3] VIII.10.2. [4] II.1.7.
[5] II.26.9, VII.5.9. See above, p. 10 n. 54.
[6] II.27.6. [7] V.20.8. See below, pp. 178–80.
[8] X.8.4. It is disputed whether it was Augustus who raised the number from the traditional number of twenty-four (G. W. Bowersock, *Augustus and the Greek World* [Oxford 1965], 97–98) or one of the later emperors (G. Daux, *CRAI*, 1975:358ff.; also in *Etudes sur l'antiquité grecque offertes à André Plassart par ses collègues de la Sorbonne* [Paris 1976], 59ff.).
[9] X.34.5. See above, p. 9 n. 50. [10] V.1.2. See above, p. 9.
[11] The expressions are ἐς ἡμᾶς (35), ἐς ἐμέ (35), ἐς τόδε (29), καὶ νῦν ἔτι (22), ἔτι καὶ νῦν (8), ἄχρι γε ἐμοῦ (4), ἄχρι ἡμῶν (2), μέχρι γε καὶ ἐμοῦ (1).

at which he lived, the second century A.D. The sheer number of these references to contemporary conditions, events, or persons would be hard to explain in a book that was, in fact, not much else but an unoriginal copy of earlier writers' work. These references, by themselves, are another argument against such views that have once been held.

More important, the first of the passages quoted above shows that Pausanias could refer to an event of the first half of the twenties of the second century as having happened in his own time.[12] It is therefore possible that he could, in the same manner (κατ᾽ ἐμέ), refer to an event of A.D. 129. The passage in question is V.20.8, which reads:

> The following incident occurred in my time. A Roman senator had won an Olympic victory, and desiring to bequeath as a memorial of his victory a bronze statue with an inscription, he dug to make a foundation; and when the excavation was carried near to the pillar of Oenomaus, the diggers found there fragments of arms and bridles and curb-chains. I saw them excavated myself.[13]

Long ago, W. Gurlitt proposed to connect with this account the inscription on the base *IOlympia* 236, which was made to receive a chariot.[14] The text has been restored as follows: [Λούκιος Μινίκιος] Νατᾶλις στρατηγικὸς Ὀλυμπιάδι σκζ ἅρματι τελείῳ νεικήσα[ς ἀνέ]θηκεν τὸ ἅρμα, ὕπατος, ἀνθύπατος Λιβύης. This is a chariot dedicated in reminiscence of an Olympic victory won by the *vir praetorius* Lucius Minicius Natalis in A.D. 129, but dedicated much later, after Natalis had been consul and proconsul of Africa, that is to say, not earlier than A.D. 153.[15] It is by no means uncommon that a victory statue at Olympia was erected so many years after the victory,[16] and a date in the fifties of the second century, after Natalis had received the governorship of Africa, would fit well into Pausanias' chronology: he was present at the time when the foundations for the monument were dug.

---

[12] See above, n. 2.

[13] Somewhat different is V.21.15, where two statues made in A.D. 125 are described as "works of the present age" (τέχνης τῆς ἐφ᾽ ἡμῶν), but this passage, too, lends support to the view that the twenties were part of what Pausanias regarded as his own time.

[14] Gurlitt, p. 421 n. 37.

[15] The earlier assumption that he was proconsul of Africa in A.D. 139 was disproved by the diploma *CIL* XVI.175, which shows that in that year he was, in fact, *consul suffectus*. It follows that his proconsulate ought to have come in A.D. 153 or 154 (R. Syme, *REA* 61 [1959]: 314; W. Eck, "Minicius," in *RE*, suppl. 14 [1974], 283; A. Deman and M. Th. Raepsaet, *Antcl* 42 [1973]: 185ff.).

[16] Pausanias VI.10.3, 10.4, 16.6 and elsewhere; G. Lippold, "Siegerstatuen," in *RE* (1923), 2269.

Gurlitt's suggestion has been called "attractive" even by those who have reservations about it or are opposed to it.[17] Two objections have been raised: first, that the mention of the consulate and the proconsulate are later additions, since Natalis could not have said that he dedicated the monument as a *vir praetorius* if he was already a *vir consularis*;[18] second, that Pausanias' words ought to mean the statue of the victor, but cannot easily mean the dedication of a chariot.[19] The first objection seems pointless, since the text can (and must) be understood as to say "victorious as *vir praetorius*," so that στρατηγικός has to be connected with νεικήσας, not with ἀνέθηκεν, whereas the act of dedication (ἀνέθηκεν) came only during or after the governorship of Africa.[20]

As for the second objection, E. Groag has already doubted its force by saying that Pausanias might very well have been content to describe somewhat loosely the specific form of a monument that was of no interest to him.[21] Moreover, it is possible that Natalis, as other victors in the chariot race at Olympia did,[22] dedicated two monuments, a statue of his own (Pausanias' εἰκών) and the chariot from which the inscription survives.

Since neither of the objections to Gurlitt's suggestion seems valid,

[17] Commentary to *IOlympia* 236: "ist auf den ersten Blick ansprechend"; E. Groag, "Minicius," in *RE* (1932), 1842: "an sich ansprechende Hypothese."

[18] W. Dittenberger, n. 2 to *SIG*[2] 390 (*SIG*[3] 840): "Consulatus et proconsulatus postea additi videntur. Nam στρατηγικὸς-ἀνέθηκεν dici non licuit de eo qui cum monumentum dedicaretur iam consul fuerat." Accepted by Groag (above, n. 17), p. 1842, and L. Moretti, *Olympionikai* (Rome 1957), 163, no. 846.

[19] Commentary to *IOlympia* 236: "Denn dieser [Pausanias' Ausdruck] lässt sich ungezwungen nur auf eine einfache Statue des Siegers deuten, wie sie seit dem vierten Jahrhundert v. Chr. auch bei Wagensiegen zuweilen vorkommen . . . , während für Minicius Natalis die Inschrift und der Umfang der Basis eine Darstellung des Gespannes bezeugen."

[20] Commentary to *IOlympia* 236: "Die Titulatur στρατηγικός [*praetorius*] kann sich, da der Dedikant nachher noch Konsul und Prokonsul von Afrika geworden, und die Erwähnung dieser Würden Z. 2 nicht erst nachträglich hinzugefügt ist, nicht auf die Zeit der Errichtung des Denkmals, sondern nur auf die des Sieges selbst beziehen."

[21] Groag (above, n. 17), p. 1842: "Indes besteht die Möglichkeit, dass der Perieget keinen Wert darauf gelegt hat, die Beschaffenheit des Denkmals, das für ihn ohne jedes Interesse war, genauer zu bezeichnen." *PIR*[2] (1983) M.620 is not helpful.

[22] Pausanias VI.10.6, on Cleosthenes: "Along with the statue of the chariot and horses he dedicated statues of himself and the charioteer." Different is the monument of Cynisca, sister of King Agesilaus, where on a single base of stone there was "a chariot and horses, a charioteer and a statue of Cynisca herself" (Pausanias VI.1.6); different again the dedication of Euagoras: "only a chariot without a figure of Euagoras himself in it" (Pausanias VI.10.8).

there is certainly a good chance that *IOlympia* 236 is, in fact, part of a dedication made by L. Minicius Natalis Quadronius Verus, consul A.D. 139, in memory of his Olympic victory of A.D. 129, sometime in the 150s. The incident of which Pausanias speaks as occurring in his time (p. 178) seems, after all, to be not the Olympic victory itself but the digging necessary for the erection of the monument and the finding of the weapons, and therefore, if the attribution of the monument to Minicius Natalis is correct, an event of the fifties of the second century A.D.

In one of the many passages where Pausanias says that certain things continue to exist down to his day, he speaks of the return of the Messenians into their land in 370/369 B.C., after an exile of 287 years, and says, "In all that time they are known to have dropped none of their native customs, nor did they unlearn their Doric tongue; indeed, they speak it to this day with greater purity than any other of the Peloponnesians." [23] It might seem that this passage was written not later than the reign of the emperor Antoninus Pius (A.D. 138–61), since the Messenians seem to have abandoned the use of the dialect during his reign. Wilhelm Dittenberger observed long ago from dedications of the city and of Messenian individuals at Olympia that the dialect gave way to the so-called Koine during the time of the emperor. [24] This, however, did not necessarily affect the way the language was spoken, neither in Messenia itself nor by Messenians abroad.

[23] IV.27.9–11; the quotation is from IV.27.11.
[24] W. Dittenberger, comments on *IOlympia* 445; Th. Schwertfeger, *Olympiabericht* 10 (1981): 250 n. 3; cf. A. Thumb, *Handbuch der griechischen Dialekte*, vol. 1, 2d ed. by E. Kieckers (Heidelberg 1932), 103–4.

BIBLIOGRAPHY

Works marked with an asterisk are cited by the name(s) of the author(s) only.

Ackerman, R. "Sir James G. Frazer and A. E. Housman: A Relationship in Letters." *Greek, Roman and Byzantine Studies* 15 (1974): 339–64.

Ackerman, R., and W. M. Calder, III. "The Correspondence of Ulrich von Wilamowitz-Moellendorff with Sir James George Frazer." *Proceedings of the Cambridge Philological Society* 204 (1978): 31–40.

Amandry, P. "Notes d'architecture delphique." *Bulletin de correspondance hellénique* 74 (1950): 10–21.

Ameling, W. *Herodes Atticus.* 2 vols. Hildesheim 1983.

Belger, Ch. "Schliemann als Interpret des Pausanias." *Berliner Philologische Wochenschrift* 19 (1899): 1180–83, 1211–15. On Pausanias II.16.

Bischoff, H. "Perieget." In *Realencyclopädie der classischen Altertumswissenschaft,* 725–42. 1937.

Blanck, H. *Wiederverwendung alter Statuen als Ehrendenkmäler bei Griechen und Römern.* Rome 1969.

Brommer, F. "Beiträge zur griechischen Bildhauergeschichte." *Mitteilungen des Deutschen Archäologischen Instituts* 3 (1950): 80–98.

———. "Erhaltene griechische Standbilder und ihre Erwähnungen in der antiken Literatur." *Gymnasium* 59 (1952): 115–25.

Brunn, H. "Pausanias und seine Ankläger." *Fleckeisens Jahrbücher,* 1884: 23–30. Reprinted in *Kleine Schriften* 3 : 210–16. Leipzig and Berlin 1906.

Burstein, St. "The Date of the Athenian Victory over Pleistarchus: A Note on Pausanias 1.15.1." *Classical World* 71 (1977): 128–29.

Calder, W. M., III. "Wilamowitz on Schliemann." *Philologus* 124 (1980): 146–51.

————. "Alexander's House (Pausanias 8.32.1)." *Greek, Roman and Byzantine Studies* 23 (1982): 281–87.

Callaghan, P. "The Medusa Rodanini and Antiochus III." *Annual of the British School at Athens* 76 (1981): 59–70.

Casson, L. *Travel in the Ancient World*. London 1974.

Chamoux, F. "Pausanias géographe." In *Mélanges Dion*, ed. R. Chevallier, 83–90. Paris 1974.

Clairmont, Ch. "Sparta's 'Golden Phiale' at Olympia." *Zeitschrift für Papyrologie and Epigraphik* 48 (1982): 79–85.

Comfort, H. "The Date of Pausanias, Book II." *American Journal of Archaeology* 35 (1931): 310–14.

Cordano, F. "I 'Messeni dello stretto' e Pausania." *La Parola del Passato* 195 (1980): 436–40.

Daux, G. *Pausanias à Delphes*. Paris 1936.

————. "Les Empéreurs romains et l'amphictionie." *Comptes rendus de l'Académie des inscriptions et belles-lettres*, 1975 : 348–62.

————. "La Composition du Conseil amphictyonique sous l'Empire." In *Etudes sur l'antiquité grecque offertes à André Plassart par ses collègues de la Sorbonne*, 59–79. Paris 1976.

Deicke, L. "Quaestiones Pausanianae." Diss., Göttingen 1935.

Despinis, G. "Ein neues Werk des Damophon." *Archäologischer Anzeiger*, 1966 : 378–85.

Diller, A. "The Authors Named Pausanias." *Transactions of the American Philological Association* 86 (1955): 268–79. Reprinted in *Studies in Greek Manuscript Tradition*, 137–48. Amsterdam 1983.

————. "Pausanias in the Middle Ages." *Transactions of the American Philological Association* 87 (1956): 84–97. Reprinted in *Studies in Greek Manuscript Tradition*, 149–62. Amsterdam 1983.

————. "The Manuscripts of Pausanias." *Transactions of the American Philological Association* 88 (1957): 169–88. Reprinted in *Studies in Greek Manuscript Tradition*, 163–82. Amsterdam 1983.

Donnay, G. "Damophon de Messène et les φαιδρυνταί d'Olympie." *Bulletin de correspondance hellénique* 91 (1967): 546–51.

Ebeling, H. L. "Pausanias as an Historian." *Classical Weekly* 7 (1913): 138–41, 146–50.

Engeli, A. *Die oratio variata bei Pausanias*. Berlin 1907.

Fingarette, A. "The Marmaria Puzzles." *American Journal of Archaeology* 74 (1970): 401–4.

Follet, S. "La Datation de l'archonte Dionysios." *Revue des études grecques* 90 (1977): 47–54.

Fontenrose, J. "The Hero as an Athlete." *California Studies in Classical Antiquity* 1 (1968): 73–104.

Forte, B. *Rome and the Romans As the Greeks Saw Them*. Rome 1972.

Fossey, J. M. "The Cities of the Kopais in the Roman Period." In *Aufstieg und*

Niedergang der Römischen Welt, ed. H. Temporini, vol. 2, pt. 7, pp. 549–91. Berlin 1979.

* Frazer, J. G. *Pausanias's Description of Greece.* 6 vols. London 1898. Roman numerals refer to the Introduction, vol. 1, pp. xiii–xcvi.

Gallavotti, C. "Le copie di Pausania e gli originali di alcuni iscrizioni di Olimpia." *Bollettino del Comitato per la preparazione dell'edizione nazionale dei classici greci e latini,* n.s., 26 (1978): 3–27, 28–38.

———. "Iscrizioni di Olimpia nel sesto libro di Pausania." *Bollettino del Comitato per la preparazione dell'edizione nazionale dei classici greci e latini,* n.s., 27 (1979): 3–29.

Gross, W. H. "Die Periegese des Pausanias." In *Allgemeine Grundlagen der Archäologie,* ed. U. Hausmann, 402–8. Munich 1969.

* Gurlitt, W. *Über Pausanias.* Graz 1890.

Hamdorf, F. W. "Zur Weihung des Chairedemos auf der Akropolis von Athen." In Στήλη εἰς μνήμην Νικολάου Κοντολέοντος, 231–35. Athens 1980.

* Heberdey, R. *Die Reisen des Pausanias in Griechenland.* Vienna 1894.

* Heer, J. *La Personnalité de Pausanias.* Paris 1979.

Hejnic, J. *Pausanias the Periegete and the Archaic History of Arcadia.* Prague 1961.

Herrmann, H.-V. *Olympia: Heiligtum und Wettkampfstätte.* Munich 1972.

Hirschfeld, G. "Pausanias und die Inschriften von Olympia." *Archäologische Zeitung* 40 (1882): 97–130.

Hitzig, H. "Zur Pausaniasfrage." In *Festschrift des philologischen Kränzchens in Zürich zu der in Zürich tagenden 39. Versammlung deutscher Philologen und Schulmänner,* 57–96. Zurich 1887.

* Hitzig, H., and H. Blümner. *Des Pausanias Beschreibung von Griechenland, mit kritischem Apparat herausgegeben von Hermann Hitzig, mit erklärenden Anmerkungen versehen von Hermann Hitzig und Hugo Blümner.* 3 vols. Leipzig 1896–1910.

Hohlfelder, R. L. "Pausanias II 2, 3: A Collation of Archaeological and Numismatic Evidence." *Hesperia* 39 (1970): 326–31.

Imhoof-Blumer, F., and P. Gardner. *A Numismatic Commentary on Pausanias.* Pts. 1–3. *Journal of Hellenic Studies* 6 (1885): 50–101; 7 (1886): 57–113; 8 (1887): 6–63. New edition, edited and enlarged by Al. N. Oikonomides, published under the title *Ancient Coins Illustrating Lost Masterpieces of Greek Art: A Numismatic Commentary on Pausanias.* Chicago 1964.

Jordan, D. "Two Inscribed Lead Tablets from a Well in the Athenian Kerameikos." *Mitteilungen des Deutschen Archäologischen Instituts, Athenische Abteilung* 95 (1980): 225–39.

Jost, M. "Pausanias en Mégalopolitide." *Revue des études anciennes* 75 (1973): 241–67.

———. "Sur les traces de Pausanias en Arcadie." *Revue archéologique,* 1974–75: 39–46.

Kahlo, G. "Pausanias als Beispiel der Wertung alter Überlieferungen." *Ziva antica* 11 (1961): 57–65.

Kahrstedt, U. *Das wirtschaftliche Gesicht Griechenlands in der Kaiserzeit.* Bern 1954.

* Kalkmann, A. *Pausanias der Perieget: Untersuchungen über seine Schrift-stellerei und seine Quellen.* Berlin 1886.

Kroll, J. H. "The Ancient Image of Athena Polias." *Hesperia,* suppl. 20 (1982): 65–76.

Lacroix, L. *Les Représentations des statues sur les monnaies grecques.* Liège 1949.

LeRoy, Ch. "Pausanias à Marmaria." *Bulletin de correspondance hellénique,* suppl. 4 (1977): 247–71.

* Levi, P. *Pausanias, Guide to Greece.* 2 vols. Baltimore 1971.

Lévy, Ed. "Sondages à Lykosoura et date de Damophon." *Bulletin de corre-spondance hellénique* 91 (1967): 518–45.

Lévy, Ed., and J. Marcadé. "Au musée de Lycosoura." *Bulletin de correspon-dance hellénique* 96 (1972): 967–1004.

Meyer, E. *Peloponnesische Wanderungen.* Zurich and Leipzig 1939.

———. *Pausanias: Beschreibung Griechenlands. Neu übersetzt und mit einer Einleitung und erklärenden Anmerkungen versehen.* Zurich 1954.

Moretti, L. *Olympionikai: I vincitori negli antichi agoni olimpici.* Rome 1957.

———. "Supplemento al catalogo degli Olympionikai." *Klio* 52 (1970): 295–303.

Muller, A. "Megarika." *Bulletin de correspondance hellénique* 104 (1980): 83–92; 105 (1981): 203–25; 106 (1982): 379–407; 107 (1983): 157–79; 108 (1984): 249–66.

Nörenberg, H.-W. "Untersuchungen zum Schluss der Περιήγησις τῆς Ἑλλά-δος des Pausanias." *Hermes* 101 (1973): 225–52.

Palm, J. *Rom, Römertum und Imperium in der griechischen Literatur der Kai-serzeit.* Lund 1959.

Pape, M. "Griechische Kunstwerke aus Kriegsbeute und ihre öffentliche Auf-stellung in Rom." Diss., Hamburg 1975.

Parke, H. W. "Pausanias' Description of the Temple of Delphi." *Hermathena* 24 (1935): 102–5.

* Pasquali, G. "Die schriftstellerische Form des Pausanias." *Hermes* 48 (1913): 161–223.

Pearson, L. "Pausanias on the Temple of Poseidon at Isthmia (2, 1, 7)." *Hermes* 88 (1960): 498–502.

* Petersen, E. "Pausanias der Perieget." *Rheinisches Museum* 64 (1909): 481–538.

Pétracos, B. "La Base de la Némésis d'Agoracrite (rapport préliminaire)." *Bul-letin de correspondance hellénique* 105 (1981): 228–35.

Pfundtner, I. O. "Pausanias Periegeta imitator Herodoti." Diss., Königsberg 1866.

Piccirilli, L. "Psyttalos di Elide olimpionico e arbitro (Paus. 6, 16, 8)." *Annali della R. Scuola Normale Superiore di Pisa, Sezione di Lettere,* n.s., 2 (1972): 479–84.

Piérart, M. "Deux notes sur l'itinéraire argien de Pausanias." *Bulletin de correspondance hellénique* 106 (1982): 139–52.

Pouilloux, J., and G. Roux. *Enigmes à Delphes*. Paris 1963.

Preisshofen, F. "Kunsttheorie und Kunstbetrachtung." In *Le Classicisme à Rome aux I^{ers} siècles avant et après J.-C.*, ed. H. Flashar, 263–77. Entretiens sur l'antiquité classique, vol. 25. Geneva 1979.

Pritchett, W. K. *Studies in Ancient Greek Topography*. Pt. 2, *Battlefields*; pt. 4, *Passes*. Berkeley 1969, 1982.

Réardon, B. P. *Courants littéraires grecs des IIe et IIIe siècles après J.-C.* Paris 1971.

*Regenbogen, O. "Pausanias." In *Realencyclopädie der classischen Altertumswissenschaft*, suppl. 8, 1008–97. 1956.

*Robert, C. *Pausanias als Schriftsteller: Studien und Beobachtungen*. Berlin 1909.

Robinson, D. M. "A Plea for Pausanias." *Classical Weekly* 37 (1943–44): 165–66.

*Rocha-Pereira, M. H. *Pausaniae Graeciae Descriptio*. Edited by M. H. R.-P. 3 vols. Leipzig 1973, 1977, 1981.

Roux, G. *Pausanias en Corinthie (II 1–15)*. Paris 1958.

Roy, J. "The Sons of Lycaon in Pausanias' Arcadian King-List." *Annual of the British School at Athens* 63 (1968): 287–92.

Rumpf, A. "Der Westrand der Agora von Athen." *Jahrbuch des Deutschen Archäologischen Instituts*, 1938: 115–24.

Schöll, R. "Zur Thukydides-Biographie." *Hermes* 13 (1878): 433–51.

Segre, M. "Pausania come fonte storica." *Historia* (Milan) 1 (1927): 202–34.

———. "La fonte di Pausania per la storia dei Diadochi." *Historia* (Milan) 2 (1928): 217–37.

———. "Note storiche su Pausania periegeta." *Athenaeum*, n.s., 7 (1929): 475–88.

Settis, S. "Il ninfeo di Erode Attico a Olimpia e il problema della composizione della Periegesi di Pausania." *Annali della R. Scuola Normale Superiore di Pisa, Sezione di Lettere*, ser. 2, 37 (1968): 1–63.

*Strid, O. *Über Sprache und Stil des Periegeten Pausanias*. Stockholm 1976.

Szelest, H. *De Pausaniae clausulis*. Warsaw 1953.

Thompson, H. A. "Odeion of Agrippa or Sanctuary of Zeus?" *Revue archéologique*, 1961, pt. 1: 1–3.

Thompson, H. A., and R. E. Wycherley. *The Agora of Athens*. Agora, vol. 14. Princeton 1972.

Travlos, J. "The West Side of the Athenian Agora Restored." *Hesperia*, suppl. 8 (1949): 382–93.

Trendelenburg, A. *Pausanias in Olympia*. Berlin 1914.

Treu, G. "Vermischte Bemerkungen." *Archäologische Zeitung* 40 (1882): 59–76.

Vanderpool, E. "The Route of Pausanias in the Athenian Agora." *Hesperia* 18 (1949): 128–37.

————. "The Agora of Pausanias I 17, 1–2." *Hesperia* 43 (1974): 308–10.

Vatin, C. "Monuments votifs de Delphes." *Bulletin de correspondance hellé-nique* 105 (1981): 227–53.

Vidal-Naquet, P. "Une Enigme à Delphes: A propos de la base de Marathon (Pausanias 10, 10, 1–2)." *Revue historique* 91 (1961): 281–302.

Wace, A. J. B. "Pausanias and Mycenae." In *Neue Beiträge zur klassischen Al-tertumswissenschaft: Festschrift B. Schweitzer*, ed. R. Lullies, 19–26. Stutt-gart 1954.

Wachsmuth, C. "Über eine Hauptquelle für die Geschichte des Achäischen Bundes." *Leipziger Studien* 10 (1887): 269–98.

Waele, J. A. de. "The Athena of Endoios in Erythrai: A crux in Pausanias (7, 5, 9)." *Platon* 32–33 (1980–81): 263–64.

Wernicke, C. *De Pausaniae Periegetae studiis Herodoteis*. Berlin 1884.

Wilamowitz-Moellendorff, U. von. "Die Thukydideslegende." *Hermes* 12 (1877): 326–67.

————. Ἐλευθέριον Ὕδωρ. *Hermes* 19 (1884): 463–65.

————. "Reiseerlebnisse des Pausanias." *Forschungen und Fortschritte* 7 (1931): 50–51.

————. *Der Glaube der Hellenen*. 2 vols. Berlin 1931, 1932.

Williams, Ch. K., II. "The Route of Pausanias" (at Corinth). *Hesperia* 44 (1975): 25–29.

Wiseman, J. "Corinth and Rome I: 228 B.C.–A.D. 267." In *Aufstieg und Niedergang der Römischen Welt*, ed. H. Temporini, vol. 2, pt. 7, pp. 438–548. Berlin 1979.

Wünsche, R. "Der 'Gott aus dem Meer.'" *Jahrbuch des Deutschen Archäo-logischen Instituts* 94 (1979): 77–111.

Wycherley, R. E. "Pausanias in the Agora of Athens." *Greek, Roman and By-zantine Studies* 2 (1959): 21–44.

INDEX OF PASSAGES CITED

PAUSANIAS

GREEK AND LATIN AUTHORS

GREEK INSCRIPTIONS

PAPYRI

GENERAL INDEX

INDEX OF SIGNIFICANT GREEK WORDS